# PATTON'S
# PRAYER

## ALSO BY ALEX KERSHAW

*Against All Odds*
*The First Wave*
*Avenue of Spies*
*The Few*
*The Bedford Boys*
*The Longest Winter*
*Escape from the Deep*
*The Liberator*
*The Envoy*
*Blood and Champagne*
*Jack London*

# PATTON'S PRAYER

A True Story of Courage,
Faith, and Victory in
World War II

# ALEX KERSHAW

**DUTTON**

**DUTTON**

An imprint of Penguin Random House LLC
penguinrandomhouse.com

Maps by Chris Erichsen Cartography.

All insert photographs courtesy of the National Archives except where noted.

LIBRARY OF CONGRESS CATALOGING-IN-PUBLICATION DATA
Names: Kershaw, Alex, author.
Title: Patton's prayer: a true story of courage, faith, and victory in
World War II / Alex Kershaw.
Description: [New York]: Dutton, [2024] | Includes bibliographical
references and index.
Identifiers: LCCN 2023054915 (print) | LCCN 2023054916 (ebook) |
ISBN 9780593183779 (hardcover) | ISBN 9780593183793 (ebook)
Subjects: LCSH: Patton, George S. (George Smith), 1885–1945—Military
leadership. | Patton, George S. (George Smith), 1885–1945—Religion. |
United States. Army. Airborne Division, 101st—History. | Ardennes,
Battle of the, 1944–1945. | World War, 1939–1945—Campaigns—Western Front. |
Generals—United States—Biography.
Classification: LCC E745.P3 K47 2024 (print) | LCC E745.P3 (ebook) |
DDC 940.54/219348—dc23/eng/20240215
LC record available at https://lccn.loc.gov/2023054915
LC ebook record available at https://lccn.loc.gov/2023054916

Printed in the United States of America

1st Printing

*For Kady*

# CONTENTS

# PATTON'S PRAYER

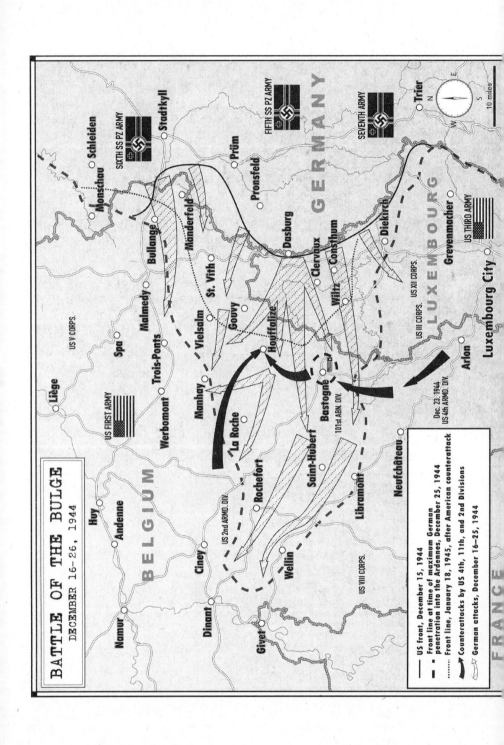

# BATTLE OF THE BULGE
## DECEMBER 16-26, 1944

N
W ——— E
S

10 miles

---

US front, December 15, 1944

Front line at time of maximum German penetration into the Ardennes, December 25, 1944

Front line, January 18, 1945, after American counterattack

Counterattacks by US 4th, 11th, and 2nd Divisions

German attacks, December 16-25, 1944

---

**GERMANY**

**BELGIUM**

**LUXEMBOURG**

**FRANCE**

SIXTH SS PZ ARMY

FIFTH SS PZ ARMY

SEVENTH ARMY

US THIRD ARMY

US FIRST ARMY

US V CORPS.

US VIII CORPS.

US III CORPS.

US V CORPS.

US XII CORPS.

US 2nd ARMD. DIV.

Dec. 23, 1944
US 4th ARMD. DIV.

101st ABN. DIV.

Schleiden

Monschau

Stadtkyll

Prüm

Pronsfeld

Dasburg

Clervaux

Consthum

Diekirch

Trier

Grevenmacher

Luxembourg City

Arlon

Neufchâteau

Libramont

Wellin

Saint-Hubert

Bastogne

Wiltz

Houffalize

Gouvy

Vielsalm

St. Vith

Büllange

Manderfeld

Malmedy

Trois-Ponts

Spa

Werbomont

Manhay

La Roche

Rochefort

Ciney

Dinant

Givet

Namur

Andenne

Huy

Liège

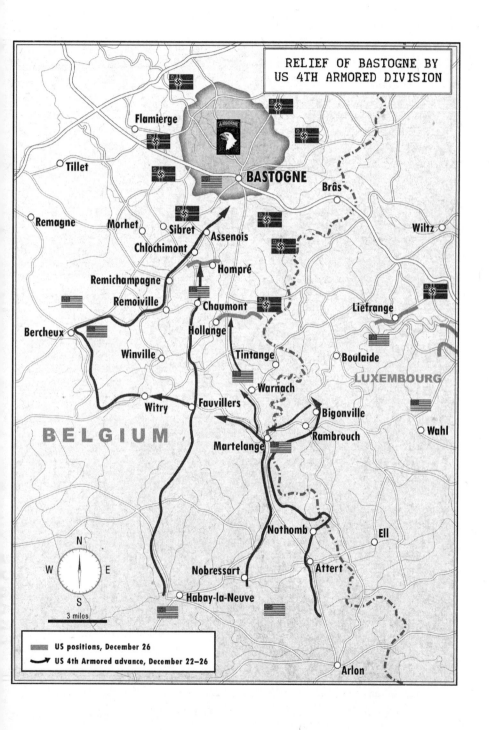

RELIEF OF BASTOGNE BY
US 4TH ARMORED DIVISION

BASTOGNE

Flamierge

Tillet

Brâs

Wiltz

Remagne

Morhet

Sibret

Assenois

Chlochimont

Hompré

Remichampagne

Chaumont

Liefrange

Remoiville

Boulaide

Bercheux

Hollange

Winville

Tintange

LUXEMBOURG

Warnach

BELGIUM

Fauvillers

Bigonville

Wahl

Witry

Rambrouch

Martelange

Nothomb

Ell

Nobressart

Attert

N
W        E
S

Habay-la-Neuve

3 miles

Arlon

US positions, December 26
US 4th Armored advance, December 22–26

TO THE RHINE

Utrecht

Arnhem

ARMY GROUP H.

FIRST PARA. ARMY

Waal

Grave

Rees

FIRST ARMY

Goch

Wesel

Maas

Xanten

NETHERLANDS

Geldern

Dortmund

Essen

Ruhr

Eindhoven

SECOND ARMY

Venlo

Duisburg

The Ruhr

Düsseldorf

FIFTH PZ. ARMY

Roermond

Rhine

GERMANY

US NINTH ARMY

Jülich

Cologne

ARMY GROUP B

Maastricht

Aachen

Düren

FIFTEENTH ARMY

Bonn

US FIRST ARMY

Liège

Remagen

Malmedy

SEVENTH ARMY

Koblenz

BELGIUM

St. Vith

Prüm

Bastogne

LUX

Moselle

Rhine

Bitburg

SEVENTH ARMY

Diekirch

US THIRD ARMY

N

Arlon

Trier

W        E

Luxembourg City

S

20 miles

— · — Front line, February 7, 1945

■ ■ ■ Front line, March 7, 1945

➤ Allied attack

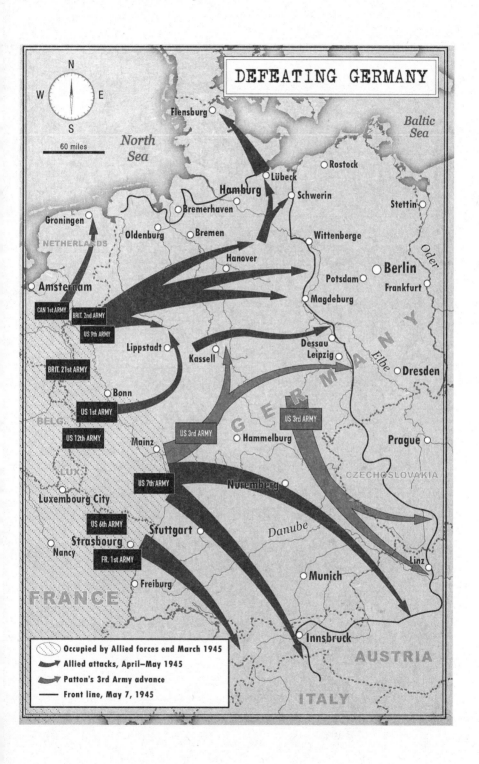

# DEFEATING GERMANY

Baltic Sea

North Sea

Flensburg

Rostock

Lübeck

Hamburg

Schwerin

Stettin

Bremerhaven

Wittenberge

Groningen

Oldenburg

Bremen

NETHERLANDS

Hanover

Berlin

Potsdam

Amsterdam

Magdeburg

Frankfurt

CAN 1st ARMY

BRIT. 2nd ARMY

US 9th ARMY

Oder

Lippstadt

Dessau

Kassell

Leipzig

BRIT. 21st ARMY

Elbe

Dresden

Bonn

BELG.

US 1st ARMY

GERMANY

US 12th ARMY

US 3rd ARMY

US 3rd ARMY

Prague

Mainz

LUX.

Hammelburg

CZECHOSLOVAKIA

US 7th ARMY

Luxembourg City

Nuremberg

US 6th ARMY

Stuttgart

Danube

Strasbourg

Nancy

FR. 1st ARMY

Linz

Freiburg

Munich

FRANCE

Innsbruck

AUSTRIA

ITALY

60 miles

Occupied by Allied forces end March 1945

Allied attacks, April–May 1945

Patton's 3rd Army advance

Front line, May 7, 1945

# Introction

IT HAD BEEN *a glorious if bloody summer. After the successful landings in Normandy on June 6, 1944, and bitter fighting through July, the Allies had broken out of Normandy, then liberated Paris on August 25. They had also landed in southern France that August and pushed up the Rhône Valley toward the Third Reich. By the early fall, it was widely believed that the war in Europe would be over by Christmas.*

*Then the weather changed. Cold rain dampened spirits. Mud clogged tank tracks. The Germans regrouped and put up a spirited defense, notably at Aachen, the first German city the Allies tried to liberate. Supply lines were overstretched, gasoline shortages became acute, and there was a woeful, deeply concerning lack of fresh troops.*

*As winter set in, along a broad front stretching from Holland to Italy, the Allies stalled. The failure to cross the Rhine in Holland that September was both demoralizing and costly, because it had stripped valuable resources from General George Patton's Third Army and others.*

*The mood darkened. Berlin would not be taken by Christmas. Meanwhile, Adolf Hitler was hatching a daring plan for a massive counterattack, hoping to catch the Allies off guard, inflict a humiliating defeat, and change the entire outcome of the war.*

# PART ONE

## Watch on the Rhine

If we take the generally accepted definition of bravery as a quality which knows not fear, I have never seen a brave man. All men are frightened. The courageous man is the man who forces himself, in spite of his fear, to carry on. Discipline, pride, self-respect, self-confidence, and the love of glory are attributes which will make a man courageous even when he is afraid.[1]

—GENERAL GEORGE S. PATTON

# CHAPTER 1

---

# Stuck in the Mud

**Metz, France**
**November 25, 1944**

THE WEATHER WAS ATROCIOUS. Valleys were flooded and roads were coated in cloying mud. Every day it rained. But he knew his troops had to keep advancing, whatever the conditions. Berlin was still a long way away. The poor, sodden bastards under his command had to push on as winter closed in and the days grew shorter.

Dead Germans lay piled neatly along the rain-lashed road as a mud-splattered dark green jeep drove past. A white-haired man in the jeep, face reddened from cold and wind, had an ivory-handled pistol strapped to his waist. Three stars were emblazoned on the side of the vehicle and on his polished helmet. Just a couple of weeks ago, on Armistice Day, November 11, he had marked his fifty-ninth birthday. He was the most controversial American general of World War II, George S. Patton, known to some of his more than two hundred fifty thousand men in the Third Army as "Old Blood and Guts."

A quarter of a century before, he'd spent his thirty-third birthday in France, at the very end of the war to end all wars, as the Great War had been described. He had earned the Distinguished Service Cross and a Purple Heart while leading the US 1st Provisional Tank Brigade as a lieutenant colonel. "Peace looks possible," he had written to his wife, Beatrice, toward the end of hostilities, "but I rather hope not for I would like to have a few more fights. They are awfully thrilling like steeple chasing only more so."[1]

Patton had courted Beatrice throughout his time at the US Military Academy at West Point, New York, where he'd had to repeat a year after failing in mathematics. Their marriage in 1910 had drawn high society from across her native Massachusetts and beyond.[2] She would remain utterly devoted to her husband, despite rumors of him having an affair with the daughter of Beatrice's half sister, let alone the considerable challenges of being married to such a mercurial, hard-driving man.

Now George S. Patton—born into privilege and wealth, a superb fencer, the designer of his very own saber, a 1912 Olympic athlete, and a believer in reincarnation—was a three-star general with an entire army and several hundred tanks at his disposal. And he was in a grim mood indeed, that November 25, 1944, as he was driven in his jeep past dead Germans toward the city of Metz. He wanted his troops to see him. He "got out where it is unhealthy oftener than any other general," as he put it, but not too frequently lest he became a nuisance.[3]

Patton knew it was important to be seen heading toward the sound of the guns.[4] George S. Patton had never been considered a shirker from any danger. Ever since he'd first seen action, chasing after the revolutionary Pancho Villa in Mexico in 1916, he'd always been up for the fight.

The current Lorraine campaign had been his least successful, bringing heartache and frustration. The Germans themselves would later criticize his tactics, arguing that attacking forts in Lorraine and the city of Metz had been too costly. He should have bypassed them and headed straight for Luxembourg. He was, after all, a master of mobile armored warfare. But the terrain and weather had not permitted it.

Above all, Patton cursed the weather. It explained all of his problems. He was convinced of it. That was why he was "stuck in the mud."[5]

*If it only won't rain we will go places.*

That was what he'd written to his dear wife, Beatrice.

*If it only won't rain we will go places.*[6]

Allied Supreme Commander Dwight Eisenhower had expected Patton to "carry the ball all the way" and push through Lorraine to Germany. Patton had hoped to declare victory by his birthday, but that had not happened. There had been a desultory party and his staff had presented him with "field expedient" Armored Diesels, cocktails usually containing bourbon or rye but now spiked with any liquor that could be found. And still the rain poured down.

Trench foot was rampant. In one division, Patton recalled, there were an extraordinary three thousand cases. It could hardly be avoided when men had to wade across flooded fields up to their waists in muddy water. It didn't matter how much a soldier dubbed his boots or how many pairs of dry socks he hoarded; everything that dismal November got wet.

Lieutenant Colonel Albin F. Irzyk, one of Patton's most able tank officers, recalled how Patton's 4th Armored Division, to which Irzyk belonged, had finally gotten bogged down after thundering across France. "We had traveled 328 miles . . . in twelve days. . . . We were sixty miles from the German border and another eighty miles to the Rhine River. . . . We'd already gone 328 in twelve days."

According to Irzyk, Patton had declared: "We'll be at the Rhine in ten days."

Twenty-seven-year-old Irzyk, commander of the 8th Tank Battalion, was a slim and handsome graduate of the University of Massachusetts and the proud son of Polish immigrants. He had had no reason to disbelieve Patton, given the 4th Armored's rapid progress. But then Irzyk recalled, "Patton ran out of gasoline." Or rather it had been taken from him, Patton believed. Eisenhower, Irzyk claimed, had given the British "priority supplies," which were used for Operation Market Garden, an attempt to cross the Rhine in Holland in September, which had ended in disaster. In any case, that fall of 1944, the Third Army had stalled. "Patton, the great offensive weapon," remembered Irzyk, "sat for five weeks as it rained and rained and rained."[7]

Patton's men had slogged on. His tanks had crawled forward, tracks caked in mud. The air support had done its best. But the Germans had fought hard in retreat, even though "motley and badly equipped"; they had been helped above all by the appalling weather: the heavy fogs, the flooding downpours, the thick blankets of gray cloud cover.[8]

Patton's commanders were now tired, nervy, pushed to the breaking point. Some were doing nothing but fighting the weather. It was one thing to storm across the flat, lush farmland between Brittany and Paris, but quite another to fight through the forests and rugged, hilly countryside of Lorraine and then conduct siege warfare as worn-out units seized the series of thirty-five forts that protected Metz.

The rain kept falling. A few days earlier, sodden soldiers from Patton's Third Army had finally managed to capture some four thousand enemy soldiers, the last holdouts in the city of Metz itself. It was a bitter victory. The defenders had fought tenaciously from underground chambers and tunnels, and the combat had been up close and costly.

Now a dejected Patton arrived in a hospital near the shattered city. Inside the hospital, Patton went over to a soldier, one of the hundreds from his Third Army who had been wounded each day that dark November in the depressing and gruesome fighting, described by Omar Bradley, Patton's immediate superior, as "a ghastly war of attrition."[9]

Had the soldier heard that Metz had finally been taken?

The soldier said he had and smiled.

Patton, white bushy brows above piercing eyes, smiled back.

"Tomorrow, son," said Patton in his high-pitched voice, "the headlines will read, 'Patton Took Metz,' which you know is a goddam lie. You and your buddies are the ones who actually took Metz."[10]

Patton left the hospital and then went to question a captured SS major general, 39-year-old Anton Dunckern, a dedicated Nazi who'd taken part in the infamous Beer Hall Putsch of 1923 in Munich. Captured by Patton's troops on November 19, he was the highest-ranking member of the SS to have been seized in Patton's area of command since November 1942, two long years earlier, when Patton's war had begun in North Africa.[11]

Sentries stood watch over Dunckern.

An interpreter was close by.

"You can tell this man," the thin-lipped Patton told the interpreter, "that naturally in my position I cannot demean myself to question him, but I can say this, that I have captured a great many German generals, and this is the first one who has been wholly untrue to everything; because he has not only been a Nazi but he is untrue to the Nazis by surrendering."[12]

Patton had enormous contempt for members of the SS. He'd fought the Germans in the First World War, in the deserts of North Africa, the mountains of Sicily, and all across France in the Second. They were often a formidable enemy. They'd killed nearly ten thousand of his men in the Third Army since August. He'd kept a careful count. But Hitler's most fanatical supporters, the SS, notorious for killing civilians and unarmed prisoners and committing other atrocities, were "special sons-of-bitches," as Patton called them.[13]

"If he wants to say anything, he can," said Patton, "and I will say that unless he talks pretty well, I will turn him over to the French. They know how to make people talk."

Dunckern most likely did not want to be handed over to the French.

"I received orders to go in the Metz sector," the German said, "and defend a certain sector there, and the reason I did not perish was that I could not reach my weapons and fight back."

Patton was not buying that.

"He is a liar!"

"There was no possibility to continue fighting," said Dunckern. "The door was opened and they put a gun on me."

Patton was disgusted.

"If he wanted to be a good Nazi," said Patton, "he could have died then and there. It would have been a pleasanter death than what he will get now."

"It was useless to do anything about it under the circumstances. . . . I consider myself a prisoner of war of the American forces, and I have not been captured by the French forces."

Patton pointed out that Dunckern had belonged to the Gestapo, Nazi Germany's feared secret police, known for torture and murder.

Dunckern protested that he had not done "anything against the rules of humanity or human treatment."[14]

Patton was done with him.

"Have the guards take him outside and have his picture taken," ordered Patton, "and then we'll see what we will do with him. Also tell him that those bayonets on the guards' guns are very sharp."

Patton later described Dunckern, a "Gestapo General," as "the most vicious looking human being I have ever seen, and who, after I got through talking to him, was unquestionably one of the most scared. He is the first man I have ever brow-beaten, and I must admit I took real pleasure in doing it."[15]

Soon after, Patton finally stood before the troops who had suffered most to take the city. They belonged to the 5th Division.

"I am very proud of you," declared Patton. "Your country is proud of you. You are magnificent fighting men. Your deeds in the battle of Metz will fill the pages of history for a thousand years."[16]

THE LORRAINE CAMPAIGN had unnerved Patton. The attrition that November left him wondering whether he had lost his touch. More than ever, he knew, he would have to "push people beyond endurance to bring this war to an end."[17]

Patton's Third Army was thinly spread across a wide area. Many more divisions were needed to adequately man the front lines. His own force of three armored and six infantry divisions needed more than ten thousand replacements.

Patton's rifle companies were at two-thirds strength or less. "We are having one hell of a war," he wrote to an old friend, Major General Alexander Surles, "and the lack of ammunition and replacements is getting more and more serious. I don't know what the young manhood of America is doing, but they're certainly not appearing over here."[18]

The Germans were far from a spent force. Patton wrote in his diary that it was "highly probable that the Germans [were] building up" east of American forces in the Ardennes, the mountainous, thickly forested area in Belgium through which Hitler had launched his Blitzkrieg in 1940.[19]

Patton's unease was based on intelligence reports provided by his staff, namely forty-seven-year-old Colonel Oscar W. Koch, who had served with Patton in the European Theater since the invasion of North Africa in 1942. He'd actually been Patton's G-2, his primary intelligence officer, since Patton had commanded the 2nd Armored Division in 1940.

Koch was indispensable after more than four years of close collaboration.[20] Rarely did Patton make a move without involving Koch and his crack team of intelligence gatherers. "In Patton's commands," Koch recalled, "intelligence was always viewed as big business and treated accordingly."[21]

The soft-spoken Koch had noted suspicious movement of German troops. What was more, along the Third Army's front, there was a notable absence of German armored divisions. Koch knew that the Germans were stockpiling gasoline and ammunition. From air reconnaissance, he had learned that trains loaded with tanks were moving west.

Why?

Koch believed a "powerful striking force, with an estimated 500 tanks" could be deployed against US forces, and he duly informed Patton.[22]

This troubling information did not interrupt Patton's current plans for a decisive strike across the Rhine, which would begin on December 19, with the primary target being Frankfurt. In the coming offensive, he instructed his commanders, "there is no purpose in capturing these manure-filled, water-logged villages. The purpose of our operations is to kill or capture the German personnel and vehicles . . . so they cannot retreat and repeat their opposition."[23]

Patton still had a war he wanted to win, and he was eager to get his Third Army moving again after the depressing debacle in Lorraine, which had resulted in the Third Army's greatest losses. In the last three months, his men had moved just fifty miles and incurred fifty thousand casualties—a third of the total the Third Army would suffer during the whole war.[24]

# CHAPTER 2

## Dark December

**Nancy, France**
**December 8, 1944**

EARLY THAT DECEMBER, as Patton regrouped his Third Army, the weather worsened. "There is about four inches of liquid mud over everything," he wrote to Beatrice, "and it rains all the time, not hard but steadily."[1]

It was high time, he decided, to muster some divine intervention.

Around eleven o'clock on December 8, Patton picked up the telephone in his office in the Caserne Molifor, an old French Army barracks in the city of Nancy that was being used as Third Army headquarters.[2]

Patton called the chief chaplain of the Third Army, James H. O'Neill.

Fifty-two-year-old O'Neill hailed from Chicago. He had

attended Loyola University in Chicago, gaining a master of arts degree before being ordained a Roman Catholic priest in 1915. He had then become a priest in the Diocese of Helena, Montana, where he had also worked as a college physics professor before entering the US Army Chaplain Corps in 1926. Before joining Patton's staff earlier in 1944, he had served in positions around the United States, in the Philippines, and with the Sixth Army in the European Theater. He would end the war having served Patton in five campaigns.

According to O'Neill, Patton had "all the traits of military leadership, fortified by genuine trust in God, intense love of country, and high faith in the American soldier. He had no use for half-measures. He was true to the principles of his religion, Episcopalian, and was regular in Church attendance and practices, unless duty made his presence Impossible."

When O'Neill was on the phone, Patton got straight to the point.

"This is General Patton," announced the Third Army commander. "Do you have a good prayer for weather? We must do something about those rains if we are to win the war."[3]

This was, of course, a highly unusual request, even from a character as unpredictable and quixotic as Patton.

O'Neill told Patton he would look for a suitable prayer. He couldn't find one, so he created his own, jotting it down on a card:

*Almighty and most merciful Father, we humbly beseech Thee, of Thy great goodness, to restrain these immoderate rains with which we have had to contend. Grant us fair weather for Battle. Graciously hearken to us as soldiers who call upon Thee that, armed with Thy power, we may advance from victory to victory, and crush the oppression and wickedness of our enemies and establish Thy justice among men and nations.*

O'Neill added a Christmas prayer to the troops for good measure, hoping it would also find favor with Patton.

*To each officer and soldier in the Third United States Army, I Wish a Merry Christmas. I have full confidence in your courage, devotion to duty, and skill in battle. We march in our might to complete victory. May God's blessings rest upon each of you on this Christmas Day. G.S. Patton, Jr, Lieutenant General, Commanding, Third United States Army.*

O'Neill pulled on his overcoat, walked across the barracks, and then stood before Patton.

O'Neill held out a card.

Patton took the card and examined it.

Patton was pleased.

"Have 250,000 copies printed," he said, "and see to it that every man in the Third Army gets one."

O'Neill was surprised by the number: "This was certainly doing something about the weather in a big way."

"Very well, sir!" replied O'Neill, who then showed Patton the Christmas prayer he had also created.

"Very good," said a smiling Patton.

"If the General would sign the card, it would add a personal touch that I am sure the men would like."

Patton signed it.

"Chaplain, sit down for a moment; I want to talk to you about this business of prayer."

O'Neill did as he had been ordered.

Patton "rubbed his face in his hands" and then went over to a window, where he stood with his back to O'Neill, looking out at the dreary weather.

O'Neill recalled: "As usual, [Patton] was dressed stunningly, and his six-foot-two powerfully built physique made an unforgettable silhouette against the great window."

O'Neill had grown to admire Patton.

The general cared that his men got hot meals whenever possible, that they had dry socks.

O'Neill had once seen Patton looking after a wounded man, injecting him with morphine, remaining with him until an ambulance arrived.

"Chaplain, how much praying is being done in the Third Army?" asked Patton.

"Does the General mean by chaplains, or by the men?"

"By everybody."

"I am afraid to admit it, but I do not believe that much praying is going on. When there is fighting, everyone prays, but now with this constant rain—when things are quiet, dangerously quiet, men just sit and wait for things to happen."

O'Neill said it was difficult to find places to congregate for prayer.

"Both chaplains and men," he added, "are removed from a special building with a steeple. Prayer to most of them is a formal, ritualized affair, involving special posture and a liturgical setting. I do not believe that much praying is being done."

Patton returned to his desk and sat down.

"Chaplain," said Patton, "I am a strong believer in Prayer. There are three ways that men get what they want—by planning, by working, and by praying. Any great military operation takes careful planning, or thinking. Then you must have well-trained troops to carry it out: that's working. But between the plan and the operation there is always an unknown. That unknown spells defeat or victory, success or failure."

Patton added: "Up to now, in the Third Army, God has been very good to us. We have never retreated; we have suffered no defeats. . . . This is because a lot of people back home are praying for us. We were lucky in Africa, in Sicily, and in Italy. Simply because people prayed. But we have to pray for ourselves, too."

Patton continued: "A good soldier is not made merely by making him think and work. There is something in every soldier that goes deeper than thinking or working—it's his 'guts.' It is something that he has built in there: it is a world of truth and power that is higher than himself."

Patton concluded the meeting by telling O'Neill that soldiers should pray wherever they found themselves; if they didn't, they'd sooner or later go to pieces—"crack up."

O'Neill returned to his quarters and issued a directive, in Patton's name, that would be distributed to the Third Army's 486 chaplains, representing thirty-two denominations, and senior officers in more than twenty divisions:

"Pray when driving. Pray when fighting. Pray alone. Pray with others. Pray by night and pray by day. Pray for the cessation of immoderate rains, for good weather for Battle. Pray for the defeat of our wicked enemy whose banner is injustice and whose good is oppression. Pray for victory. Pray for our Army, and Pray for Peace."[4]

THE FOLLOWING DAY, December 9, Koch met with Patton and briefed him on the latest intelligence: Of the fifteen panzer divisions in the west, only five remained at the front.

What were the Germans up to?

There had also been a massive movement by rail of German forces to the north of the Third Army: more than two hundred trains rolling on one day alone.

A new force, the Sixth Panzer Army, had also been formed.

Some kind of offensive was clearly in the making.

Patton continued with preparations for his attack due to begin on December 19. But he also told his staff to draw up plans in case the Germans launched a major strike to the north.

"We'll be in a position to meet whatever happens," Patton wrote in his diary.

Two days later, on December 11, Koch's Third Army G-2 report stated: "The massive armored force the enemy has built up in reserve gives him the definite capability of launching a spoiling offensive to disrupt the Allied drive."[5]

Under cover of darkness that very day, two hundred thousand German troops began to gather in the Ardennes, known to GIs as a "sleepy corner"—a "Ghost Front." The first of more than twenty-five hundred armored vehicles were driven to jump-off positions in the area where Hitler's forces had stormed toward France in 1940.

Hitler knew that American forces in the Ardennes were inexperienced and understrength, woefully unprepared for a major offensive, spread thin in difficult terrain. The 106th and 99th divisions were green, untested in combat, and two other divisions, the 4th and 28th, were licking their wounds after a terrible mauling that fall in the Huertgen Forest, around one hundred miles to the northeast.

That same day, December 11, Hitler briefed his senior generals on his planned strike in the west, code-named Wacht am Rhein. He did so at the Adlerhorst, a series of bunkers based around a castle at Ziegenberg, around 125 miles from the border of Luxembourg. The day for his massive surprise offensive had already been decided: December 16, 1944.

Hitler had arrived that morning accompanied by a large motorcade of black Mercedes. Security was tight. It had been at a similar meeting of his Wehrmacht senior generals on July 20, 1944, that Count von Stauffenberg had managed to plant a bomb that had badly injured Hitler. Indeed, he had been fortunate to survive the assassination attempt, and so the generals gathering at the Adlerhorst that day were searched, sworn to secrecy, and made to hand over their sidearms before being allowed into Hitler's presence.

It was 6 P.M. when Hitler finally limped onto a stage and took a seat at a table between Field Marshal Wilhelm Keitel and General Alfred Jodl, arguably his most trusted staff.

Hitler was in a shocking state. He had a tremble in his left arm, an aftereffect of the July explosion. He was also abusing a wide array of drugs, all manner of pharmaceuticals. For those generals who had not seen the Führer in some time, his haggard appearance was unnerving.

Field Marshal Hasso von Manteuffel, commander of the Fifth Panzer Army, remembered how the leader of the Third Reich was now but "a stooped figure with a pale and puffy face, hunched in his chair . . . his left arm subject to twitching which he did his best to conceal. A sick man . . . When he walked he dragged one leg behind him."[6]

Hitler gave a rambling lecture on the state of the war and its origins.

"We must allow no moment to pass," said Hitler, "without showing the enemy that, whatever he does, he can never reckon on [our] capitulation. Never! Never!"[7]

Hitler then explained his plan of attack. At 5:30 A.M. on December 16, "Null Hour," three armies would attack through the Ardennes, punch a hole in the Allied lines, and then storm toward Antwerp, sowing such terror and chaos that the Allies would consider a negotiated peace in the west. That would enable Hitler to then concentrate all his forces in the east to confront the Soviets. The Third Reich might yet survive.

The commander of the Sixth Panzer Army, Sepp Dietrich, listened as Hitler outlined the offensive. It was an ambitious plan indeed, to be carried out, as Dietrich later complained when not in Hitler's presence, at "the worst time of the year through the Ardennes when the snow is waist-deep and there isn't room to deploy four tanks abreast, let alone armored divisions. When it doesn't get light until eight and it's dark again at four and with re-formed divisions made up chiefly of kids and sickly old men—and at Christmas."[8]

Manteuffel's Fifth Panzer Army would seize vital road junctions in the towns of Bastogne and St. Vith and then protect Dietrich's southern flank. The Seventh Army, commanded by Erich Brandenberger, would strike to the south to block an American counterattack.

If all went according to plan, the Allies would be in utter disarray and Hitler's armies would indeed reach Antwerp, cutting off the Canadians and British in the north from the Americans to the south.

"This battle," Hitler stressed, "is to decide whether we shall live or die. I want all my soldiers to fight hard and without pity. The battle must be fought with brutality and all resistance must be broken in a wave of terror. In this most serious hour for the Fatherland, I expect every one of my soldiers to be courageous and again courageous. The enemy must be beaten—now or never! Thus lives our Germany."[9]

That evening, Hitler's generals gathered to celebrate Field Marshal Gerd von Rundstedt's sixty-ninth birthday. The mood was far from joyous. No one dared discuss the imminent attack—even mentioning it had been forbidden on penalty of death.

Hitler's generals dutifully set off for their commands, resigned to carrying out their Führer's orders as best as they could. Hopefully, the weather gods would cooperate. Several days of thick cloud cover and fog would be ideal. Then the Allied air forces would be grounded and Wacht am Rhein might stand a chance.

Despite Hitler's decrepit appearance, which was hardly

inspiring, Manteuffel was confident of some kind of success. "Everything was right for the attack: the plans, ammunition, supplies, etc.," he recalled. The surprise offensive would be "made on a wide front, with elements of all the panzer divisions in the assault wave. My theory was that if we knocked on ten doors, we would find several open."[10]

THAT SAME DAY, December 11, Patton wrote in his diary: "I had the Army Chaplain direct all chaplains to pray for dry weather. I will publish this prayer with a Christmas greeting on the back of it to all members of my command."[11]

The following day, Patton ordered his chief of staff, Brigadier General Hobart Gay, and his operations officer, Colonel Halley G. Maddox, to devise a plan in case the Germans did indeed attack to the north of his Third Army.

Final preparations were meanwhile being made for Wacht am Rhein. More than three million gallons of fuel had been assigned. But even that amount would not be nearly enough. Each German tank would be able to advance some eighty miles. Then the fuel supply would run dry. Tankers would have to scavenge if they wanted to roll farther, seizing what they could from abandoned American depots. Antwerp was considerably farther than eighty miles from the German jump-off line. If tanks were to reach the port, they would be running on fumes unless American supplies could indeed be found.

It was remarkable that so many men and so much matériel could be gathered literally under the noses of the Americans without the senior Allied command being aware of the extent of the buildup. By day, roads in the German sector of the Ardennes were "lifeless and deserted," recalled one German officer, "and it was not until nightfall that obscure, cautious and silent movement set in. Huge quantities of ammunition . . . camouflaged . . . were dumped everywhere. Guns were placed in the forests and long columns of vehicles on the edges."[12]

The Luftwaffe flew low over Allied lines to mask the noise of German armor. Troops used charcoal to avoid smoke from campfires being detected. They carried ammunition by hand. Artillery units were not allowed to fire practice rounds. Straw was strewn along roads to muffle the sound of tank tracks.

Later that day, December 12, Patton paid a visit to the 4th Armored Division in Domnon-lès-Dieuze, "a tiny, wet, muddy and depressing French village about 40 miles northeast of Nancy," recalled tanker Albin Irzyk. Patton "arrived at high speed in his jeep, with a wide, crooked grin and all his stars blazing. He was jolly, animated and interested in how we were doing."[13]

Patton jumped down from the jeep, then walked "along the entire length of the small town. He stopped at every vehicle, talked with every cluster of soldiers and had something to say to each—a question, a word of encouragement or appreciation, a compliment, a wisecrack, a good-natured dig. He was a master at this kind of rapprochement. His visits were brief, and he kept moving. But in 30 minutes or so, he had worked his magic—he had 'touched' virtually every man in that battalion."[14]

This was Patton at his best.[15] "We soon learned that the 8th Tank Battalion was the only battalion in the division that he

visited," remembered Irzyk. "Although the troops had no in-
kling of the momentous events that lay just ahead, Patton was
apparently aware that an attack might be in the offing. After
visiting the three other divisions of the XII Corps that day, he
wrote in his diary that he had decided to put the 6th Armored
Division and the 26th Infantry Division into the III Corps because 'if the enemy attacks the VIII Corps of the First Army, as
is probable, I can use the III Corps to help.'"[16]

It was indeed a sensible precaution. On December 14, a Third
Army G-2 Periodic Report was emphatic: "It is evident from
the determined hoarding of Sixth Panzer Army units that the
enemy is making every effort to employ this armor in a coordinated effort."[17]

That same day, the last of Patton's prayer cards was distributed to the men of his Third Army. Father O'Neill later recalled
how the "664th Engineer Topographical Company, at the order
of Colonel David H. Tulley, C.E., Assistant to the Third Army
Engineer," had toiled around the clock to print a quarter million
copies, which had been delivered to Patton's forces in just forty-
eight hours.[18] The timing of their delivery could not have been
better.

The following day, December 15, the Germans began to observe radio silence, an ominous sign. Patton told his chief of staff
"to start making plans for pulling the Third Army out of its eastward attack, change the direction ninety degrees, moving to
Luxembourg and attacking north."[19] Alone among senior Allied
generals, Patton had prepared a response to what was about to
be unleashed in just a few hours—the greatest surprise attack on
US forces in Europe during the war.[20]

———

THAT EVENING, German officers addressed their frontline troops. They had been forbidden to brief their men until the eleventh hour. One officer in the 26th Volksgrenadier Division declared: "In twelve or fourteen days we will be in Antwerp—or we will have lost the war. . . . Whatever equipment you may be lacking, we will take from American prisoners."[21]

Many soldiers were exultant, even ecstatic, full of hope of saving the Fatherland. Others were not so ebullient. "The mood was really grim," recalled twenty-year-old Lieutenant Wingolf Scherer, a company commander in the 277th Volksgrenadier Division. "We all knew that this was our last chance to put another twist in the tale of the war. But none of us knew if we would make it out alive."[22]

An SS soldier wrote to his sister: "I write during one of the great hours before an attack, full of unrest, full of expectation for what the next days will bring. Everyone who has been here the last two days and nights (especially nights), who has witnessed hour after hour the assembly of our crack divisions, who has heard the constant rattling of panzers, knows that something is up and are looking forward to a clear order to reduce the tension. We are still in the dark as to 'where' and 'how' but that cannot be helped!"

The soldier added that "some believe in big wonders, but that may be shortsighted! It is enough to know we attack, and will throw the enemy from our homeland. That is a holy task! I do not want to talk or write much now—but wait and see what the hours ahead will bring!"[23]

Others in the SS actually believed they were about to repeat the glorious Blitzkrieg of spring 1940, also launched through the Ardennes, and then storm into Paris in a few weeks' time.

How on earth would the Allies be able to stop them? Dietrich's Sixth Panzer Army had more than five hundred tanks and more than a hundred thousand men, backed by at least a thousand artillery pieces.

Yet, even among the SS, there were skeptics. One officer later remembered feeling that the war was pretty much lost but he and others would never think of "not doing their duty." They had to try to defend their homeland.

If Hitler's last gamble did not fully succeed, reasoned another SS stalwart—a sergeant—then perhaps the offensive would end with him and others "gaining as much territory as possible to embarrass the Americans and demonstrate success to the German people."[24]

It was almost midnight.

Wacht am Rhein would begin in just a few hours.

Officers read out a final exhortation from Field Marshal Gerd von Rundstedt:

"Soldiers of the Western Front! Your great hour has come. Large attacking armies have started against the Anglo-Americans. I do not have to tell you more than that. You feel it yourself. We gamble everything! You carry with you the holy obligation to give all to achieve superhuman objectives for our Fatherland and our Führer!"[25]

# CHAPTER 3

# Blitzkrieg

**Allied Front Lines, the Ardennes**
**December 16, 1944**

THE UNEASY SILENCE was suddenly broken as tank engines began to cough and growl.

"Null Hour" was nigh.

The 1st SS Panzer Regiment was about to roll.

"All batteries ready to fire!"

Exhaust fumes billowed into the black night.

"Good-bye, Lieutenant," exclaimed one soldier, "see you in America!"

"Fire!"[1]

Miles away, an American soldier looked at the sky and spotted "countless pinpoints of light"—flashes from more than a thousand German artillery pieces that had opened fire.

It was 5:20 A.M. on December 16, 1944, and thousands of

shells thundered toward American positions in one of the heaviest barrages of the war. Mortars screamed and the ground shook underfoot. The flashes from shells exploding lit up the dark sky, which quickly turned red from fires that began to rage in farms and villages.[2]

Along the "Ghost Front," young Americans cowered, quivering with shock, hands over their ears in their foxholes, or taking refuge wherever they could. One soldier in the 99th Division "could clearly hear shell fragments falling like a hailstorm, slicing into hard, frozen ground" beside his foxhole. "Anyone outside of a log-covered, deep hole would be dead in seconds, bleeding from numerous body wounds."[3]

German officer Lieutenant Wingolf Scherer recalled: "The German artillery barrage was frightening and awe-inspiring at once. I just thought, maybe we can do this after all. . . . We knew nothing about the enemy we were up against and we were essentially attacking into the blue."[4]

5:30 A.M.

Thousands of German soldiers moved through the mist like ghosts, many clad in heavy gray overcoats.

Hitler's last great gamble had begun.[5]

Some Germans were singing and shouting. Some wore white camouflage, which flashed red as flares soared into the sky.

Chaos and panic spread fast. GIs sheltering from the long, frigid night—sixteen hours of darkness enveloped the Ardennes at this time of the year—found their farmhouses direct targets, and they frantically pulled themselves out of their sleeping bags, snatched weapons, and ran outside and then for their lives.

The clouds above were bathed in bright light from German

searchlights, and below, because of the reflection, in some areas it was as bright as day.

The Battle of the Bulge had indeed begun. It would become the greatest ever fought, in terms of the number of US troops involved, in US military history.

Everything was at stake.

*Es geht um das Ganze.*

6:30 A.M.

The German barrage finally ended. German troops, backed by tanks, stormed through American lines. "Time appeared to stand still," remembered one officer in the inexperienced 99th Division, now confronting thousands of seasoned SS troops. "My mind seemed to reject the reality of what was happening, to say it was all make-believe."

It was all too real. The officer saw a young lieutenant perform "a rubber-legged jig as he twisted slowly, making the bullet hole between his eyes clearly visible. One moment our battalion chaplain and his assistant were kneeling beside their disabled vehicle. The next moment they were headless, decapitated by an exploding shell as if by the stroke of a guillotine."[6]

At Patton's Third Army headquarters in Luxembourg, some thirty miles south from the German onslaught, professorial Colonel Oscar Koch began his daily intelligence briefing, unaware that the German attack had begun in full fury.

Patton was seated as usual in the front row, amid his staff officers. Outside it was still dark. It would not get light until after 8 A.M.

One of Koch's staff, an intelligence officer, Captain John J. Helfers, addressed the assembled officers.

Helfers believed a large number of German troops were on the move.

Were the Germans moving toward the Third Army?

"What do you make of it, Koch?" asked Patton.

Koch reached for his notes, jotted on small index cards, and was about to speak when he was handed a message.

The bespectacled Koch read the message and then announced that the Germans had "gone on radio silence."[7]

Patton looked at Koch.

"Well," asked Patton, "what do you make of that?"

"I don't know what it means when the Germans go on radio silence," Koch replied. "But when we place one of our units in radio silence, it means they're going to move. In this particular case, sir, I believe the Germans are launching an attack, probably at Luxembourg."

"If they attack us," said Patton, "I'm ready for them. But I'm inclined to think the party will be up north. VIII Corps has been sitting still—a sure invitation to trouble."[8]

That same morning, at Patton's headquarters, Colonel Paul Harkins received a call from Leven C. Allen, chief of staff for Omar Bradley, commander of the US Twelfth Army Group.

The Third Army was to send the 10th Armored north to support the VIII Corps.

When Patton was informed, he was furious. He did not want to lose the division. He was, after all, in the final stages of planning his upcoming December 19 attack.

Patton called Bradley and protested at the loss of his division.

Bradley—Eisenhower's most trusted subordinate, a baseball

star on the 1914 team at West Point—was having none of it. He said the 10th Armored needed to move as soon as possible. It was needed urgently to help push back a German strike.

Patton argued further, but fifty-one-year-old Bradley then gave, he would later remember, "a direct, unequivocal order to get his 10th Armored moving."

Time was short.[9]


BY 8:30 A.M., as it started to get light, Hitler's three armies were back waging war, on the offensive once more. Manteuffel's Fifth Panzer Army, attacking positions held by the US 28th and 106th Divisions, made rapid progress, maximizing the Germans' greatest advantage: complete surprise. The Americans were massively outnumbered. More than a hundred thousand German troops, from seven divisions, had stormed into the 28th "Bloody Bucket" Division's thinly manned lines, which stretched for some thirty miles.[10]

One regiment from the 28th Division, the 110th, took the full brunt of the German attack. Corporal Bob Bradicich remembered the utter shock and confusion that morning: "This was not just a small German patrol and we were spread out too thin to stop a large German attack."

Bradicich wondered what his unit should do.

An officer said the men should "try and get back" or surrender.

Bradicich and others wanted to fight.

"No" came the answer to the mention of surrender.[11]

Other such groups of soldiers from the 28th Division stayed in the fight, even attacking the Germans as they tried to avoid capture, in some places making heroic last stands.

The Sixth Panzer Army, spearheaded by the formidable Lieutenant Colonel Jochen Peiper, was heading toward the Losheim Gap in the direction of the Belgian city of Liège. There was unexpectedly fierce resistance from elements of the 99th Infantry Division, however, which prompted the Sixth Panzer Army's commander, Sepp Dietrich, to commit more tanks earlier than had been planned.

Meanwhile, the most senior Allied commanders went about their usual business, ignorant of the extent of the German attack. Allied Supreme Commander Dwight Eisenhower was that morning a guest at the wedding of his valet in Versailles. Omar Bradley was taking time out to order a custom shotgun. British general Sir Bernard Montgomery, commanding the Twenty-First Army Group, was playing golf and had made plans to return to England to celebrate Christmas, believing the Germans could no longer counterattack in force.

That day's intelligence summary for Montgomery's Twenty-First Army Group stated: "The enemy is at present fighting a defensive campaign on all fronts; his situation is such that he cannot stage major offensive operations."[12]

But by lunchtime, the once sleepy "Ghost Front" in the Ardennes was hell on earth. "Fear reigned," recalled one US soldier. "Once fear strikes, it spreads like an epidemic, faster than wildfire. Once the first man runs, others soon follow. Then, it's all over; soon there are hordes of men running, all of them wild-eyed and riven by fear."[13]

Some outnumbered GIs, such as those in the "Bloody Bucket" Division, did manage to delay the German onslaught in a few places, but most did whatever it took to stay alive. "We were not really retreating," remembered one platoon sergeant, "but simply doing our best to stay out of the enemy's way until we could figure out what was happening and what we could do about it. Dodging and praying—fighting only when necessary—we looked for any friendly unit we could hook up with."[14]

Men did their best to avoid capture, hiding as the Germans stormed westward. One GI recalled German tanks rolling past him: "After a while, the squeaking of the tank tracks really got to me. I was so close that, had I had one, I could have touched the armored giants with a fishing rod as they passed."

The GI saw a man fire his rifle at a German tank. "The next tank in line fired a shell in our direction as if to say, 'Get the hell out of the way.' Somehow, we convinced ourselves that if we couldn't see them, they couldn't see us. I'm sure they knew we were there, but they were more interested in keeping to their schedule."[15]

The spearheads of the SS forces were under particular pressure to stay on track. The veteran SS commander twenty-nine-year-old Lieutenant Colonel Peiper, leading "Kampfgruppe Peiper," which comprised more than a thousand men and dozens of formidable seventy-ton Tiger II tanks, knew he had just forty-eight hours to reach the river Meuse or his mission would fail. And so Peiper barked orders to his tankers, knowing every minute counted.

"You will go ahead at full speed on the assigned road," Peiper had stressed to his commanders before their panzers rolled into battle. "Your task will be fulfilled after you have been blown up."

The tank behind would take the destroyed one's place.

"If shooting has to be done," Peiper had ordered, "it will be done while moving. There will be no stopping for anything. No booty will be taken, no confiscated enemy vehicles are to be examined."

This would be war without mercy, employing the tactics of Blitzkrieg that Peiper had practiced on the Eastern Front, where he'd earned the sobriquet "Blowtorch Peiper" after leaving villages ablaze.

"It is not the job of the spearhead to worry about prisoners of war," added Peiper.[16]

Maximum violence was required. Speed was indeed of the essence, but in densely forested areas and along narrow winding roads that crossed small bridges, his force could go only so far, so fast. Delays because of broken-down or destroyed tanks became increasingly infuriating.

A Tiger II would block a narrow lane and stall dozens of others, leaving Peiper's forces trailing behind for hundreds of yards, offering up stationary targets. Thankfully, for the time being, thick cloud cover protected Peiper's forces from what they knew would be savage Allied attacks from the air.

By afternoon on December 16, German forces had pushed more than ten miles into Allied territory. Lieutenant Tony Moody of the 28th Infantry Division, in the center of the Allied line in the Ardennes, recalled how panic spread as more and more Germans stormed through American lines, leaving his and other units stranded: "If you feel you're surrounded by overwhelming forces, you get the hell out of it. I was demoralized, sick as a dog. . . . You just want to die. We felt the Germans were much better trained, better equipped, a better fighting machine than us."[17]

LATER THAT DAY, Omar Bradley met with Eisenhower at the Supreme Headquarters Allied Expeditionary Force (SHAEF), at Trianon Palace Hotel in Versailles, and finally learned of the extent of the German offensive.

Bradley still didn't consider it a serious threat.

His boss did.

"That's no spoiling attack," said Eisenhower.[18]

The planned December 19 strike toward the Rhine, which had preoccupied Patton and others, would clearly have to be called off.

A very different battle now had to be won.

It would fall to Bradley to tell Patton.

Bradley said Patton would not be pleased. He was bound to protest.

"Tell him that Ike is running this damn war," snapped Eisenhower.[19]

Bradley returned to his headquarters in Luxembourg. "I finally got to bed around midnight," he recalled. "But I could not sleep. I lay awake most of the night mulling over the impact of this massive attack. We had been caught flat-footed."[20]

WHILE BRADLEY FRETTED that night of December 16–17, at his headquarters at the Adlerhorst, Hitler was on the telephone to

Hermann Balck, commander of Army Group G, which was south of the Ardennes.

Hitler was exultant—Dietrich's Sixth Panzer Army was rolling toward the Losheim Gap, and the strategically vital town of Bastogne was within the Fifth Panzer Army's grasp.

Providence had indeed been kind—there was thick cloud cover.

The Allied air forces were no threat.

"Balck! Balck!" exclaimed Hitler. "Everything has changed in the West! Success—complete success—is now in our grasp!"[21]

# CHAPTER 4

## Blood and Iron

**Malmedy, Belgium**
**December 17, 1944**

THE WEATHER was indeed on Hitler's side. According to an Eighth Air Force B-17 pilot, Charles "Mac" McCauley of the 385th Bomb Group, that morning of December 17, "fog [had] rolled in over the battlefield and air power was grounded. . . . We read the news, knowing the bombers could be rushed in to change the flow of German ground forces. The fog was so heavy we couldn't see fifty feet."[1]

German tank commanders looked to the skies in gratitude. The SS veteran leading arguably the most critical spearhead, Lieutenant Colonel Jochen Peiper, had been delayed the day before and was now desperate to make up for lost time. If he didn't reach his first critical objective, the Meuse River, within twenty-four hours, he believed Hitler's entire offensive would flounder.

That morning, his force made steady progress and reached the village of Malmedy in Belgium. Men from several American units were herded into a field after being captured, among them Harold Billow, a twenty-one-year-old soldier serving with the 285th Field Artillery Observation Battalion.[2]

Germans belonging to Peiper's unit, recalled Billow, set up two machine guns in the field where he and more than a hundred others were made to stand.[3]

A German officer pulled out a pistol and shot a man to Billow's right and another to his left. Then machine guns opened up on Billow and others in the field.[4]

Billow and another soldier, Jim Mattera, were lucky to survive the ensuing massacre, in which at least eighty Americans were murdered.

Finally, the firing ceased and the German executioners left, but then tanks in Kampfgruppe Peiper approached.

Mattera could hear the "tanks and half-tracks winding up, rrmmmm, rrmmmm. Down the road they come. Everyone who went by opened up with a machine gun. . . . Brrep! Jesus Christ, I thought they'd never stop. Finally, no more hollering. I'm laying there, about ten degrees that afternoon. Jesus Christ, my heart is in my mouth."

He guessed he had not been hit. "I couldn't feel nothing burning. I kinda surmised when you're shot you're gonna hurt. When I hit the ground, my helmet flew off. I was twenty and had plenty of hair. I'm laying there bareheaded. Finally, I thought I heard somebody walking, there was maybe an inch or two of snow. Somebody's here, I thought. Thank God I didn't open my eyes to look. I was too scared to open them."

Mattera lay still as men from the 1st SS Panzer Regiment finished off any wounded soldier whom they believed was still alive. They spent twenty minutes doing so, some shouting: "You sons of bitches."[5]

The SS kicked GIs in the groin to see if they were still breathing, and if they were, the Germans then shot them in the head. Mettera recalled: "Finally I got enough nerve to open my eyes and looked at all the bodies laying there all which away." Eventually, Mattera managed to get back to American lines.

Another soldier, Bill Merriken, of Battery B of the 285th Field Artillery Observation Battalion, had also been lined up in the field.[6] "The fellow on top of me was completely out of his head," recalled Merriken. "I was trying to keep still, [trying] not to make any noise. But he was in such extreme pain that he started rolling over. I was face down, so I couldn't see what was going on. But he rolled over . . . drawing the attention of two German soldiers."

The SS men walked over to where Merriken lay. "I sensed they were right over us. Then they shot him with a pistol. The bullet went through him into my right knee. He didn't move anymore. I kept perfectly still. I don't know how I did it. But I did. Then I lost all sense of time. I was flat down, my head turned to the left and my left arm covering my eyes and head and face."

Merriken knew that if the Germans saw his frosty breath, he would be killed. "It was so cold that day, just fifteen degrees. If your mouth was exposed, the Germans would see the vapor and they'd know you were alive, so I lay perfectly still. I heard the Germans smashing men's heads with the butts of their guns."[7]

Merriken lay as motionless as possible for two hours, then

crawled to a farmhouse where locals tended to him. He too finally made it to the American lines and would then spend four months in a hospital recovering from his wounds.

News of what had happened at Malmedy, first brought by the few survivors, spread fast through the American lines. One soldier recalled: "Somehow during combat news such as that travels throughout the troops with lightning-like speed."[8]

The massacre incensed the American soldiers who heard about it. Many vowed to show no mercy.

"American troops are now refusing to take any more prisoners," it was noted in the US Ninth Army's war diary, "and it may well spread to include all German soldiers."[9]

Jewish GIs had particular reason to be afraid of being captured, given the reputation of the SS after the Malmedy Massacre. One soldier, Ray Leopold, a replacement in the 28th Division, remembered being approached by his Jewish sergeant less than an hour after he learned what had happened at Malmedy, which was just a few miles away.

"Ray," said the sergeant, "why don't you do what I'm doing? Take your dog-tag with the big letter 'H' on it, wrap it around your hand, put your glove back on. If by chance you're ever forced to surrender . . . as you raise your hand, throw the glove together with the dog-tag into the snow and step on it. . . . If you are captured and identified as Jewish, from what we know that has happened just a short distance away, you will not live."[10]

Leopold did as he was advised and survived the war.

Elsewhere that day, the Waffen SS committed another atrocity, torturing and then murdering eleven men from the African American 333rd Field Artillery Battalion near the village of

Wereth. Sadly, this incident, although investigated by the same unit that examined the crimes committed at Malmedy, was not officially recognized in the US until 2017.[11]

Jochen Peiper's men in the 1st SS Panzer Regiment pushed on, killing civilians as well as yet more defenseless GIs and prisoners of war, practicing a particularly merciless form of Blitzkrieg.

PEIPER'S FORCE CONTINUED westward, growing more and more frustrated by delays: American resistance was proving surprisingly effective, even though the Germans outnumbered US troops three to one.

According to the German schedule, Manteuffel's Fifth Panzer Army was supposed to seize the town of Bastogne in Belgium that day, December 17. Three German armored divisions were in fact pushing toward it. But elements from the 28th Infantry Division and the 705th Tank Destroyer Battalion stood in the way.

Under severe pressure, outmanned and outgunned, the American units managed that day to prevent the Germans from seizing Bastogne, which had some four thousand inhabitants.[12] "We'd drop back and fire," recalled one GI. "Drop back and fire . . . apparently we were trying to protect Bastogne. I had never heard of Bastogne."[13]

For several hundred years, the market town had been protected by high walls, some of which still survived. Renowned for its timber supply and cattle fairs, it had prospered before the First World War. Surrounded by thick pine forests and lush pasture, and some fifteen hundred feet above sea level, it had been occupied by Hitler's troops for more than four years until liberated the previous September 10. Now the Germans appeared set to retake the town and surely punish those who had welcomed the Americans just a few months ago.

That day, the 28th Division's 110th Infantry Regiment had been particularly impressive in holding off the far larger German force. The commander of the 26th Volksgrenadier Division, Major General Heinz Kokott, concurred. Tasked with storming through the 28th Division's lines, he later stated: "What had not been expected to such an extent was the way the remnants of the beaten units of the 28th did not give up the battle. They stayed put and continued to block the road [to Bastogne]. Fighting a delaying battle . . . individual groups time and again confronted our assault detachments from dominating heights, defiles, on both sides of gullies and on forest paths."

These remnants had been the equal of Hitler's best troops. "They let the attacking parties run into their fire," added Kokott, "engaged them in a fire duel, made evading movements with great skill and speed and then conducted unexpected counter-thrusts into flanks and rear."[14]

IT WAS also that day, December 17, 1944, that the first reports of the German offensive in the Ardennes appeared in the American press. For several months, newspapers had tracked the seemingly inexorable Allied advance. "Arrows pointed here and there where different armies were going," remembered a newspaper delivery boy in California. "And then, all of a sudden, there was this bulge in the map that was going back the other way. . . . What's happening here? Are we losing now that we're this close?"[15]

The German counterattack was both embarrassment and humiliation for Allied Supreme Commander Dwight Eisenhower. "The morning of December 17 it became clear that the German attack was in great strength," he recalled. "Two gaps were torn through our line, one on the front of the 106th Division, the other on the front of the 28th. Reports were confusing and exact information meager, but it was clear the enemy was employing considerable armor and was progressing rapidly westward."[16]

At Patton's headquarters in Luxembourg that day, the German offensive was urgently discussed.

"The thing in the north is the real McCoy," said Patton.

One senior officer, Colonel Halley Maddox, saw a great opportunity for Patton's forces.

"If they will roll with the punch up north," said Maddox, "we can pinwheel the enemy before he gets very far. In a week we could expose the whole German rear and trap their main forces west of the Rhine."[17]

Patton agreed with Maddox. But he was skeptical about Montgomery, in command of Allied forces "up north," and about his willingness to go on the offensive so soon.

"That isn't the way those gentlemen up north fight," said Patton. "They aren't made that way. That's too daring for them. My guess is . . . we will have to go up there and save their hides."[18]

With that in mind, Patton made certain that the 4th Armored Division, which had roared across France that summer, would be available to him rather than deployed elsewhere.

Patton could count on the 4th Armored Division to get to its objectives faster than any other unit he commanded. For both the Americans and the Germans, he knew, the key to victory was covering as much ground as possible in the shortest time.

Patton's tankers knew it too.

"Speed, speed," remembered Nat Frankel with the 4th Armored. "Obsessiveness with speed permeated our lives. No one even had to tell us; there were no orders from Patton to move faster. It was understood, it was a given. . . . Put your fastest men on the fastest ground. He turned to the 4th Armored Division, and we were designated as the vanguard of the Third Army advance."[19]

Patton was bellicose and confident. By contrast, Eisenhower was increasingly concerned as more reports filtered through to him in Versailles that day. His strategy of attacking the Third Reich along a broad front appeared utterly flawed, given how thinly the Ardennes had been manned.

The German advance was indeed alarming. German tanks were just eight miles from the headquarters of the US First Army at Spa by that evening. The headquarters was quickly abandoned, like so many other American positions.

American forces needed to be rushed to the front to prevent disaster. But Eisenhower had no infantry divisions in reserve. They had all been deployed. The only men available belonged to airborne divisions—the 82nd and 101st—which were recovering from the failed attempt to cross the Rhine that September, Operation Market Garden, which had been Montgomery's brainchild.[20]

Neither division was suited to the intense ground warfare

raging in the Ardennes. But they were all Eisenhower had available, and so that very same evening of December 17, the 101st Airborne, known as the Screaming Eagles, was instructed to get to Bastogne, a hundred miles away, as quickly as possible. It was a formidable challenge—many men from the battered unit were on passes in Paris.

MPs roamed streets in the city, looking for paratroopers. One private remembered: "MPs came and called out everyone who was wearing a Screaming Eagle patch, telling us there was an emergency and we were to return to our base [in Mourmelon] at once."[21]

The private didn't even get to finish his dinner.

Another GI was in a bar when MPs entered and told him and his buddies to get on a truck immediately. There was no time to finish their drinks.

In one barracks later that night at Mourmelon in northern France, a sergeant received a phone call from an officer.

The men were to be woken and told to move out.

"Yes, sir!"

The sergeant ran into the barracks.

"Everybody up! Everybody up! We're moving out."

Many men had fought hard during Operation Market Garden. They were far from happy. They deserved a rest.

The sergeant was suddenly a target: "I was deluged with a barrage of boots—mess kits—everything imaginable. I was lucky to get out of there alive."[22]

A captain from the South gathered his unit, which he had led since April 1944 through Normandy and then Holland. He knew his men had lost many good friends. They had lived on meager rations for months and had been promised the delights of Paris.

"I can't tell you a goddamned thing about what we'll be doing," drawled the captain, "except at this time we'll be in the Corps reserve."

He knew he had to be as direct as he could with his men. He'd lose respect if he didn't tell them they were going back to combat.

"I know you've got men who can't take any more of this shit," he added, "so I want you to single them out and leave them behind. Draw ammo and rations from the supply room. Remember, it's winter. Take overcoats, overshoes, extra blankets. We leave as soon as the trucks get here, so get cracking!"[23]

It was the first time the Screaming Eagles would go to war in trucks rather than in gliders or C-47 planes.

Officers joined their men in ten-ton open-top trucks. The gusts of wind felt like razor nicks to the face. The paratroopers all had to stand up, with fifty or more men crammed into each truck. The crisis was clearly so serious that the truck drivers did not bother to dim their headlights as they drove through the darkness.

One private looked back on the column of trucks as it headed toward Bastogne. All he could see was a long line of blazing lights. "There was no way to move to the back of the truck," remembered another soldier, "and every time the five-gallon can we used as a latrine got to me, it was full."[24]

The column of trucks crawled on through the night, snaking over frozen, muddy roads toward Bastogne, before halting at the arrival of another cold gray dawn on December 18. The men poured gasoline into puddles and set them ablaze for warmth, while some, needing to boil water for coffee, filled empty C ration cans with gasoline-drenched pebbles and lit them.

Underway again, the trucks passed frightened-looking GIs from the 28th Division walking single file away from Bastogne.

Every now and again, an exasperated paratrooper would shout out from a truck, "Hey, you fellas are going the wrong way!"[25]

Meanwhile, the Germans were doing their best to reach Bastogne first.

Hans Herbst, who belonged to the "Windhund" 116th Panzer Division, recalled leaving that morning for Bastogne in a half-track in frigid temperatures.

Herbst spotted none other than Fifth Panzer Army commander von Manteuffel, who was just five feet, two inches tall. He was standing on a Panther tank, shouting at his troops as they crossed into Belgium.

*"Schneller, schneller!"*

Faster, faster![26]

Manteuffel himself recalled: "The importance of Bastogne was considerable. In enemy hands it must influence all the movements in the west, damage our supply system, and tie up considerable German forces. It was therefore essential that we capture it at once."[27]

One American paratrooper remembered passing through the town of Arlon, around twenty-five miles from Bastogne, that afternoon. "It was snowing, but the Christmas lights were on, people were shopping and it was about the prettiest scene you could ever imagine. After passing through Arlon we made a turn in the road and the truck headlights showed a sign saying 'Bastogne,' white letters on a dark blue background. I had never heard of Bastogne, but something told me that it was a name that I would never forget."[28]

The skies were still overcast that day, yet again preventing the Allies from launching effective bombing. Some Ninth Air Force fighter pilots, flying P-47s, did manage to get into action, strafing and thereby slowing the spearhead of Kampfgruppe Peiper, which had committed the Malmedy Massacre. Those pilots bought precious time for engineers to blow key bridges and further slow the SS advance.

IN LUXEMBOURG, Bradley called Patton on the telephone.

"I want you to come to Luxembourg as soon as you can," said Bradley. "I will have to tell you something that I'm afraid you won't like, but it can't be helped."[29]

Patton and three of his staff were on their way less than ten minutes later. It was an hour's journey in jeeps for Patton and his staff, beneath sullen skies.

The convoy of jeeps made its way into Luxembourg City and then to its center.

Patton's staff was met outside a brick railroad building by an MP who insisted on checking each man's identity. Germans dressed as Americans, led by the notorious SS commando Otto Skorzeny, had infiltrated behind American lines and had sown considerable confusion and panic. Paranoia ran deep.

Patton and his staff entered a crowded operations room inside Omar Bradley's headquarters.

Bradley himself waited beside a situation map that indicated his Twelfth Army Group's positions.

The map showed where the Germans had smashed through American lines and pushed into Allied territory, as far as fifty miles in the case of the Sixth Panzer Army.[30]

Seven Panzer divisions were shown on the map. Fourteen German divisions in all had been identified. This had caused Bradley to wonder "just where in hell has this sonuvabitch gotten all his strength?"[31]

It was not all doom and gloom.

The map showed that the southern and northern shoulders of the Allied line in the Ardennes were holding.

The center was another matter altogether.

Bradley recalled: "By the following morning, December 18, the center of our line in the Ardennes had been crushed. . . . Manteuffel's panzers had smashed through the 28th Division [and were headed] for Bastogne almost midway between the city of Luxembourg and Liège. To the north of the unlucky 28th, two regiments of the 106th had already been encircled in position."[32]

The German salient was some sixty miles wide—thrust into the heart of the Ardennes.

Bradley told Patton he had already taken action concerning the weak central position, ordering the 101st Airborne to Bastogne. He had also deployed the 10th Armored Division, part of Patton's Third Army—a move that had annoyed Patton but that he now understood upon examining the map.

Bradley's decision to use the 10th Armored would soon prove to be critical. The unit would be the first large force to reach Bastogne. That day, Combat Command B of the division would take up positions in three villages to the east of the town, in the hopes of further delaying the German advance, just as the 28th Infantry Division had done the previous day. With only seventy-five tanks and twenty-eight hundred men, Combat Command B succeeded in slowing the Germans—some fifty thousand troops backed by three hundred tanks—thereby buying time for the 101st Airborne to arrive and earning the Presidential Unit Citation in the process.

Bradley now had to break the bad news.

"George, I feel you won't like what we are going to do, but I fear it is necessary."[33]

He explained that Patton's planned December 19 offensive was not possible.

Patton did not protest.

He knew the situation was grave.

"What can you do to help?" asked Bradley.[34]

Patton said he'd have three divisions ready to attack within forty-eight hours.

Bradley liked the sound of that. He wanted to strike back and "hit this bastard hard."

"What the hell," said Patton, "we'll still be killing Krauts."[35]

Patton listened as Bradley outlined his next moves.

It was critical to prevent the Germans from using the roads leading west of Bastogne.

Patton said he would reposition the 4th Armored Division so that it could attack toward Bastogne. "The 80th Division can be removed from the line," he added, "and it can start for Luxembourg in the morning. The 26th Division, even though it has four thousand green replacements from headquarters units, can be alerted to move in 24 hours."[36]

Patton then telephoned his chief of staff, Hobart Gay—known as Hap—and gave him instructions to carry out what he'd just told Bradley. Patton was soon being driven back to his headquarters, not knowing how far the Germans had pushed. Might he run into the enemy?

The drive was done in total darkness without headlights. In his diary, Patton later noted: "A very dangerous operation, which I hate."[37]

Once Patton reached his headquarters, he telephoned Bradley.

"The situation . . . is much worse than it was when I talked to you," said Bradley. "You and a staff officer meet me for a conference with General Eisenhower at Verdun at approximately 11.00."[38]

"Will do," said Patton.

Patton hung up and then spoke to Hap Gay.

"I want you to call a special staff session for 0800 tomorrow."[39]

Meanwhile, American troops continued their journey toward Bastogne. Fortunately, the officer leading the 101st Airborne's advance, Lieutenant Colonel Julian Ewell, the commander of the 501st Parachute Infantry Regiment (PIR), knew where he was going. Earlier the previous month, he had visited Bastogne and therefore was familiar with the town.

Ewell was a twenty-nine-year-old graduate of West Point who had parachuted into Normandy on D Day. "During the evening of 18 December," he recalled, "I met many groups of men, Americans, coming down the roads from the north and northeast. . . . I stopped some of them."

The men fleeing the Germans had been taken utterly by surprise and stunned by the ferocity of the attack. Some units had been decimated.

"We have been wiped out," some men said.

They were lost. They didn't know where they'd been or where they were going, only that it was away from death. "It was useless to talk to them," remembered Ewell. "I tried several times and so did others around me. Finally, we realized we were wasting our time and then we paid almost no attention to them."[40]

THE COMMANDER of the 101st Airborne, Major General Maxwell D. Taylor, was not with his men as they finally made their way into Bastogne. He had been called away to attend a staff conference in Washington, DC. In his absence, command of the division had passed to the rather dour Brigadier General Anthony McAuliffe, who had been in charge of the division's artillery and had received the Distinguished Service Cross for jumping into Normandy.[41]

Forty-six-year-old Anthony Clement McAuliffe had just missed out on the First World War, after graduating from West Point in November 1918. He had become assistant division commander of the Screaming Eagles after his predecessor had been killed on D Day. By now he had clocked up more than a hundred days of combat command.[42]

McAuliffe was an unimposing figure with a broad face; he lacked the ego and vanity of Patton and the charisma of James Gavin, who led the 82nd Airborne. But soon he would become a giant. He recalled arriving in Bastogne: "I drove into town on

December 18 with Colonel Kinnard, my assistant chief of staff. We took a car and drove around for about an hour, and I showed him where every unit should be. I don't want to sound conceited, but the Lord must have led me by the hand. I had no map or anything and yet the disposition turned out just right. It permitted us to commit all our regiments to the best advantage."

Artillery would be critical. McAuliffe knew he was doomed without it. "We had about sixty guns," he remembered. "We figured the angle of the shell and time on target and we placed them in such a way that each could swing 360 degrees and zero in on any section of the battlefield. Within two minutes, we could hit any point where the Germans were breaking through."[43]

The Screaming Eagles had reached Bastogne in the nick of time. The question now was how long they could hold the town. Facing an enemy force five times larger and without winter clothing or adequate supplies of food, ammunition, and medicine, the paratroopers confronted seemingly insurmountable odds. They had surely been sent on a fool's errand that could end only one way—in bloody tragedy.

AT MIDNIGHT THAT December 18, German civilians all across the Third Reich listened to the news on their radios.

There were uplifting reports on the great new battle being waged in the Ardennes:

*The speedy collapse of every organized Allied defense has considerably eased our tasks!*

*We have all been asking ourselves why is the Führer so silent.*

*Perhaps he is ill? Now we can tell you. The Führer is enjoying excellent health, but he is preparing this new offensive down to the minutest details. His silence has been worth it. The enemy has received a shock!*

*We must force the enemy to throw in the sponge. He must realize that the battle no longer pays!*[44]

Germans heard the news with relief. There was cause for hope. All was not lost. The Third Reich might yet be saved.

# CHAPTER 5

---

# Crisis at Verdun

**Verdun, France**
**December 19, 1944**

GENERAL GEORGE S. PATTON was seated once more in the front row at his daily staff meeting, which began at 8 A.M. sharp. He had slept soundly the night before, despite the troubling news of the German advances in the Ardennes.

One of Patton's staff gave details of the German attack.

Patton got to his feet.

"Gentlemen," he said, "what has occurred up north is no occasion for excitement. As you know, alarm spreads very quickly in a military command. You must be extremely careful in a critical situation such as this not to give rise to any undue concern among the troops."

Patton paused for effect.

"Our plans have changed! We're going to fight, but in a different place. Also, we are going to have to move very fast!"

Patton's staff had not forgotten the heady days of summer, when they had barreled across France, nor the bitter slog through Lorraine. Movement was always welcome. The quicker the better.

"We pride ourselves on our ability to move quickly," added Patton. "But we're going to have to do it faster now than we've ever done before. I have no doubt that we will meet all demands made on us. You always have and I know you will do so again this time. And whatever happens, we will keep right on doing as we have always done—killing Germans wherever we find the sons of bitches."[1]

Patton explained how the Third Army would now attack on "three possible axes."

A formidable challenge confronted Patton and his staff. They had to turn nine divisions ninety degrees during a battle, using a poor road network in icy and wet conditions that would complicate matters. Patton would need to make sure his Third Army was also adequately supplied, which was difficult at the best of times.

At that morning's meeting was Colonel Karl R. Bendetsen, Omar Bradley's chief combat liaison officer.

"Bendetsen," said Patton, "there's something you can do for me and I believe you can do it if you really want to."

"Sir, anything you request is an order. I will give it all I've got."

"I need a freight train. . . . You know where more supplies and equipment and transportation gear are located in France than anybody else I know. . . . I do not know whether there are any freight trains immediately available; nevertheless I want one and I call upon you to provide it by all means, fair or foul."

Bendetsen was a canny operator and later recalled managing to "steal a freight train" for Patton.[2]

IT WAS ALMOST 9 A.M. The briefing had lasted exactly an hour.

"Gentlemen," Patton concluded, "I'm going to Verdun to see the Supreme Commander. I want you to polish up the plan separately for each of the axes. I'm leaving a code name for each eventuality with General Gay. Be ready to jump with the one whose code name I'm going to phone back."[3]

Patton left the room and was soon on his way, in a jeep driven by his driver, John Mims; he left his headquarters in Nancy at 9:15 A.M.

It was a dreary, overcast day, which meant the Allied air forces again could do little. Patton's prayer for good weather had yet to be answered. "The weather was so terrible," recalled Otto P. Weyland, commanding general of the XIX Tactical Air Command. Snowfall was particularly frustrating. "It was white when you looked down," added Weyland, "white when you looked up, white when you looked [ahead]. Tanks and trucks were painted white. It was a most difficult situation."[4]

A B-17 pilot in England noted in his diary: "Boy, what a fog there is this morning. We were going to bomb a marshalling yard right behind the lines to try to stop the Nazi drive back to Belgium. I guess they're really driving the boys back. We could have done them a lot of good, if we could have taken off today."[5]

Patton's destination was a barracks in Verdun, some seventy miles away. That was where Eisenhower's senior generals were to gather later that morning of Tuesday, December 19, for a crisis conference.

Eisenhower arrived in a bulletproof Cadillac, having been driven from his headquarters at Versailles. He was accompanied by a small convoy of aides and security staff.

Bradley and Patton were on time, and they gathered with their entourages in a squad room around 11:30 A.M. before filing upstairs to take their seats at a long table in a drab room on the second floor of the stone barracks.

A single potbellied stove gave off feeble heat.

Patton's aide Colonel Charles Codman, a decorated World War I pilot, watched as the meeting began: "I have seldom seen longer faces. General [Kenneth] Strong got up before a situation map and gave a short exposé of the picture. It was grim. When he sat down, General Eisenhower spoke."[6]

"The present situation," said Eisenhower, "is to be regarded as one of opportunity for us and not of disaster. There will be only cheerful faces at this conference table."

Patton needed no cheering up.

"Hell, let's have the guts to [let the Germans] go all the way to Paris. Then we'll really cut 'em off and chew 'em up."

Eisenhower smiled but then told Patton that the Germans would "never be allowed to cross the Meuse."[7]

"George," Eisenhower told Patton, "I want you to go to Luxembourg and take charge."

"Yes, sir."

"When can you start up there?"

"Now."

"You mean today?"

"I mean as soon as you have finished with me here."[8]

Some generals laughed. Others sat up, backs straight, in their chairs.

Bradley and Eisenhower seemed impressed.[9]

"Don't be fatuous, George," cautioned Eisenhower. "If you go that early, you won't have all three divisions ready and you'll go piecemeal. You will start on the twenty-second, and I want your initial blow to be a strong one! I'd even settle for the twenty-third if it takes that long to get three full divisions."[10]

Patton pulled out a cigar and lit it. He looked at Bradley and gestured toward the situation map on a nearby wall showing the German advances.

"Brad, this time the Kraut's stuck his head in a meat-grinder."

Patton clenched his fist and then twisted it.

"And this time I've got hold of the handle."[11]

The meeting ended.

As Eisenhower was leaving the barracks, he showed Patton the five stars on his shoulder.

"Funny thing, George," said Eisenhower, "every time I get promoted, I get attacked."

"Yes," replied Patton, "and every time you get attacked, I bail you out."[12]

Eisenhower grinned.

They shook hands.

Bradley's aide Major Chester Hansen looked on. In his diary,

Hansen later wrote of Eisenhower: "There's something about the guy, the way he brushes along, the way he breaks out in a big grin, the way his voice, harsh and loud, cracks out, that disarms all within his vicinity. That's the way he is, gay, loud, democratic, dynamic, thinking fast, acting fast, spreading confidence."[13]

Patton contacted his headquarters before leaving Verdun and gave instructions.

"Everyone is a son-of-a-bitch to someone," Patton stressed. "Be better sons-of-bitches than they are."[14]

With Patton was Codman and another aide, Colonel Paul Harkins. He told Harkins to contact his chief of staff, Hap Gay.

"Telephone Gay. Give him the code number [sic], tell him to get started. . . . You know what to do."

"Yes, sir."

"Codman, you come with me. Tell Mims we start in five minutes—for Luxembourg.

"Telephone General Walker," Patton added, "and tell him I will stop and see him in Thionville on the way."

Walton Walker was in command of the Third Army's XX Corps and had previously led the 3rd Armored Division.[15]

Patton's orders that morning were carried out with astonishing speed. The Third Army was already on the move, as Bradley saw for himself as he returned to Luxembourg and passed a convoy of Patton's III Corps trucks.


EISENHOWER MIGHT have appeared confident and decisive, but it was Patton who was the most effective that day. His aide

Charles Codman remembered that within an hour of the meeting in Verdun, Patton had his Third Army primed: "Everything had been thrashed out—the divisions to be employed, objectives, new Army boundaries, the amount of our own front to be extricated for a counterattack in the Ardennes."[16]

Patton's journey to Walker's headquarters in Thionville, some fifty miles to the east, would probably take several hours in a jeep, given the woeful state of the roads. Mims did his best, squeezing past a steady stream of tanks and trucks. Patton didn't speak. He was all business, one ivory-handled pistol tucked in his waistband and another "strapped to his parka."[17] Destiny called louder than ever before.

Patton had immense faith in his own abilities. Those qualities would now be sorely needed. Before the Allied invasion of North Africa, Operation Torch, in November 1942, he had written in his diary: "I can't decide logically if I am a man of destiny or a lucky fool, but I think I am destined. . . . I feel that my claim to greatness hangs on an ability to lead and inspire. . . . I am a genius—I think I am."[18]

In May 1940, with his nation imperiled, Winston Churchill felt upon becoming prime minister that all his "past life had been but a preparation for this hour and for this trial."[19]

For Patton now, his own entire life had led to this moment.

Now too was Patton's hour.


THE SITUATION that morning in Bastogne was desperate, even though many men from the 101st Airborne had arrived to help the elements of the 10th Armored, which had slowed the German advance, ensuring that Bastogne remained in US hands.[20]

Twenty-year-old Phil Burge belonged to the 10th Armored. He recalled that morning of December 19, as snow fell and yet more Screaming Eagles arrived in Bastogne.[21]

The paratroopers were marching into town as other American troops beat a hasty retreat.

"Run! Run!" cried some panicked men.

"They'll murder you!"

"They'll kill you! They've got everything, tanks, machine guns, air power, everything!"[22]

The arriving paratroopers were short on everything they needed to hold Bastogne.

"Where's the ammo?" one paratrooper asked. "We can't fight without ammo."

"Got any ammo?" asked another Screaming Eagle.

"Sure, buddy," replied one retreating soldier, "glad to let you have it."[23]

An officer from the 7th Tank Destroyer Group encountered an American artillery unit pulling back, southwest of Bastogne.

"Where are you going?" asked the officer.

"We're retreating, sir."

"The hell you are. This is where you turn around and fight."[24]

ELSEWHERE IN the Ardennes that afternoon, tragedy was unfolding. By 3:30 P.M., thousands of men in the 106th Division were surrounded. The 422nd Infantry Regiment, commanded by Colonel George Descheneaux, came under terrible attack by panzers in a wooded area.

Officers gathered with Descheneaux in a trench.

"We're like fish in a pond," he said.[25]

The regiment was fast running out of ammunition, water, and medical supplies.

The Germans were shelling the regiment's positions relentlessly.

One of Descheneaux's company commanders, Captain James Perkins, had his leg blown off, with blood "pouring from the stump."[26]

Other men were crying out in pain.

"My God," said Descheneaux, "we're being slaughtered!"

He didn't "believe in fighting for glory" if it meant many more men being killed for no good reason.

"It looks like we'll have to pack it in."[27]

Descheneaux asked a group of officers for their views.

None wanted to surrender. But there seemed little option.

One officer, the commander of the 589th Field Artillery Battalion, Lieutenant Colonel Thomas Kelly, argued that it would be dark in an hour and they could then try to escape.

Descheneaux disagreed.

"As far as I'm concerned," he said, resigned to surrender, "I'm going to save the lives of as many men as I can, and I don't care if I'm court-martialed."

According to one account, men "began to break their weapons against the tree trunks" in an effort to keep them out of German hands. Meanwhile, Descheneaux began to cry "like a baby." Looking up from his slit trench, the colonel saw several young officers staring down with a mixture of pity and contempt.

"Do you want me to take the white flag?" asked one officer, Major William J. Cody Garlow, grandson of the famous frontiersman Buffalo Bill Cody.[28]

Descheneaux said he should.

Less than a mile away, Colonel Charles Cavender, the commander of the 423rd Regiment, had come to the same conclusion—it was futile to fight on. Like Descheneaux, he gathered his officers and explained the situation.

"I was a GI in the First World War," Cavender told his men, "and I want to see things from the soldier's standpoint."

Fighting on was pointless, most agreed.

"Gentlemen, we're surrendering at 1600."[29]

Lieutenant Alan Jones Jr., also of the 423rd Infantry Regiment, remembered: "A runner came to me with a message. All weapons were to be rendered inoperable. And all units were to stand fast. While the number of casualties had piled up . . . I was surprised that we weren't given the option to try to scatter and infiltrate our way out."

Jones and others might have been able to get back to Allied lines but it would have been a considerable challenge, given the overwhelming superiority of the German troops in the vicinity. Jones did not attempt to escape imprisonment, he recalled, because he thought he should stay with his men and make sure they were not abused by their captors. "That was dumb," he remembered bitterly. "The Germans, just as we did, separated officers and noncoms from the rest of the prisoners. There is no way to take care of your men or exert control over the situation."[30]

SOME THREE THOUSAND men from the division surrendered that afternoon. One of them was a chaplain, Father Paul Cavanaugh of the 422nd Infantry Regiment.

Patches of snow dotted a cornfield as Cavanaugh and others pulled back beneath dark clouds.

Cavanaugh was trudging through the snow at the rear of a column, praying for the men in his regiment who had been killed, when he heard gunfire.

Trucks had stopped ahead of him.

Chaos and panic ensued as men jumped out of vehicles and took cover. Then there was the snarl of enemy machine guns.

From cover, Cavanaugh could see four German tanks in the distance firing on the column.

Bullets hit the ground nearby.

Cavanaugh began to pray out loud: "Mary, my Mother, help me."

He realized he was not afraid to die.[31]

The tanks kept firing. He had lost his sense of time when he heard a soldier cry out: "*Kamerad!*" [comrade].

Cavanaugh lifted his head from the ground and saw an American medic waving a white flag. "With tears of shame and frustration in our eyes," he remembered, "we raised our hands over our heads and advanced slowly toward the tanks."

Weapons were seized and men were lined up and searched.

Medics were soon busy tending to the injured. Then Cavanaugh saw Germans grabbing supplies from jeeps.

Cavanaugh left the line of prisoners and ran over to the Germans.

"I am a priest! A priest!" he shouted. "Let me go to take care of the wounded."[32]

The Germans were surprised, but quickly realized that he was a priest from the markings on his helmet and a brassard on his sleeve.

"*Ja, ja,*" said a German. "*Priester, Katholisch!*"

"*Ja, ja,*" Cavanaugh replied. "Let me go to the wounded in the field."

From a pocket Cavanaugh produced "oil stocks containing the oleum infirmorum"—holy oil with which he intended to anoint wounded soldiers.

A German soldier tried to take it from his hand.

"No . . . oleum sanctum—holy oil!" Cavanaugh said, making the sign of the cross and gesturing toward a field of dead and wounded.

The German relented.

Cavanaugh soon found a soldier with a bullet wound to his head on the verge of death.[33] Cavanaugh reached for the man's dog tag, which read: *Harold Greenspan, Hebrew.* Within seconds, the man died in the priest's arms.

Then in a column, five men abreast, Cavanaugh and the other POWs were led away toward the Third Reich.

A teenage German soldier, having seen Cavanaugh was a priest, moved over to him as the POWs walked. The teenager

CRISIS AT VERDUN                    69

was carrying cartons of American cigarettes, freshly seized booty.

"Here, you are a good priest."

Cavanaugh said thank you and took the cigarettes, knowing his fellow prisoners would soon be desperate for some kind of relief.[34]

MEANWHILE, THREE DIVISIONS from the Fifth Panzer Army pressed toward Bastogne. Screaming Eagle Pfc. Robert Wickham remembered that the fog was so thick that he couldn't see more than thirty yards. "We hadn't gone far," he recalled, "when we met a man from the 28th Infantry Division retreating. He had a bazooka, which I confiscated since he obviously had no use for it. He said he had knocked out a tank shortly before and had no more ammo."

Wickham and his men rounded a bend in the road and then "all hell broke loose. A tank was sitting just around the corner and it opened fire, demolishing a jeep, and then another jeep came back in reverse faster than it had passed us just a moment before . . . bullets were buzzing by so thick."

It seemed to take just seconds for Wickham to frantically dig a hole, and then a scout joined him. He saw the German tank move forward, then turn a corner. Wickham asked the scout to load the bazooka with some new ammo so he could try to take out the tank.

"It's all set to go, don't miss him!" said the scout.

Wickham had never used a bazooka. But the scout had, and

he grabbed the bazooka from Wickham and fired at the tank. There was a loud explosion but the bazooka shell had missed the tank by a few feet. To Wickham's surprise, the tank ground to a halt. "[The driver] may have thought he'd hit a mine," remembered Wickham, "but we didn't touch him. He was later knocked out and our main line of defense developed from [that] spot."[35]

The Screaming Eagles were taking casualties. Captain Willis P. McKee, a surgeon with the 101st Airborne, set up a field unit outside Bastogne. McKee knew a sizable enemy force was headed toward Bastogne because of the steady flow of refugees who passed by, escaping from the German advance.

That afternoon, McKee left the field unit and went to division headquarters in Bastogne to ask if his men could return to the town because they risked being captured by the Germans, who were clearly advancing at some speed. McKee found General McAuliffe and discussed the situation with him.

McAuliffe was insistent.

McKee was to stay where he was.

McAuliffe was confronting the full brunt of German forces led by forty-eight-year-old General Heinrich Freiherr von Lüttwitz, a former Olympic equestrian and the bespectacled commander of the 47th Panzer Corps.

"Go on back, Captain," McAuliffe ordered, "you'll be alright."[36]

It was an unfortunate command with serious consequences. Lüttwitz's forces would soon attack McKee's 326th Airborne Medical Company, whose tents had been set up northwest of Bastogne. The medical unit had no option but to surrender.

The Germans seized vital supplies such as morphine.

American casualties would now have to be treated in stables and cellars and garages in Bastogne with few trained medical staff on hand and with very little medicine. There were no cots, so men would have to be bedded on blankets on straw. The badly wounded would not last long.[37]

Yet spirits remained surprisingly high. One corporal with a leg wound entered an aid station in Bastogne crammed with casualties. He had never seen so many.

"Hey, how come you got so many wounded people around here?" he asked a medic. "Aren't we evacuating anybody?"

"Haven't you heard?" replied the medic.

"I haven't heard a damn thing."

"They've got us surrounded—the poor bastards."[38]

LATER THAT AFTERNOON, Patton arrived in the town of Thionville. General Walker was waiting in a jeep in the main square, and he led the party to his headquarters, where Patton proceeded to issue brisk orders.

It was dark by the time Patton was done. He wanted to get back to his headquarters in Luxembourg, more than forty miles to the south. Walker advised against it, warning that the road was dangerous at night. He should wait until daylight.

"All right," Patton said. "If you will lend me pajamas and a toothbrush I will spend the night and make an early start in the morning."[39]

Patton wrote in his diary that evening: "When it is considered that Harkins, Codman, and I left for Verdun at 9.15 and that between 0:800 and that hour we [held] a Staff meeting, planned three possible lines of attack, and made a simple code in which I could telephone General Gay . . . it is evident that war is not so difficult as people think."[40]

Patton knew war in the raw and relished it. One day, more than any other, had prepared him for the rigors and stress of leadership in the most challenging circumstances: September 26, 1918. Patton had been a thirty-two-year-old lieutenant colonel, serving in northern France with a newly created tank corps during the Meuse–Argonne offensive, a bloodbath that claimed twenty-six thousand American lives. That day, under the cover of fog, Patton and his soldiers had advanced beyond the security of their tanks when the mist cleared and they came under intense German machine-gun fire. Men around him jumped into a trench to avoid the bullets, and some begged Patton to join them.

"To hell with them—they can't hit me!" he roared.

Patton rallied his soldiers, shouting orders and cursing, and soon led some hundred fifty men forward. At the crest of the next hill, they again came under withering fire. Patton shook with fear, but continued to lead.

"It is time for another Patton to die," he declared.

He turned to his men.

"Who is with me?" he shouted.[41]

Patton advanced once more, followed by a few brave men. Before long, only Patton and his orderly could carry on—the others had been killed or wounded.

A bullet then hit Patton and he too fell to the ground, bleeding profusely. Before he was eventually taken to a field hospital, he insisted on making a report at division headquarters.

"I do not know of a better way to die than to be facing the enemy," Patton stated decades later before a gathering of men under his command. "I pray that I will fall forward when I am shot. That way I can keep firing my pistols!"[42]

WHILE PATTON was busy rallying his troops that afternoon of December 19, Eisenhower sent a telegram to General Montgomery: "HAVE JUST RETURNED FROM CONFERENCE WITH BRADLEY CMA PATTON. . . . PATTON MOVES NORTH WITH SIX DIVISIONS AND TAKING OVER EIGHTH CORPS TEMPORARILY WILL ORGANIZE MAJOR COUNTER BLOW."[43]

The following morning, Eisenhower made a key decision, opting to transfer command of the US First and Ninth Armies from Omar Bradley to Montgomery. The switch made sense strategically, given that the First and the Ninth were closer to Montgomery's headquarters in the north.

Eisenhower called Montgomery and got straight to the point.

"Monty, we are in a bit of a spot."

"So I gathered," replied Montgomery.

"How about taking over in the north?"

"Right."[44]

When Eisenhower's chief of staff, General Walter Bedell Smith, informed Bradley that morning, Bradley chafed at the loss of his forces to a British rival but nevertheless replied: "Bedell, it's hard for me to object. Certainly, if Monty's were an American command, I would agree with you entirely."

Eisenhower himself spoke with Bradley by telephone later that morning. By then, Bradley had changed his tune. Now he was enraged.

"By God, Ike," he shouted. "I cannot be responsible to the American people if you do this. I resign."

Eisenhower was angry and taken aback, but remained calm.

"Brad, I—not you—am responsible to the American people. Your resignation therefore means absolutely nothing."

Bradley was still not happy but did not insist on resigning.

"Well, Brad, those are my orders," Eisenhower said before hanging up.[45]

Meanwhile, Patton met with his staff to discuss the updated orders.

"Gentlemen," said Patton, "this is a hell of a Christmas present, but it was handed to me and I pass it on to you. Tonight, the Third Army turns and attacks north. I would have much preferred to have continued our attack to the east as planned, but I am a soldier. I fight where I am told, and I win where I fight!"

Patton added: "There is one encouraging factor in our favor, however. The bastards will be easier to kill coming at us above ground than they would be skulking in their holes. You have all done a grand job so far, but I expect more of you now."

Warrant Officer Fred Hose, who worked in Patton's G-2 section, recalled that Patton "announced very matter-of-factly what we were going to do, and that we were going to kick the shit out of the Germans." Patton was "excited": "This was right up General Patton's alley! He was in hog heaven. Hog heaven!"[46]

Among those listening was James O'Neill, Patton's head chaplain. The monsignor knew that he too would now see plenty of action. Patton believed chaplains were critical to victory. "He wanted a chaplain to be above average in courage, leadership and example, particularly the example of his life," recalled O'Neill. "And in time of battle, he wanted the chaplains up front, where the men were dying. And that's where the Third Army chaplains went—up front. We lost more chaplains, proportionately, than any other group."

That day, after addressing his staff, Patton called out: "Padre, are you back there?"

"Yes, sir," replied O'Neill.

"Now you get to work," ordered Patton.[47]

Patton never doubted that God was on his side. Brigadier General Harry H. Semmes served with Patton in both World Wars, and he knew better than most how much Patton relied on prayer and drew strength from his own faith. "From his adolescence," wrote Semmes, "he had always read the Bible, particularly the life of Christ and the wars of the Old Testament. He knew by heart the order of morning prayer of the Episcopal Church. His thoughts, as demonstrated daily to those close to him, repeatedly indicated that his life was dominated by a feeling of dependence on God. . . . General Patton was an unusual mixture of a profane and highly religious man."[48]

Omar Bradley concurred, writing of Patton: "He was profane, but he was also reverent. He strutted imperiously as a commander, but he knelt humbly before his God."[49]

PATTON LEFT his headquarters and headed to visit Major General Troy Middleton, commander of VIII Corps, at Arlon, some twenty miles west of Luxembourg. Patton did so only after he had made it clear to his staff that "everyone in this army must understand that we are not fighting this battle in any half-cocked manner. It's either root hog—or die. Shoot the works. If those Hun bastards want war in the raw then that's the way we'll give it to them!"[50]

In Arlon, Patton discussed the situation in Bastogne with Middleton.

Patton and the bespectacled fifty-five-year-old Middleton were old friends, having been classmates at the Army's Command and General Staff School at Fort Leavenworth in the 1920s. Middleton had, like Patton, served with distinction during the First World War.

"George," said Middleton, "just look at that map with all the roads converging on Bastogne. Bastogne is the hub of the wheel. If we let the Boche take it, they will be in the Meuse in a day."[51]

"All right, Troy," said Patton, "if you were in my position, where would you launch [an] attack?"[52]

They considered options, and Patton decided to attack from Arlon toward Bastogne. The road leading north from Arlon to Bastogne was best suited to tanks, and the terrain between the two towns was the least inhospitable.

Patton then left Middleton to return to Luxembourg.

Later that afternoon, Middleton talked over the radio with McAuliffe in Bastogne.

"There are three divisions in your area," said Middleton. "And the 116th Panzer is on its way. You're going to have a rough time staying there."

"Hell," replied McAuliffe, "if we pull out now, we'd be chewed to pieces."

"Well, I certainly want to hold Bastogne," Middleton replied. "But in view of recent developments I'm not sure it can be done."

"I know we can hold out for at least forty-eight hours," said McAuliffe.

"Good luck, Tony," said Middleton.[53]

That day in Bastogne, McAuliffe held a staff meeting. Fred MacKenzie from the *Buffalo Evening News*, the sole reporter in Bastogne, watched as McAuliffe "moved to the center of the room and stood alone. The easy familiarity that characterized most of Tony McAuliffe's relationships with the staff fell away for a moment."

McAuliffe looked at the faces staring back at him.

"I am staying."[54]

It was a statement of defiance, intended to stiffen resolve and prepare his staff for the hard fighting and loss of life that lay ahead.

Meanwhile, at Eisenhower's headquarters, the tension was also palpable. According to Eisenhower's personal assistant and driver, Kay Summersby, "Intelligence reported a suicide squad of at least three score Germans headed toward Versailles. . . . Their single mission, to be accomplished with ruthless, frantic zeal: the assassination of General Eisenhower."

The Allied supreme commander was, it appeared, a prime target for Hitler's best commandos. "To say the report upset the

SHAEF staff is pure understatement," added Summersby. "Security officers immediately turned headquarters compound into a virtual fortress. . . . The atmosphere was worse than that of a combat headquarters up at the front, where everyone knew how to take such a situation in stride."[55]

Eisenhower would soon lose patience. He couldn't abide being held captive in his own headquarters.

"Hell's fire," he snapped. "I'm going out for a walk. If anyone wants to shoot me, he can go right ahead. I've got to get out."[56]

By contrast, Patton the warlord was in his element. "I visited seven divisions," he boasted in his diary, "and regrouped an army alone."[57] At one point, driver John Mims allegedly said to Patton: "General, the Government is wasting a lot of money hiring a whole General Staff. You and me [have] run the Third Army all day and done a better job than they do."[58]

Patton himself noted: "It was quite a day. . . . Destiny sent for me in a hurry when things got tight. Perhaps God saved me for this effort."[59]


THE GERMAN VISE was meanwhile closing on Bastogne. By 1 P.M., all seven of the roads leading out of the town had been cut off by the Germans. That afternoon, elements from three divisions managed to encircle the town. Darkness had fallen when, at his headquarters in Bastogne, the 101st Airborne's operations officer, Lieutenant Colonel Harry Kinnard, was asked over the radio to sum up how things were going.

"Visualize the hole in the doughnut," he replied. "That's us!"[60]

After the ordeals of Normandy and Market Garden, many

Screaming Eagles were used to the idea of being stranded and isolated, with the enemy looming all around. On the outskirts of Bastogne that evening, a paratrooper from the 101st Airborne returned to his foxhole, having learned at battalion headquarters that Bastogne was now cut off.

"Welcome home!" another paratrooper called out to him in the darkness. "So, what's new?"

"We're surrounded."

"So, what's new?"[61]

# PART TWO

# Days of Thunder

I don't want to hear of any soldier under my command being captured unless he has been hit. Even if you are hit, you can still fight back.[1]

—GEORGE S. PATTON

# CHAPTER 6

## "Drive like Hell"

**SHAEF, Versailles, France**
**December 21, 1944**

"THIS IS THE SHORTEST DAY," wrote Eisenhower in his diary on Thursday, December 21, 1944, the winter solstice—not only the first day of winter but also the year's shortest span of daylight. "How I pray that it may, by some miracle, mark the beginning of improved weather."[1]

Eisenhower's prayers would not be answered that day. As was so often the case in the Ardennes during winter, when low-pressure systems could settle in for weeks on end, thick cloud cover and dense fog shrouded the battlefield yet again. One company commander recalled that it was "so foggy that one of our men found himself ten yards from a German machine-gun before he knew it. . . . Everyone had been pushed about as far as he could be. Nerves were being broken on men whom one might have thought would never weaken."[2]

Back in the United States, the now days-old crisis in the Ardennes was finally big news. A *New York Times* headline blared: "NAZI PUSH MOUNTS IN POWER, 13 DIVISIONS USED; FOG BALKS AIR BLOWS AT RAMPAGING COLUMNS."[3]

The battle for Bastogne had intensified too.[4] The market town had around eighteen thousand defenders, but they were now confronting forty-five thousand enemy troops. And the Germans were meanwhile closing on another vital objective, the Meuse River, some twenty miles west of Bastogne. Thus far, Hitler's gamble was paying off.

It all added up to arguably the greatest crisis Eisenhower had faced as Allied supreme commander, and still he could hear the clomp of armed guards' boots above his head at his Versailles headquarters as his protectors paced back and forth on the roof above, eyes searching for German commandos.

Eisenhower issued an order of the day: "By rushing out from his fixed defenses the enemy may give us the chance to turn his great gamble into his worst defeat. . . . Let everyone hold before him a single thought—to destroy the enemy on the ground, in the air, everywhere—destroy him!"[5]

In Luxembourg, Omar Bradley also fretted at his HQ. "Each day our gloom had deepened," he recalled, "as the Ninth Air Force's youthful meteorologist opened the daily briefing with his dismal repetitious report. And each morning [General Hoyt] Vandenberg [commanding officer of the Ninth Air Force], in a chair next to mine, pulled his head a little tighter into his leather flying jacket."

On over a hundred airfields, pilots of more than four thousand planes waited for a break in the weather.[6]

At the Hotel Alfa in Luxembourg, where both Bradley and Patton were staying, staff officers were readying for the worst. Patton's aide Charles Codman noted: "Papers collected, ready to be destroyed. Personal effects packed. Vehicles gassed up and ready to go."

Codman remembered that Patton, in contrast to others in the Allied senior command, was "the best of tonics. His mere presence has already begun to dissipate the prevailing miasma of dismay. For the last forty-eight hours he and Sergeant Mims, without benefit of staff, baggage, or even a toothbrush, have been charging up and down the fluid lines visiting corps and division commanders, pushing, pulling, relocating, cannibalizing, galvanizing."[7]

Patton believed, as he put it, that the "more senior the officer who appears with a very small unit at the front, the better the effect on the troops. If some danger is involved in the visit, its value is enhanced."[8]

It wasn't only the troops' morale that he had influenced: Patton's entire Third Army now had pivoted and was ready to attack. Moving more than a hundred thousand troops and thousands of tanks and trucks more than a hundred miles in atrocious weather was a considerable achievement, arguably Patton's greatest. Amid many other challenges, an entire communications network had to be set up, which required laying almost twenty thousand miles of wire.

One armored unit moved 161 miles in just twenty-two hours. A tanker remembered "pushing so hard we were virtually maniacal. . . . We didn't even stop to piss. Individual soldiers would squeeze into the turrets and urinate down the sides of the tanks. Sometimes two men were back-to-back, their cocks bent over a metallic ridge. An odd phenomenon, as if the tanks themselves were running with yellow sweat."[9]

Now Patton was ready to wage all-out war. "As usual on the verge of an attack, they [his staff] were full of doubt," he noted in his diary. "I seemed always to be the ray of sunshine, and by God, I always am. We can and will win, God helping. . . . I wish it were this time tomorrow night. When one attacks it is the enemy who has to worry. Give us the Victory, Lord."[10]

Patton also wrote a letter to his wife, Beatrice, that day:

> Though this is the shortest day of the year, to me it seems interminable. We shoot the works on a chestnut pulling expedition in the morning. I am very confident that a great success is possible and I hope certain. . . . I have a room in a very nice hotel with heat and a bath which is fine.

> The Bosch landed a lot of para troops in our uniforms for the purpose of murdering Ike, Brad, me, etc. . . . Remember how a tarpon always makes one big flop just before he dies.

> We should get well into the guts of the enemy and cut his supply lines.[11]

> Destiny sent for me in a hurry when things got tight. Perhaps God saved me for this effort.[12]

———

Patton was confident. He later recalled that he received "quite a few telephone calls from various higher echelons, expressing solicitude as to my ability to attack successfully with only three divisions. I maintained my contention that it is better to attack with a small force at once, and attain surprise, than it is to wait and lose it."[13]

Omar Bradley would settle scores after the war and be less than complimentary about his fellow Allied commanders. But he was full of praise for Patton during this period. Patton was "magnificent." His maneuvering the Third Army in such harsh conditions so quickly was one of the most "brilliant performances by any commander on either side in World War II."

Bradley added: "It was absolutely his cup of tea. . . . He relished every minute of it, knowing full well that this mission, if nothing else, would guarantee him a place of high honor in the annals of the U.S. Army."[14]

That evening, over dinner at the Alfa Hotel, Bradley congratulated Patton.

"All the credit," replied Patton, "all of it, one hundred per cent, goes to Third Army Staff."

Patton finished his meal and then instructed Colonel Codman: "Be ready for an early start tomorrow. We attack with Third Corps at six."[15]

"DRIVE LIKE HELL!" That was Patton's order for the tankers of his 4th Armored Division who had been tasked with reaching

Bastogne. On December 22, at 6 A.M., still under the cover of darkness, the greatest offensive of his military career began. Less than seventy hours since he had made his bold promise to Eisenhower at Verdun, three divisions under his command moved out to strike back at the Germans: the 4th Armored Division to the east of the 26th Infantry Division, and on the right flank the 80th Infantry Division.

Gears ground and eight-cylinder Ford engines roared as Patton's 4th Armored forces advanced along a twenty-mile front. Long columns of Shermans stretched like giant centipedes into the darkness—dawn came at 8:34 A.M., and so for the first few hours the progress was slow because a blackout had been ordered and drivers, burning through almost two gallons per mile, were careful not to crash into the vehicles lumbering ahead of them.

It was snowing. Flakes the size of silver dollars, one man recalled, drifted down, and soon the thirty-six-ton green behemoths, a white star emblazoned on each side of the turret, were grinding through a blizzard. Whenever they reentered combat, the vast majority of men among the tanks' five-man crews felt greater fear than the last time they'd gone into action. War got worse and worse. Many by now found prayer to be most helpful in allaying a sense of helplessness.

Men crossed themselves when they returned to hell. They held tight to lucky charms and other talismans: rings, rabbits' feet, even small stones that gained in importance the longer men survived.

"God help me" would no doubt have been whispered or said out loud in many a tank. It was often automatic, a reflex as the stomach tightened, the heart pounded violently, and cold sweat trickled down the back.[16]

Always there was the fear, suppressed or not, of being spotted at a standstill and becoming the twenty-foot-long-by-nine-foot-wide target of an experienced German gunner in a Tiger or the more common Panther. This was the nightmare of every experienced 4th Armored tanker who'd seen other tanks "brew up"—explode—after being hit by a high-velocity 88mm shell fired by a Tiger or from an artillery piece.

Even if a shell glanced off a tank by some miracle, or did limited damage by exploding close by, every man inside the tank knew that, having been targeted, they had perhaps just a few seconds at most before another shell came roaring, like a demented express train, toward them.

When a crew was going up against another tank, getting off the first shot was critical, and Shermans always had to get close to a Tiger—within a hundred yards—to pierce its flank armor; even at point-blank range, a Sherman's 76mm gun could not blast through a Tiger's frontal armor.

If tankers survived being hit, they had very little time to get out of their burning vehicles. Once outside their turrets, however, they might not get far—snipers could be lurking, ready to put slugs through their heads or hearts with the squeezes of triggers and the resulting cracks.

One veteran American officer had seen his fair share of Shermans get hit and the horrific consequences: "long searing tongues of orange flame" belching from each hatch as sometimes more than a hundred fifty gallons of high-quality gasoline ignited. It was indeed an infernal blaze as ammunition—Shermans carried seventy-one rounds of 76mm ammunition at full load—would begin to explode, and as sparks erupted "from the spout of the [tank's] barrel like the fireballs of a Roman candle."

As Nat Frankel of the 4th Armored recalled: "It takes twenty minutes for a medium tank to incinerate; and the flames burn slowly, so figure it takes ten minutes for a hearty man within to perish. . . . Steel coffins indeed!"

After the rubber tracks and lubricating oil had burned off, spewing black clouds, the steel coffins might be opened. Inside would lay the charred remains of five men, sometimes looking like charcoal dolls a couple of feet high.[17]

OUTSIDE THE HOTEL ALFA in Luxembourg, staff officers and General Bradley watched as Patton's forces rolled through the city, headed to the front lines. One officer recalled that the men "looked cold, bundled in brown against the winter wind that tore through their open vehicles, sitting stone-facedly on the piles of baggage in their trucks as they rode through town, staring back vacantly at the civilians who looked earnestly at them."[18]

Snow also fell that morning in Luxembourg as other troops filed toward the front, passing the headquarters for the Ninth Air Force. Their heavy footsteps could be heard inside the gloomy building. The white flakes, visible through the windows, were yet another dismal reminder of how the weather continued to frustrate the Allies' plans. Heavy snow made patrolling and supply difficult for the Germans too, as roads leading back toward Germany needed to be plowed. But the dense cloud cover still provided invaluable protection from Allied airpower.

At a headquarters in Luxembourg City that morning, Major Stuart Fuller, a meteorologist, briefed General Hoyt Vandenberg, commander of the Ninth Air Force, on the godforsaken weather. There would be mist, snow, and fog across the Ardennes. Yet again.

Vandenberg did his best to lift his men's spirits as snow continued to fall outside.

"Do you think Hitler makes this stuff?"

Later that morning, Vandenberg called Fuller to his office.

"How much longer is this going to last?" asked Vandenberg.

During the war, forecasters had become increasingly accurate by employing radar and weather balloons, thus helping commanders to make critical decisions, notably Eisenhower's postponement of the Normandy invasion the previous June.

Fuller knew from detailed reports that "stagnant" high-pressure systems lay tantalizingly to the east and the west of the Ardennes. If the systems shifted, then the skies could clear. But that wasn't predicted for another four days.

"Suppose it's clear tomorrow," asked Vandenberg, "what are you going to do?"

Clear skies so soon would mean Fuller's predictions had been terribly wrong.

"Shoot myself," Fuller muttered to himself as he turned away.[19]


BY DECEMBER 22, it had been more than a week since men in the Third Army had received Patton's prayer cards with Monsignor O'Neill's exhortation and plea for fair weather.[20]

The prayer card, which included Patton's florid signature,

featured a string of red-berried mistletoe along the left margin. It had been read by many a weary and scared tanker and infantryman, some of whom kept it folded in their jacket pockets and no doubt consulted it when in particular need of faith and inspiration.

GIs were issued pocket Bibles, which many kept close to their hearts in gold-colored steel "Protecto" Shields; soldiers often had the shields etched with phrases such as "May God Be with You" or "To My Loved One." But not every man carried one or was religious enough to make room for the Psalms when a packet of cigarettes or extra rations could seem more sustaining than biblical verse. Now, at least, for those who wanted to pray, there were O'Neill's words at hand and on just one paper card.

Among the most devout serving under Patton was Episcopal priest George Metcalf, a Minnesota native who helped supervise the four-hundred-odd chaplains in the Third Army. He worked alongside O'Neill as his deputy and, when O'Neill was looking for suitable words for Patton's prayer, had even consulted an Anglican "Petition for Fair Weather" in a 1928 edition of the American *Book of Common Prayer*.

Metcalf had held services, being the "No. 2 Chaplain" for the Third Army, for Patton himself. "My personal relations with George Patton as a communicant of the church were always pleasant," he recalled. "But I never knew when he was going to explode. It was like sitting on a time bomb."

Metcalf now prayed for good weather, as did many others on Patton's and Vandenberg's staffs and at headquarters across the Ardennes and beyond. If the skies cleared, the last great battle in the west would surely be won. "There is no question in my mind," Metcalf would insist fifty years later, "that anything there is a good need for can be taken to the Lord in prayer. What he does with it is another matter."[21]

What would God do with Patton's prayer? It seemed inconceivable that the Almighty would ignore it and side with Hitler. But that December 22, as the winter weather got even worse, Patton and so many of his men were still waiting for a sign from the Lord, which they hoped to receive sooner rather than later.

# CHAPTER 7

## The Hole in the Doughnut

**Bastogne, Belgium**
**December 22, 1944**

AS PATTON'S TANKS ground forward, McAuliffe visited a road-block on the outskirts of Bastogne, knowing his men were under severe pressure and needed all the encouragement they could get.

McAuliffe, remembered a sergeant called Robert Bowen, "individually congratulated the men. . . . He was an extremely gracious person who was loved by his troops."[1] McAuliffe knew help was on the way. The question was, would it arrive in time? Ammunition was running low, and food was so scarce that it had to be taken from civilians.

The snow kept falling. Only half the men had protective over-shoes, as the Screaming Eagles had yet to be issued winter combat clothing. But the troopers proved remarkably adaptable and found white tablecloths and fashioned them into camouflage, while some worked out how to insulate their boots.[2]

The locals did their best to help. In one village near Bastogne, the mayor was contacted with a request for sheets. An American captain then met with him and an old man who'd witnessed invasion by the Germans twice before. They'd taken his village in 1914 and 1940.

"Come," the mayor told the captain, who then followed him to the village church, where the old man tolled the church bell.

"The people will know," said the mayor. "The ringing is a signal for them to come."[3]

The pealing bell stirred villagers to action, and within thirty minutes, they had brought more than a hundred sets of sheets to the church. Paratroopers were soon cutting them up to wrap around machine-gun and rifle barrels and helmets. They looked a ghoulish bunch, mummies in a frozen desert, but at least they had some camouflage protection.[4]

Later that morning of December 22, around 11:30, Pfc. Charles Kocourek of the 327th Glider Infantry Regiment heard three shots ring out from his unit's position.

"Germans—way out there!" cried a GI.

Kocourek spotted four Germans walking down a road toward him.

One was carrying a white flag.

"Three shots and we've got four Germans—not bad!" said a paratrooper.

"Why would four Germans at four hundred yards' distance

from our positions want to give up?" asked Kocourek. "It doesn't make sense."

A staff sergeant, Carl Dickinson, approached the Germans.[5]

"According to the Geneva and Hague Conventions," said one of the Germans in English, "we have the right to deliver an ultimatum."

Each of the Germans had a handkerchief to be used as a blindfold.

"We want to talk to your commanding general," said one of the Germans.[6]

The enemy soldiers were blindfolded and taken before the commander of the 327th, Colonel Joseph Harper, who then telephoned Lieutenant Colonel Ned Moore, McAuliffe's chief of staff.

The Germans, said Harper, had a message they wanted delivered to the commander of American forces in Bastogne.

That afternoon, Harper arrived at McAuliffe's headquarters with the Germans' message.

"What is it?" asked McAuliffe.

"It's an ultimatum, sir," said Harper.

"What does it say?" McAuliffe asked.

"They want you to surrender."

"Aw, nuts!" said McAuliffe.[7]

The message read:

*December 22nd 1944.*

*To the U.S.A. Commander of the encircled town of Bastogne.*

*The fortune of war is changing. This time the U.S.A. forces in and near Bastogne have been encircled by strong German armored units. More German armored units have crossed the river Ourthe near Ortheuville, have taken Marche and reached St. Hubert by passing through Hompre-Sibret-Tillet. Libramont is in German hands.*

*There is only one possibility to save the encircled U.S.A. troops from total annihilation: that is the honorable surrender of the encircled town. In order to think it over a term of two hours will be granted beginning with the presentation of this note.*

*If this proposal should be rejected one German Artillery Corps and six heavy A. A. Battalions are ready to annihilate the U.S.A. troops in and near Bastogne. The order for firing will be given immediately after this two hours' term.*

*All the serious civilian losses caused by this artillery fire would not correspond with the wellknown American humanity.*

**The German Commander**[8]

McAuliffe was in no mood to consider surrender for a second. He knew his men were performing well in battle, and some were insisting that the Germans were getting, as he later put it, "one hell of a beating." The Germans had failed to break through his defenses. Had they been able to launch a coordinated, all-around attack, Bastogne might well have fallen. But they had not, and McAuliffe had plenty of troops left, on the line and in reserve. His artillery had performed superbly, stopping German attacks by concentrating fire from most batteries on one area.

The crisis at Bastogne was not one of morale or fighting capability or commitment, but of supply, most critically of ammunition and medicine.[9]

The demand for surrender, said McAuliffe, was "way out of line."

He was also annoyed by the German reference in the ultimatum to saving civilian lives. They'd shown not the slightest inclination to do so in their own pursuit of victory.

McAuliffe picked up a pencil. He was seated in a cubicle next to his operations room. His staff stood nearby.

Several minutes passed.

"Well," McAuliffe finally said, "I don't know what to tell them."

"That first crack you made would be hard to beat, General," said Harper.

"What was that?"

"You said 'Nuts!'"

"That's it."

McAuliffe wrote: "To the German commander: Nuts! From the American Commander."

"Will you see that it's delivered?" McAuliffe asked Harper.

"I will deliver it myself. It will be a lot of fun."

"Don't go into their lines," McAuliffe warned.

Harper duly delivered the paper to the German delegation, who were under guard at the command post for F Company of the 327th Glider Regiment.

"I have the American commander's reply," said Harper.

"Is it written or verbal?" asked one of the German officers.

"It is written. I will stick it in your hand."

He did so.

"The answer is 'Nuts!'"

The Germans were confused.

"Is that reply negative or affirmative?" asked one of them. "If it is the latter, I will negotiate further."

"If you don't understand what 'Nuts!' means," said Harper, "in plain English it is the same as 'Go to hell!' And I will tell you something else; if you continue to attack, we will kill every goddam German that tries to break into this city."

"We will kill many Americans," replied one of the Germans. "That is war."

"On your way," replied Harper, "and good luck to you."

The Germans walked back the way they had come.[10]


IN THE TOWN of Arlon, officers in Patton's III Corps kept up a frantic pace as they issued orders from their headquarters in a girls' school. It was five minutes past four when Patton arrived for a meeting with Major General John Millikin, commander of III Corps, and Major General Hugh Gaffey, who led the 4th Armored Division. Patton was concerned that both generals, recently appointed to command their respective units, might not be up to the task of relieving Bastogne. He reasoned that they could use all the encouragement and chivying they could get.

Millikin updated Patton on III Corps's progress.

Then Patton faced both commanders. He smacked his gloves in his palm.

"No gasoline will be captured," said Patton. "It will be destroyed by us in case capture appears imminent. No ordnance equipment will be captured by the enemy. They will be destroyed. This includes vehicles. No units must be surprised. Necessary security measures will be taken by all commanders. This means that field officers must be gotten up in the line. In case we have to withdraw, roads will be doubly barricaded."

Both commanders nodded their understanding and occasionally responded with "Yes, sir."

Patton looked at Gaffey.

"Lead off with tanks, artillery, tank destroyers, and engineers. Keep main body of infantry back. When Jumbo tanks are available put them in the lead. [The Jumbo was better armed and had thicker protection than the average Sherman.] . . . In this operation we must be the utmost ruthless. Make all tanks fire."[11] So destroy—and if the campaign were to fail, destroy anything that could be of value to the Germans.

All three men believed that III Corps would get to Bastogne within twenty-four hours.


AS IT GOT DARK that evening, defenses along the perimeter around Bastogne were still holding.[12] But there was by now a serious shortage of artillery shells, which greatly concerned McAuliffe. One regimental commander asked for artillery support only to be told by McAuliffe: "If you see 400 Germans in a 100-yard area and they have their heads up, you can fire artillery at them, but only two rounds!"[13]

Casualties mounted. In one church in Bastogne, which served as the 501st's aid station, bloodied men lay shoulder to shoulder on the floor. Medics and surgeons could barely find space to move between the wounded.

MEANWHILE, TANKERS FROM the 4th Armored Division pushed northward for Bastogne. There was to be no stopping for rest. That day, the attack had advanced a respectable seven miles but not nearly enough as far as Patton was concerned. He ordered that the 4th Armored press on through the night toward Bastogne, even though he knew it was a formidable challenge and probably asking too much of men who had already been pushed to the limit.

Albin Irzyk, the commander of the 8th Tank Battalion, recalled learning of Patton's order to keep on through the darkness: "[The men] were just in the process of settling in for the night, when they were slapped hard in the head. That brought them awake in a hurry."

There would be no sleep.

The orders were simple.

"Move all night!"

As far as Irzyk saw it, "[Patton] was using his spurs and riding crop. . . . Patton had ordered the night move with the very optimistic, but completely unrealistic, belief that the forces could reach Bastogne by daylight."[14]

But if any unit could do it, it was the 4th Armored. Patton had great faith in the division. Indeed, it was his favorite. "The 4th Armored was the spear point of the Third Army," recalled Jacob Devers, the second-highest-ranking American general in the European Theater. "They were the ones who got things done."[15]

Yet the 4th Armored was no longer the slashing, potent force it had been the previous summer when it had stormed across France.[16] Tanks were prone to breaking down. Some had been repaired time and time again and had far exceeded their expected mileage limits. The electrical traverse in some turrets no longer worked, so men had to crank the turrets around by hand.

Green troops lacking combat experience filled the ranks, and the division was under General Hugh Gaffey, an inexperienced Texan with "boots you could use as a mirror," according to one account.[17] Thankfully, there were old hands who were still in fine form—leaders like Irzyk who would fight until the very last tank was blasted from under them.

JUST AFTER MIDNIGHT, back at the Ninth Air Force headquarters in Luxembourg, the meteorologist Major Stuart Fuller examined a weather report. Good news at last—the report indicated that to the east of the Ardennes the barometric pressure was finally rising.

Fuller knew only too well that the low pressure that had existed since the opening salvos of the Battle of the Bulge had created the snow, fog, and mist—active, turbulent weather. When there is low pressure, the air is lighter than adjacent air masses, so it rises and this is what creates rain and snow—specifically, when air rises, it causes water vapor to condense, which leads to cloud formation.

Major Fuller was not the only meteorologist to read the report and receive a much-needed boost to his morale. At his headquarters in Reims, France, the commander of the 9th Bombardment Division of the Ninth Air Force, thirty-eight-year-old General Sam Anderson, was awoken by the shrilling of a telephone.

Anderson answered.

"General," said a meteorologist on his staff, "you won't believe this, but it is going to be clear tomorrow."

The North Carolina native and 1928 West Point graduate, who wore a trim mustache, couldn't believe what he was hearing. He climbed out of bed and looked out of his window. The fog was as thick as ever.

"I can't see across the street," said Anderson.

The meteorologist explained the weather report predicting high pressure moving in from the east.

Anderson contacted Ninth Air Force headquarters in Luxembourg. Indeed, he learned, the weather was about to change.

There were new reports coming in to Major Fuller. In spots along the front lines, the fog was lifting. A "Russian high" was closing in from the east and would soon banish remaining cloud cover and fog. Temperatures would plunge yet the skies would clear.

Major Fuller and his fellow meteorologists worked deep into the night. More reports confirmed the dramatic, unexpected change in the weather.

"Notify the general," declared one officer. "Tell everybody that it's almost certain we'll fly tomorrow."[18]

Duly informed, the head of the Ninth Air Force, General Vandenberg, seized the moment. His staff was alerted and soon orders were ticking out of teleprinters at bases in France, Belgium, Holland, and England. Ten of the eleven groups under Vandenberg's command would receive the Presidential Unit Citation by war's end; now they were being summoned to arguably their most decisive action. They should be ready to hit targets as soon as ordered.

The weather had mostly aided Hitler so far in the battle, although snow had hampered supply of ammunition and replacement tanks to his forward units. Now it was in German-occupied territory in the Ardennes, to the east of Luxembourg, that the changing weather—the plunging temperature—was first felt. German airfields that had been shrouded by gray clouds and mist were stripped of their protection by gusting winds. That meant one thing for certain. The *"Amis"*—as the Americans were known—would soon be paying a call in their P-47 fighters, their much-feared "Jabos."

The long night drew to a close. Dawn broke in the Ardennes. As the sun rose, it burned through what was left of the infernal fogs, the misty gray blankets of cloud. In Luxembourg, one of Patton's chaplains, Episcopal priest George Metcalf, was awake that dawn. He would never forget his reaction to the clear skies:

"Thank God!"[19]

# CHAPTER 8

——————————————

# Blue Skies

**Third Army Headquarters, Luxembourg**
**December 23, 1944**

THE DAWN SKIES were a glory to behold. In the words of one GI, "It was the war's most beautiful sunrise."[1]

On the morning of December 23, Patton was at his headquarters in Luxembourg, looking out of his window, delighted to see blue above, not gray. His prayer for good weather had indeed been answered.

"What a glorious day for killing Germans!" he would note in his diary.[2]

Air controllers at Allied air bases announced "visibility unlimited."[3] A massive armada could finally take to the air. It was the Allies' chance to halt Hitler's forces and destroy their supply lines.

Patton would soon call for his deputy chief of staff, Colonel Paul Harkins. When Harkins arrived, Patton apparently exclaimed: "God damn! That O'Neill sure did some potent praying. Get him up here, I want to pin a medal on him."[4]

Father O'Neill was brought to see Patton.

"Chaplain, you're the most popular man in this headquarters," said Patton. "You sure stand in good with the Lord and soldiers."[5]

Patton then pinned the Bronze Star Medal on O'Neill's chest—he was the only man to be awarded a medal in World War II for writing a prayer.

O'Neill recalled: "As General Patton rushed his divisions . . . to the relief of the beleaguered Bastogne, the prayer was answered. . . . To the consternation of the Germans and the delight of the American forecasters who were equally surprised at the turn-about . . . the rains and the fogs ceased. . . . General Patton prayed for fair weather for Battle. He got it."[6]

AT THE NINTH Air Force HQ in Luxembourg, men stood at windows looking to the heavens, as did civilians in the streets. Soon, American fighter planes—P-38 Lightnings and P-47 Thunderbolts—passed high above, looking like flocks of tiny silver birds, the sun glinting off their fuselages. That day, the Ninth Air Force would complete more than a thousand sorties.

The clear skies offered fighter pilots rich pickings. Twenty-six-year-old Colonel David Schilling was among the most aggressive that day. He had flown his P-47 Thunderbolt plane, *Hairless Joe*, since July 1944 and now headed the 56th Fighter Group.

That morning, Schilling tried to find enemy planes to attack, going in search of them three times. On his fourth attempt, he was successful, spotting more than ninety German planes while at twenty-eight thousand feet.

Schilling and his unit attacked, and in the ensuing melee, which lasted more than half an hour, he took down one German plane after another. He recalled destroying one of his victims: "I gave about a five-second burst and began getting strikes all over him. The pilot immediately bailed out and the ship spun down to the left, smoking and burning, until it blew up at about 15,000 feet."[7]

It was an extraordinary feat: That day, Schilling shot down five German planes to become one of thirty-eight US Army Air Force "Ace in a Day" pilots. He would survive the war and in 1950 became the first pilot to fly nonstop across the Atlantic in a jet fighter.

As the day progressed, the skies became even more magnificent to behold to many on the ground. War reporter Alan Moorehead recalled: "If you turned your back to the ruined villages and forgot the war for a moment, then very easily you could fancy yourself to be alone in this radiant world where everything is reduced to primary whites and blues; a strident, sparkling white among the frosted trees, the deep blue shadows in the valley, and then the flawless ice-blue of the sky."[8]

Germans also looked up at the clear sky, which was raining punishment. "Airplanes everywhere," noted a German tank officer. "Thousands. Shitting all over us. I didn't see a single Luftwaffe plane."[9] An American P-47 pilot recalled: "Targets all over the place. Our air controllers zeroed in on hundreds of fat targets. We caught them out of fuel. . . . Hundreds and hundreds of vehicles; tanks, trucks, lined up on the road in a traffic jam."[10]

MEANWHILE, THE push toward Bastogne continued. But the pace had slowed.

Patton telephoned III Corps headquarters.

"There is too much piddling around," Patton complained.[11]

The opposite was in fact the case. The 8th Tank Battalion, for one, was battling hard to reach Bastogne—there was no piddling around, far from it. The increasingly battered battalion's leader, Lieutenant Colonel Albin Irzyk, had by now shared his tank with four others since he arrived in the killing fields of Normandy six long months ago. He was proud to belong to Patton's favorite division in the Third Army because he believed Patton was a superlative combat commander. Indeed, the "Allies' most effective, offensive weapon [was] Patton."[12]

In the village of Chaumont, around seven miles south of Bastogne, Irzyk's unit came under ferocious attack from some five hundred German infantrymen and at least four Tiger tanks that had spotted the Americans and enjoyed the benefit of surprise and higher ground. The Tigers, the deadliest and therefore the most feared and respected of Hitler's panzers, quickly wreaked havoc. A Tiger's cannon could pierce the front of a Sherman over a mile away. Slow and cumbersome, the Tiger could be outmaneuvered by canny tankers like Irzyk but not easily in this moment, with the Americans disorganized and unprepared.

German tank rounds exploded among Irzyk's force. Irzyk

had seen his fair share of combat but the German onslaught that day was the most traumatic yet: "It was the frightening, demoralizing, intimidating, unreal sounds, screeches, and screams of high velocity tank gun rounds hitting, crashing, exploding, and ricocheting all around. . . . It shook, staggered, numbed, alarmed and unnerved."[13]

Elsewhere in Chaumont, there was pandemonium as shells from Tigers landed with terrifying accuracy. Explosions were deafening. High-velocity rounds zipped through the air. Men and tanks began to pull out of the village but, tragically, to the south the terrain was exposed and sloped upward, making escape just as dangerous as staying put. One company from Irzyk's battalion, Baker Company, trapped along narrow village roads, was torn apart. It was impossible to call in American artillery fire because the situation was so frantic.

Irzyk had no choice but to retreat. He told his driver to reverse his Sherman as his gunner fired as fast as he could. A few minutes later, the tank was reversing up a hill along a road. In the receding distance, Chaumont was aflame.

Surely, they had escaped just in time? But then there was, in Irzyk's words, "a low, loud, deafening, earsplitting sound, followed by a terrible, horrible, powerful, frightening blow. . . . It was as though the tank had been hit in the back by a huge sledgehammer, and picked up and thrown forward by a superhuman hand." The three men in the Sherman's turret were thrown around like "rag dolls," but—amazingly, it must have seemed—no one was killed and Irzyk and his crew, stunned and bruised, were able to get back on their feet.

"Keep moving!" shouted Irzyk.[14]

A German shell had hit Irzyk's tank turret and ricocheted off.

For Irzyk, it was "a minor miracle—that they had been spared and uniquely blessed by the Supreme Being." It was as if Irzyk had "received a tap on his shoulder from the back, reassuring him that someone was behind him, protecting him . . . an unreal, mystical feeling."[15]

Others were not so lucky. After reaching an area southeast of Chaumont that provided cover, Irzyk learned that he'd lost eleven tanks in the surprise German counterattack on Chaumont. Among the soldiers of the 10th Armored Infantry Battalion, which had fought valiantly beside Irzyk's tankers, there had been terrible casualties—A Company had lost every one of its officers, and more than sixty other men had been killed or wounded.

The Germans, having also suffered high casualties and needing reinforcement, did not advance beyond Chaumont that day. Meanwhile, Irzyk's force had to be reorganized. One thing was clear: When it came to stopping the American relief force, the Germans were not "piddling around." The Allied route to Bastogne led through an icy hell.

PATTON HAD left his headquarters by noon and headed to the front. A sergeant, from atop his tank destroyer, spotted the general "along the side of the road waving us on. I don't know how he got ahead of us all the time, but he did. Patton was right there breaking it up and getting things moving again. . . . Patton had a theory that the Germans didn't shoot as well on the run. That's why he never wanted to stop. The only time he stopped in the field was when he ran out of gas."[16]

Indeed, Patton seemed to be everywhere that day, constantly on the move. From his tank, Nat Frankel of the 4th Armored remembered hearing a voice call out, "'Look, there goes Lucky 6.' [That] was the radio code for General Patton. Sure enough, his jeep was passing by with Old Blood and Guts sitting in the right front seat behind a machine gun mounted on the dash before him."[17]

Frankel's column of tanks had stalled, and Patton had arrived to find out why. As the general's jeep pulled up close to Frankel's Sherman, his first thought was *My God, we failed to salute and he's going to bawl us out.*

Frankel and any other crewmen within sight stood to attention and snapped off salutes. Patton bounded out of the jeep and strode toward them. "Gesturing with his right hand, in his high-pitched voice [Patton] said, 'Man, von Rundstedt's nuts are in the meat grinder and I have the handle in my hand,'" repeating what by now was surely his favorite wisecrack. Frankel remembered Patton's eyes, "glowering like two jewels planted into a Polynesian idol. His arms were waving, randomly but not frantically. He was the very picture of total energy combined with godlike self-control."

"What's wrong?" shouted Patton.

A tank was stuck.

"Goddamn! This is no time to get stuck! Get this goddamn thing rolling!"

"Yessir!"

News of Patton's presence "passed up and down [our] column [and] one could see clearly in the posture and expression of every soldier that any previous doubt . . . had been summarily erased," recalled Frankel. "We had them licked, by God. That pistol-packin', swaggerin', Hun-killin' son of a bitch had just said so in unmistakable terms!"[18]

Patton also found time while inspiring his troops to stay in contact with Allied Supreme Commander Dwight Eisenhower. Many years later, Eisenhower would remember that Patton contacted him almost every day during the push toward Bastogne.

"General, I apologize for my slowness," Patton told Eisenhower on one occasion. "This snow is God-awful. I'm sorry."

"George, are you still fighting?" Eisenhower asked.

Patton said he indeed was.

"All right then, that's all I've asked of you. Just keep at it."[19]

# CHAPTER 9

|——————————————|

# Manna from Heaven

**Bastogne, Belgium**
**December 23, 1944**

THE BRIGHT BLUE skies also meant that the men of Bastogne could more easily be resupplied from the air. Ahead of flocks of C-47s that duly headed toward Bastogne that day were pathfinder planes, sent to drop men who would mark zones for the vital supplies that later would be landed by parachute.

Pfc. John Agnew, aboard the lead pathfinder, was worried about friends on the ground: "We heard they had gone into Bastogne with no more than two or three clips of ammo, little clothing and food."

And then there was the risk to the flights themselves. Piloting Agnew's plane was Lieutenant Colonel Joel Crouch, who, as the lead pathfinder for the 101st Airborne Division on D Day, was no stranger to spearheading dangerous missions.[1] Crouch had taken off from England for Bastogne at 6:45 A.M., his plane loaded with pathfinders and their beacons, which would later guide waves of C-47s carrying vital supplies. Now, more than three hours later, Private Agnew was in the back of Crouch's C-47. As it approached a drop zone, he saw a light inside the plane, the signal for him and others to hook up. He heard guns open up below and saw tracer fire through the plane's windows.

Crouch reacted fast, diving on a German gun position. The soldiers manning it clearly thought the C-47 was going to crash into them, so they ran away. Crouch stayed in control and soon had the plane back at the right height for men to make a jump.

"Luckily," recalled Agnew, "we all recovered our balance just as the green light came on and out the door we went."[2]

Agnew dropped to the ground and set up a CRN-4 radio beacon on a large pile of bricks. At noon, more than two hours after the pathfinders had flown over Bastogne, Screaming Eagles, huddled in foxholes, heard overhead the thunder and roar of dozens more C-47s, which dropped resupply loads that dangled from brightly colored parachutes.

A radio operator aboard one of the planes remembered: "The first thing you saw, coming toward Bastogne, was a large, flat plain completely covered with snow, the whiteness broken only by a few trees and some roads and, off in the distance, the town itself. Next, your eye caught the pattern of tank tracks across the snow. We came down lower and lower, finally to about 500 feet off the ground, our drop height."[3]

Staff Sergeant Ben Obermark recalled looking down on Bastogne: "I couldn't believe an army of men could be trapped down there in what looked like nothing but wide fields of snow. At first, I couldn't see any men at all. We pushed out the parapacks through the open door and then I lay down on the floor looking out the door and sort of squinting against the glare of the snow; that way, I could see men running toward the stuff we had dropped and dragging it away to their still invisible foxholes."[4]

For the men on the ground, it was as if the heavens had delivered the perfect early Christmas present. Soldiers cheered wildly as the cargo descended.

It seemed to be an act of divine intervention. One Bastogne defender described it as "the most beautiful sight in the world, when those clouds opened up and we saw all that material coming down."[5] Pfc. Ben Rous recalled: "As we retrieved bundles, first we cut up the paper bags to wrap around our feet, then took the supplies back to their proper areas. What a great feeling to have warm feet!"[6]

Hopes of survival surged. Another soldier, Phil Burge, later insisted that the resupply saved his life: "If that had not happened, I would not be here today. That was a miraculous sight. It was an act of God."[7]

The journalist Fred MacKenzie was at the 101st Airborne's headquarters that morning. "Five days had passed without visible evidence that anywhere outside Bastogne were beings who did not want to destroy [us]," he recalled.[8] At the news that help had finally arrived, men gathered in a courtyard of the barracks. They looked up, according to MacKenzie, "transfigured with rapture."

The C-47s seemed to be "great immortal carriers of goods

from heaven." But there was also antiaircraft fire from the Germans, and when two planes were hit and exploded in flames, the men watching were "aghast."

In Bastogne, civilians stood in the streets, necks craned toward the sky. As the colorful chutes came down, townspeople cried and clapped their hands. They had not been forsaken. By nightfall, some hundred fifty tons of invaluable supplies had been dropped by 241 planes. In the next three days, eight hundred fifty more tons would arrive, courtesy of more than nine hundred aircraft.

Some of the men who had risked their lives to resupply Bastogne would not make it back to England. Captain Paul W. Dahl, a pilot, was just four minutes from his assigned drop zone at Bastogne when two antiaircraft shells hit his plane. His navigator and copilot were both hit and he was wounded in the arm.

There was considerable damage to instrument panels. Somehow, Dahl was able to carry on to the target and drop his load. As he started back toward England, another round of antiaircraft fire hit his plane on the nose. The cockpit was soon in flames.

Dahl had no choice but to order his crew to bail out. He set the controls so the plane would glide down, giving his men and him valuable seconds to escape. Dahl couldn't find his own parachute but then found a spare. Because of his wound, he couldn't get it on properly. "I placed my arms through the shoulder straps of the seat-type chute and jumped and hung on by my arms until I reached the ground," he remembered.[9]

Dahl came down in Allied territory. He had lost two of his crew; as they drifted down, their parachutes were holed by machine-gun fire from Germans on the ground, and both fell to their deaths.[10]

ONE MAN PERHAPS more than any other was vital to the resupply mission's success that day—Ninth Air Force radio expert Captain James Parker.[11] He had trained as a fighter pilot and served in the Pacific, where he shot down three Japanese Zeros, but that day he controlled communication from the ground in Bastogne to the supply planes.[12]

Four days earlier, Parker had arrived in Bastogne, an hour before the last road was cut off. He'd then tried to find a high-frequency radio. He had scoured the 101st Airborne's headquarters but had come up empty-handed before finally finding one in a jeep and another in a tank belonging to the 10th Armored Division, elements of which were fighting alongside the 101st Airborne in Bastogne.

All that day, as C-47s approached, Parker was busy with his switchboard, directing supply planes as well as Thunderbolts, the first of which he sent to the west and northwest to strike the enemy confronting the 327th Glider Infantry and the 502nd PIR.

Artillery fire from the 101st had failed to stop the advancing Germans. Thankfully, tracks in the snow led the Thunderbolts, initially guided by Parker, to their prey hidden in wooded areas. The Thunderbolts dropped napalm, setting trees ablaze. They also hit German troops in villages to which Parker had directed them.[13]

GIs were delighted to see the formidable P-47 Thunderbolts, armed with no less than eight machine guns, making them deadly indeed when strafing troops or columns of vehicles. A corporal in an artillery unit spotted several of the planes and a big cheer went up. But then one of the planes dived toward the corporal and his unit.

The corporal ran for a foxhole.

The Thunderbolt's guns blazed. Bullets ripped into the ground and fortunately the corporal made it to the hole and then curled up in a ball.

Not long after, a soldier arrived to check on the corporal.

"Can't you see I'm praying!" shouted the corporal, and the soldier dropped down beside him as the Thunderbolt attacked again, this time dropping a bomb that exploded nearby.

An officer bravely stood in the open and waved a cloth panel, indicating they were American troops, and the Thunderbolt thankfully moved on to German targets.[14]

There were other incidents of friendly fire that day. One sergeant, Steve Koper, remembered being in a jeep heading to pick up supplies that had been dropped. Thunderbolts suddenly swooped down and opened fire. He hopped out of the jeep and sought cover. When he returned, the jeep was riddled with bullet holes. Somehow, it was still operable and he managed to load it with vital supplies.

Despite these mishaps, the resupply from the air was highly successful and a much-needed boost to morale, but the situation in Bastogne was hardly encouraging. Above all, the defenders needed Patton's forces to break through and open a land corridor for armor and troops. They would be essential if McAuliffe's men were going to fend off increasingly violent German attacks.

———

MORE AND MORE wounded were being brought to the Belgian barracks that served as the 101st Airborne's headquarters, so many that a riding hall had been converted into a makeshift hospital. Maimed and dying men were placed beside some six hundred others already lying on litters, as well as the walking wounded and those stricken with severe combat fatigue. A chaplain made his way between the rows of gravely injured, trying to comfort soldiers, some in their last moments.

In the coming days, the chaplain would have to soothe yet more soldiers as they died. Indeed, the battle for Bastogne would grow only more ferocious as Christmas approached. Hasso von Manteuffel, commander of the Fifth Panzer Army, had ordered: "Bastogne must be taken at all costs."

Manteuffel knew that Patton's forces were on their way, fighting toward Bastogne. If there were to be any chance of avoiding humiliation and defeat, it meant seizing Bastogne as soon as possible. As the journalist Fred MacKenzie put it: "Bastogne . . . was the key."[15]

One soldier, Louis Simpson of the 327th Glider Infantry, vividly recalled the persistence of the German attacks. Atop a rise, he was trying to spot the oncoming Germans while keeping his head as low to the ground as possible.

Bullets whined overhead. Soldiers to his right fired their M-1 rifles over and over. Simpson looked down at the snow-covered slope before him. It seemed to "come alive and to be moving, detaching itself from the trees at the foot of the slope." He saw a "line of men, most of them covered in white—white cloaks and hoods. Here and there men stand out in the gray-green German overcoats. They walk, run and flop down on the snow."[16]

The Germans got to their feet and attacked again. Simpson and his unit managed, once more, to hold them at bay. But for how much longer?

God only knew.

THAT NIGHT, McAuliffe contacted the 4th Armored Division, which had moved just two miles closer that day.

"Sorry I did not get to shake hands today. I was disappointed."

A member of McAuliffe's staff followed up with another message.

"There is only one more shopping day before Christmas."[17]

# CHAPTER 10

---

# Christmas Eve

**Bigonville, Luxembourg**
**December 24, 1944**

ON A HILLSIDE to the south of the village of Bigonville, which lay fifteen miles from Bastogne, the silence was broken by the sounds of engines roaring and tank tracks clanking. Some of the Sherman tanks had been hastily daubed with white swaths of paint for camouflage. With their gloved hands holding binoculars, commanders stood in their turrets, powerful .50-caliber machine guns mounted to their left. Inside the turret of each Sherman, just in front of the commander's legs, sat a gunner ready to fire and a loader to his left. A driver sat at the front of the turret beside a bow gunner. None of the five-man crew in most tanks had been able to sleep for more than a couple of hours or so since December 21.

"Let 'er roll," ordered Creighton Abrams, riding in a Sherman that he had named *Thunderbolt VII*. Tanks named *Destruction*, *Deuces Wild*, and *Betty* followed behind.

It was around 2 A.M. on December 24 when thirty-year-old Abrams and his tankers in the 37th Tank Battalion moved out, headed toward Bastogne.

Abrams and his unit had been driving north since December 20—that day alone, the battalion under his command had covered a hundred twenty miles in some fifteen hours, a truly remarkable feat given the miserable conditions and the shortness of daylight. Roads had been slicked with ice and some tanks had slid out of control, stopping only when they crashed into buildings.

On the twenty-third, under the clear skies, Abrams's force had pushed along a winding route to the east of Lieutenant Colonel Irzyk's ill-fated 8th Tank Battalion, which had been savaged by the German counterattack at Chaumont. Abrams's battalion had also encountered fierce German resistance, with several tank commanders killed by machine-gun and rifle fire. Among those lost was C Company commander Captain Charlie Trover.

The 37th Tank Battalion had battled on, with Abrams replacing Trover with Lieutenant Charles Boggess. After reorganizing the previous evening, Abrams had ordered the battalion's Shermans in B Company to take the lead along a road that led via small hamlets, through gorges and thick forest, to Bastogne.

"Drive like hell," Patton had ordered. "We have an opportunity of winning the war."[1]

Abrams needed no urging. A West Point graduate in the class of 1936, he had led his battalion with great success and courage. His tanks had often spearheaded the Third Army's rampage across Normandy—a veritable American Blitzkrieg that had earned Patton considerable acclaim. He was probably the highest-scoring tank commander in the US Army—the top tank ace; his superb crew and he had destroyed dozens of enemy tanks and armored vehicles. Not that Abrams himself was one to keep count. That would have been unseemly.[2]

One of Abrams's men in the 37th Tank Battalion, which had the motto "Courage Conquers," remembered him "shooting tanks like the rest of the boys. He would mix in wherever the toughest battle was. It made us feel like fighting harder when you could see a great man like Abe alongside of you."[3]

Abrams had already worn through six previous tanks, but he had never had one destroyed by the enemy. He had called each one of them *Thunderbolt*, and he rode at the front of his tank columns, his head jutting from the turret as he chomped on a long black cigar, cussed, and cajoled.[4] "THUNDERBOLT" was emblazoned on his Sherman's hull in bold white letters.

Amazingly, Abrams hadn't received a scratch in many fierce engagements, which included a nine-day slugfest in September 1944, the Battle of Arracourt, to that date the biggest tank battle for American armored forces in Europe. "The Almighty was careful with Abe," remembered battalion surgeon Dr. John Scotti, "because He knew he had much to do."[5]

Abrams was Patton's kind of warrior. Patton in fact held Abrams in the highest regard: "I'm supposed to be the best tank commander in the Army, but I have one peer—Abe Abrams. He's the world champion."[6] After crossing the Seine in August 1944, Patton had singled out Abrams while talking with reporters at Third Army headquarters.

"There's a great young officer in the 4th," Patton had said.

"But if you're going to write about him, you better do it right away. He's so good, he isn't going to live long."[7]

Like Patton, Abrams was an avid believer in inflicting maximum violence upon his adversary. The aim was to kill as many of the enemy as fast as possible, thereby shortening the war and limiting American casualties. He preferred to engage the Germans rather than chase after them. "We don't want the Germans to fall back," he explained. "We want them to defend their positions so we can destroy them and their equipment. There's entirely too much emphasis on getting prisoners and not enough on destruction!"

Abrams was indeed a man cut from the same cloth as his hyperaggressive commander. "Whenever the Germans get us in the wringer they show us no quarter, so why should we?" Abrams asked, echoing the philosophy of George Patton. "We've got to set our minds on destroying them. That's the only way to get this job done, and done fast."[8]

Early that morning of December 24, Abrams chewed on his black cigar. "It looked like another gun," one of his men recalled.[9]

Abrams's tanks were rolling, their exhaust pipes belching black clouds into the frigid air. But would they be able to advance fast enough to save the thousands of defenders of Bastogne?

TELETYPE MACHINES at air bases in England stuttered out field orders.[10] Finally, the full might of the Allied air forces based there was to be deployed. Some two thousand planes would see action in one of the greatest air strikes of the Second World War.[11]

The stakes were immense. Some planes were flown even though they had been classified as unfit for long-range missions. Soon, bombers formed an immense line across the English Channel and headed for targets east and west of the Rhine.

In action that December 24 was the 4th Fighter Wing of the Eighth Air Force, led by Brigadier General Frederick Castle. On his thirtieth mission, he was flying as a copilot in a B-17 with the 487th Bomb Group, headed for an airfield target in Germany. Unfortunately, due to weather conditions, fifteen vital minutes were lost and the 487th was not joined by P-51 fighters who were supposed to provide escort.[12]

Castle was in the lead B-17. His group flew on toward the target. They were over Allied territory and the Germans rarely attacked formations in unfriendly skies. But then, diving out of the sun, came a swarm of yellow-nosed German bandits.

Castle's plane fell back with engine trouble and was soon seen as the injured among the flock, easy pickings.

The Germans belonged to JG3, one of the more formidable German fighter units led by one of the greatest fighter pilots of the war, Heinz Bär, who would by the end of 1944 have claimed more than two hundred victories.[13]

The Germans pounced.

Two of Castle's crew were hit by bullets.

Flames licked from two engines.

The B-17 was clearly doomed.

Castle knew it.

"Okay, men, we've been hit—get out."[14]

Castle managed to fly the plane straight as his crew escaped from the plane. He remained at the controls beside his copilot, and then a fuel tank blew up. Castle and his copilot were killed as the plane crashed. The brigadier general had sacrificed himself so that some of his men would be able to get out of the plane.

It was later noted, "General Castle was posthumously awarded the Medal of Honor, this incident being the last for which such an award was made to a member of the Eighth. . . . [He] had left the safety of a desk job to take over a demoralized B-17 group in the summer of 1943. . . . [He] was the highest-ranking officer in the Eighth to be awarded the Medal of Honor."[15]

ON THE GROUND, there were just nine tanks left in B Company of Creighton Abrams's 37th Tank Battalion—half the normal strength—later that morning of December 24. Abrams's unit had continued with little food or sleep but now closed on Bigonville, which had to be taken in order to reach Bastogne. A lead platoon stopped on a ridge overlooking a railroad track that led into the village.

Three German tanks accompanied by white-camouflaged troops appeared and B Company, led by Captain Jimmie Leach, went to work. But it was so cold that every time a B Company tank fired, an ice cloud formed, obscuring the gunner's view as he tried to let loose another round. After many misses, the Germans had been dealt with, their tanks destroyed.

Leach pushed his men onward. He was lucky to be alive,

having earlier been hit in the helmet by a German soldier's bullet as he stood exposed in his tank's turret. The slug had put a shallow furrow across his skull and he'd dropped, unconscious, to the bottom of his turret but had come to in time to fight on, only to be hit in the shoulder by another bullet. Abrams finally pulled Leach's company back and sent another forward to become the battalion's lead unit.

In Bigonville itself, the Germans fought with stubborn skill, expertly infiltrating back into areas cleared by Abrams's men and then firing on them from the upper stories of houses. Infantrymen had no option but to double back and clear the Germans from one house after another, a harrowing process, especially against the German 5th Parachute Division, a superb unit that Abrams's battalion had defeated that summer but had now been replenished with tough, determined fighters. These were the kind to surrender only when they'd fired their last bullets. Three hundred twenty-eight of them ultimately became prisoners in the hectic combat before Bigonville finally fell.

Dead German soldiers littered the village, their mangled corpses forming grotesque shapes. Farm animals wandered among the carnage. The village's church steeple had been riddled by gunfire, and in seemingly every street, a carpet of smashed tiles and masonry lay, overhung by torn electric wires.

Abrams's battalion moved on late that afternoon, leaving Bigonville behind in burning and smoking ruins.[16]

MEANWHILE, MCAULIFFE sent a Christmas message to the men holding Bastogne:

*What's merry about all of this, you ask? We're fighting—it's cold—we aren't home. All true, but what has the proud Eagle Division accomplished with its worthy comrades of the 10th Armored Division, the 705th Tank Destroyer Battalion, and all the rest? Just this: we have stopped cold everything that has been thrown at us from North, East, South and West.*

*We have identifications from four German Panzer Divisions, two German Infantry Divisions and one German Parachute Division. These units, spearheading the last desperate German lunge, were headed straight west for key points when the Eagle Division was hurriedly ordered to stem the advance. How effectively this was done will be written in history; not alone in our Division's glorious history but in World history. The Germans actually did surround us, their radios blared our doom. Their Commander demanded our surrender. . . . Allied troops are counterattacking in force. We continue to hold Bastogne. By holding Bastogne we assure the success of the Allied Armies. . . . We are giving our country and our loved ones at home a worthy Christmas present and being privileged to take part in this gallant feat of arms are truly making ourselves a Merry Christmas.*[17]

*/s/ A. C. McAuliffe*

**/t/ McAULIFFE,
Commanding.**

GENERAL OMAR BRADLEY, lionized by history as the "GI's general," spent that Christmas Eve safely ensconced in his headquarters in Luxembourg. Patton, by contrast, was again with his troops on the battlefield, a .45 strapped to his waist. It was more important than ever to be seen and to assess for himself conditions and the demeanor of troops and their commanders. Before the day was out, he visited the leaders of three corps and three armored divisions, covering mile after miserable mile, sitting in his winter coat, with his back straight, arms often folded, exposed to the elements in an open-top armored jeep as it sped along icy, winding roads.

And among senior German commanders, the advance of Patton's Third Army from the south was of increasing concern. Fifth Panzer Army commander Hasso von Manteuffel, the most successful German general during the offensive, contacted Alfred Jodl at Hitler's headquarters.

"Time's running out," said Manteuffel. "I expect a heavy Allied attack any moment from the south. You've got to let me know this evening what the Führer wants. The time has come for a complete new plan. I can't keep driving toward the Meuse and still take Bastogne."

"The Führer won't like the news," said a nervous Jodl.

"It's the damn truth."

"But the Führer will never give up the drive to Antwerp."

If Hitler changed strategy, Manteuffel believed, there would still be a chance of defeating the Allies in the Ardennes. But the plan to reach Antwerp should be abandoned.

"Give me reserves," stressed Manteuffel, "and I'll take Bastogne, reach the Meuse, and swing north."

"Well," replied Jodl hesitantly, "I'll speak with the Führer."

"Now. Every minute counts."[18]

BELOW THE CLEAR SKIES, as Christ's birthday approached, the last great battle waged on the Western Front continued unabated, often with haunting intensity. Sergeant Bruce Egger of the 26th Infantry Division remembered his company attacking a German-occupied hamlet as the light began to fade on Christmas Eve.

There was the familiar snarl of a German machine gun and one of Egger's men fell dead. Two others had been hit but not killed.

One of the wounded tried to get to his feet.

"Mother, Mother! Help me!" he cried.

The German machine gun opened up once more and the wounded man was killed. "That beseeching plea," remembered Egger, "on that clear, cold Christmas night will remain with me for the rest of my life."[19]

Such loss on Christmas Eve was particularly depressing for soldiers who were struggling to stay alive and who had already seen so much suffering and death. "There were two things in front of you always, the enemy and death," remembered a corporal in the 90th Division. "Sometimes morale was so low that you preferred death instead of a day-by-day agonizing existence. When you were wet, cold, hungry, lonely, death looked very inviting. It was always close at hand and I found myself being envious of a dead comrade. At least he suffered no more physically or mentally."[20]

Despite the resupply from the air, the morale of McAuliffe's staff in Bastogne was also low. The journalist Fred MacKenzie recalled: "Headquarters personnel gathered at the mess hall for the usual meager meal around sundown, more quiet than usual, thoughtful, depressed."

A mass was to be held at 7 P.M.

MacKenzie was present when some hundred men gathered in one of the barracks rooms that would serve as a chapel for a Christmas Eve service. Thankfully, McAuliffe's base of command—several basements in long, low buildings known to the Belgians as the Heintz Barracks—had survived relatively unscathed so far in the battle for Bastogne.

Sentries had been posted, and half-tracks and trucks came and went at all hours. The buildings, on the outskirts of the besieged town, were adjacent to a parade ground and skirted here and there by fir trees. Across a nearby road stood a cemetery that had also escaped severe German shelling.

With candles flickering, a young chaplain gave a brief sermon. MacKenzie described it: "The simple service and the dimly lighted room were wondrously appropriate to this place where the human spirit sometimes seemed recognizable, a naked and vibrant thing, apart from fleshy woes. It was as though one was dying, or being born, in travail."

"Do not plan," the chaplain counseled, "for God's plan will prevail."

When the chaplain finished, the men left the room and walked out into the bracing night air. The moon shone bright in the clear sky.

"Religion is a wonderful thing in a time like this," said one soldier to a comrade.[21]

That evening, the headquarters filled with more soldiers. Men wanted to be with their comrades. Hope was fragile. Faith mattered. And then came the sounds of war. As MacKenzie described them, "suddenly, three petrifying explosions, with a short interval of time between blasts, stilled all voices and movement."[22]

The Germans were bombing Bastogne. Soldiers took shelter where they could. One recorded in his diary: "It was a living hell. We have no ack-ack or machine guns to hinder them. They [the enemy] come over, drop flares, and then take their time dropping their 'bundles.'"[23]

Several bombs exploded less than two hundred yards from McAuliffe's headquarters. The blasts could be felt in a cellar where senior officers had gathered.

"Steady men, keep calm and don't crowd," said Lieutenant Colonel Ned Moore, the 101st Airborne's chief of staff.[24]

Others felt the full brunt of the Luftwaffe. Captain Gordon Geiger of the 10th Armored Division remembered: "They hit our air station, which caved into the basement. We went over and tried to get the men out. A lot of mattresses had caught fire, as well as other things. One boy was pinned down by a beam on his leg. Someone found a saw and began to cut at the beam to free him. The boy was saying, 'Shoot me! Please shoot me!' But we said, 'You'll be all right!'"

The man was rescued but many wounded were not so lucky. Among those killed was a young Belgian woman, Renée Le-Maire. She "had been taking care of our boys," recalled Geiger. "When the bomb came in, she was killed. My doctor was there and he sat down and cried like a baby. He had a daughter about the same age and the Belgian girl's death really got to him."

Captain John T. Prior was in a building near the hospital. He was planning to write a letter to the wife of a young lieutenant who was dying and set off to visit the man. "As I was about to step out of the door for the hospital," recalled Prior, "one of my men asked if I knew what day it was, pointing out that on Christmas Eve we should open a champagne bottle."

They did so and were about to take a drink when the room "became as bright as an arc welder's torch." Then came the scream of a bomb falling. Surely it had their names on it? They dived to the floor. The building shook from the force of an explosion.

Prior picked himself up and then rushed outside only to see that all that remained of the hospital was a pile of smoking rubble some six feet high, bathed in the intense light caused by magnesium flares dropped by the Germans.

A German bomber returned, flying low.

The pilot wanted to strafe bystanders and others who had rushed to the scene.

Prior and others crawled under trucks and the bomber passed over several more times. Then Prior arranged to take any surviving patients to the riding hall that was serving as the main hospital for the 101st Airborne.[25]

That same night, McAuliffe spoke with General Middleton on the phone.

"The finest Christmas present the 101st could get," said McAuliffe, "would be relief tomorrow."[26]

The Germans were not done. Bombers returned later that night and dropped not only their deadly loads but also leaflets that, recalled Master Sergeant Ralph Manley, urged the Screaming Eagles to surrender, "saying this was our pass to a warm bed."

If men wanted to see their "sweethearts" again, they should give up.

It made sense. The enemy was utterly ruthless. That evening, the Germans had killed twenty-one people in their attack on the hospital, and elsewhere along the ragged perimeter around Bastogne, casualties were mounting.

Hope was fading.

Yet no man was ready to surrender.

The leaflets, Manley remembered, were "the perfect paper for us to use to relieve ourselves."[27]

CREIGHTON ABRAMS's battalion paused that evening on high ground beyond the village of Bigonville, a victory behind them and Bastogne still ahead. The moon rose in the night sky. The soldiers in accompanying half-tracks were just as tired as the tankers. Temperatures had risen somewhat but the resulting rain and mist had made roads slippery, only increasing the men's frustration.

Patton had forbidden his tankers to advance "buttoned up"

with the hatches closed, which had made the journey so far toward Bastogne all the more arduous. But none had lost heart. If anything, the ordeal had left many fighting mad, eager to finish the job and roll into Bastogne.

"Keep your head outside the hatch," Patton had instructed tank commanders, "so you can see where the hell you're going and where the Krauts are shooting from. Give the sons of bitches a target so you can see where they are and go kill them. Never button up a tank in Third Army and blind yourself."

Patton prized aggression above all.

"When you attack be fast and violent," he had also stressed. "The more violent you are, the fewer of your men get shot. Forget everything you learned . . . about conserving ammunition. Shoot. Fire scares the Heinies. A mortar or an artillery piece that isn't firing is just junk. Shoot off your ammo. . . . A pint of sweat will save you a gallon of blood."[28]

The men waiting for Abrams's battalion shivered in foxholes all along the perimeter around Bastogne.

Some felt doomed.

As one soldier put it: "The end was at hand."[29]

One officer thought he knew why some soldiers were particularly on edge—it was "purely a nervous reaction because the men all began thinking of home at one time and it seemed to sweep through all ranks that they would not live through Christmas Day."[30]

Patton, meanwhile, was returning to his headquarters in Luxembourg after a long day.

A sentry beside a road spotted the general.

Stars shone above.

A lone Allied plane flew overhead.

Patton looked up at it.

The sentry wished Patton a happy Christmas.

"Thank you, son," Patton told the sentry. "A very Merry [Christmas] to you. Noel, Noel, what a great night to give the Nazis hell."[31]

LATER THAT NIGHT in Luxembourg City, it was snowing as civilians and soldiers walked into a small church. Chaplain Frederick A. McDonald was about to hold a candlelit service when he spotted Patton at the back of the church. He approached the general, welcomed him, and told him that Kaiser Wilhelm II had attended services in the very same church during the First World War.

"Would you, sir, like to sit in the Kaiser's pew?"

Patton smiled.

"Lead me to it."[32]

Also with Patton was his aide Colonel Charles Codman, who remembered that the church "was packed, hence not quite as cold as it might have been, but frigid nevertheless."[33]

Also among the congregation was a Red Cross worker who observed Patton and recalled his "brick-red face, with its round, receding forehead sparsely framed by silvery-white hair. . . . I saw a tired, aging man, a sorrowful, solitary man, a lonely man, with veiled eyes behind which there was going on a torment of brooding and introspection."[34]

Patton had hoped that his men would reach Bastogne on

Christmas Day, but from reports, he knew that was no longer likely. Abrams's battalion was poised to move again but had been slowed by the battle in Bigonville. It would take them at least another twenty-four hours to reach Bastogne—longer if the Germans continued to mount such stiff opposition. Earlier that day, Patton had sent a message to McAuliffe: "Xmas Eve present coming up. Hold on." It had been a mistake. McAuliffe now had the false hope that relief was only hours away from Bastogne.

Patton had also contacted General Millikin at III Corps and given clear instructions: "Bypass these towns and clear them up later. Tanks can operate on this ground now." But that had again proved to be wishful thinking. The 4th Armored's spearhead—Abrams's 37th Tank Battalion—had not been able to bypass Bigonville.[35] Valuable hours had been lost as Abrams's tankers and accompanying infantry cleared the town to avoid the risk of being attacked from the rear and cut off.

That night, Patton noted in his diary: "This has been a very bad Christmas Eve. All along our line we have received violent counterattacks, one of which forced the 4th Armored back some miles with the loss of ten tanks."

Patton had asked too much of his tankers. Day and night attacks were "all right on the first or second day of the battle and when we had the enemy surprised, but after that the men get too tired. Furthermore, in this bad weather, it is very difficult for armored outfits to operate at night."[36]

Lieutenant Colonel Irzyk's 8th Tank Battalion had done its best but had been badly bloodied at Chaumont. If any unit was going to reach Bastogne, it was Abrams's battalion. But that would now entail, it had been decided, taking a new route, hopefully one not as well defended as the roads used so far. Abrams's force would move even farther to the east, to the left flank of the 4th Armored Division, before rolling on once more toward Bastogne, the market town where seven roads met and that had already cost so much blood.

IN BASTOGNE ITSELF, as Christmas Eve drew to a close, McAuliffe passed a building where his forces held some four hundred German soldiers captive.

He could hear the Germans singing Christmas carols.

McAuliffe entered with an aide.

Some Germans who could speak English learned who their surprise visitor was.

"We'll be out of here soon, General," shouted one prisoner "and you'll be in."

There were other taunts.

"It's nice and cozy in here, General, you'll like it."[37]

"We'll be in Antwerp in a few weeks."[38]

McAuliffe, unruffled, waited for the Germans to fall silent. Then he said simply, "I just came in to wish you all a Merry Christmas."[39]

Meanwhile, Germans outside of Bastogne, tasked with taking the town, steeled themselves for combat the following day, Christ's birthday.

One German soldier wrote to his wife that Christmas Eve:

*Dearest:*

*Against expectations, the planned Christmas Eve
attack did not come off. The whole front is quiet. I
suppose the Americans will be equally glad that
everything is so peaceful on the most beautiful and
sacred evening of the year. They feel the cold even
more than we for they are lying in their holes without
having been issued winter clothes, and that is no
pleasure in this weather, I assure you. . . . Another
hour and I shall be able to go to bed. It's eleven now.
God what terrible things tomorrow may bring.*[40]

# CHAPTER 11

---

# Christ's Birthday

**Bastogne, Belgium**
**December 25, 1944**

FRED MACKENZIE AWOKE around 2 A.M. on Christmas Day. He walked out into the cold night and talked to sentries guarding an entrance to General McAuliffe's headquarters. Around an hour later, he heard planes overhead. "I told myself they were friendly planes," he recalled. "It couldn't be that Christmas morning would bring new horror to the defenders of Bastogne."

It could indeed. Bombs were falling on Bastogne. "Down, down they came and one of the sentries cried, 'In here, sir!' As I plunged into a foxhole where they stood guard with .30 caliber machine guns, bombs burst everywhere, but we were unscathed. . . . Here was the supreme moment of apprehension for me at Bastogne."

An explosion less than a hundred yards away sprayed shrapnel in all directions, and MacKenzie reached a breaking point: "I was physically and spiritually folded in one little knot of thought which ran something like this: 'Thy will be done—for how long, I do not know.'"[1]

MacKenzie survived the bombing.

The real ordeal for many others at Bastogne and across the Ardennes on Christ's birthday was about to begin.

CHRISTMAS DAY dawned cold and bright in Luxembourg, where Patton, not yet aware of the early-morning bombing of Bastogne, wrote to his wife, Beatrice: "The Lord has given us the 3 consecutive days of good weather and things are looking up but so far I am the only one attacking. I am going out now to push it. I love you and hope for the best."[2]

He would also note in his diary that day: "A clear cold Christmas, lovely weather for killing Germans, which seems a bit queer, seeing Whose birthday it is."[3]

In Bastogne, men were worried that the Germans would attack once more after the bombing and that this time they would succeed. "The appearance of German armor and infantry bearing down on the heart of the defenses seemed more and more a probability," recalled the journalist MacKenzie, still the only reporter in Bastogne with the 101st Airborne, "and if it did appear, the defense of Bastogne could deteriorate almost at once into a wild and disorganized struggle at the multiple crossroads."

According to MacKenzie, that morning, for the first time "since the start of the siege," General McAuliffe was "alarmed": "Headquarters personnel privy to the secrets of the operations room looked to the condition of their own arms and thought it probable they would be forming their own force of combative cooks, clerks, drivers and helpers."[4]

And where the hell was Patton's relief force? McAuliffe ordered a forward artillery observer to take off in a Piper Cub spotter plane and try to find the 4th Armored.

The forward observer returned, having flown over German lines south of Bastogne, and told McAuliffe about the enemy positions.

"Hell, I know that!" snapped McAuliffe. "I want to know where the 4th Armored is."[5]

The plunging temperatures were causing as many casualties, it seemed, as the Germans.[6] Paratrooper Sergeant Schuyler Jackson recalled that "there were a couple of replacements who actually froze to death while on duty. I would always have two guys go out there to keep the men awake and prevent them from freezing. When one of our planes was shot down, I took a fleece-lined jacket from the body of one of our crew. It sounds terrible but he had no more use for it."[7]

For one private in the 10th Armored, Walter Lipinski, Christmas Day "was just another day; you never knew it was Christmas Day. It didn't seem like there was ever a Christmas there. I lost track of the days of the week."[8]

Another soldier from the 10th Armored Division remembered how his battalion chaplain "held Mass on the hood of his jeep. Every soldier not on duty at the time was there, such was the feeling of dread and the thought of impending death. Perhaps this Mass would shield us all from the advancing evil!"

A tanker from the 10th recalled that "President Roosevelt promised that everyone would have turkey for Christmas, and in Bastogne a jeep pulled up and put a frozen turkey on the front of our tank. . . . [Roosevelt] did keep his promise."[9]

As for the Germans, they were determined to deliver Bastogne as a Christmas gift for their Führer. That morning, they prepared to strike, and intense shelling preceded their attack.[10] Fred MacKenzie believed the Germans "counted on smashing into Bastogne by 8 o'clock." If not, "American airpower would catch [them] on the open plains in broad daylight and end all chance of a Christmas Day victory."[11]

Vital to the defense of Bastogne that Christmas Day was air controller Captain Parker, who directed planes to targets and, according to MacKenzie, "stood by his jeep with his map spread out on the hood and chattered on the radio almost constantly to the pilots."[12]

Thanks in part to Parker, the Ninth Air Force provided vital support: "Thunderbolt fighter-bombers streaked in low over the white, cold battlefield, bombing and strafing German armor and troop concentrations."

Screaming Eagles looked up into the skies and watched the action in a "dreamlike state."[13]

While the soldiers closest to the Germans manned the perimeter defenses, they watched as the P-47s dived on German positions and grew concerned that they too might become targets.[14] In some places, men laid down markers to show that they were Americans.

MacKenzie recalled that the "blasts of the bombs and the racket of the German anti-aircraft guns furnished an audible gauge of the battlefield's dimensions. The island resisting the gray-green sea was made to seem very small and survival all the more miraculous."[15]

Before the day was over, American fighters would fly more than four thousand sorties. Oberst Ludwig Heilmann of the 5th Fallschirmjäger Division remembered "an uninterrupted trail of burning vehicles extending like a torchlight procession from Bastogne all the way back to the Westwall. . . . In my opinion, the Ardennes offensive was irretrievably lost when the Allies sent their air forces into action on 25 December, a fact that even the simplest soldier realized."[16]

Drifting snow slowed traffic along roads reaching all the way back to Germany, making the Germans' vehicles easy targets. In some places, men tried to put up snow fences to contain the drifts, but they were pulled down by freezing German troops hunting for firewood. Snowplows, including those drawn by horses, were few and far between. Colder temperatures meant that panzers could move across frozen fields and did not have to squeeze onto icy and narrow roads, but whenever the Panthers and Tigers appeared in the open, Allied planes almost inevitably, it seemed, soon arrived.

At one point that Monday, December 25, Allied planes spotted a convoy of some seventy trucks transporting gasoline. Every truck was soon ablaze, belching black smoke into the frigid air. German planes were in the skies too. But according to one account, many pilots in the Luftwaffe were losing their nerve and "were all too ready to seize on the slightest excuse for returning early from their missions. [They] had no zest for facing the heavy Allied onslaught."[17]

FIGHTING RAGED along the fragile perimeter defenses around Bastogne. It was surely only a matter of minutes or at most a few hours before the Germans finally broke through to the heart of Bastogne itself.

When enemy tanks appeared in one sector, men panicked and ran for the nearest trees.

A soldier looked up and saw his company's captain.

The captain had his arms in the air.

He wasn't running.

He was out in the open.

The soldier looked at his leader and for a moment thought he looked like Jesus Christ.

"Hold up right there!" cried the captain. "This is as far as we're going to run. Turn around, we're going back to get the bastards!"[18]

The soldiers did so and, after fighting with other units, repulsed the attack.

Elsewhere, freezing men held their positions. One battalion commander, Major John Hanlon, had never experienced such intense combat. Several times, he saw the facial expressions of German soldiers, so close was the action.

Hanlon came across one of his men, a private, draped in a white sheet for camouflage.

The private stood calmly beside a house and watched six Germans attacking from the rear of Hanlon's position.

"How do you suppose they got inside our circle?" asked Hanlon.

"Beats me," said the private, "but they'll have a hell of a time getting out."[19]

The private was true to his word.

The Screaming Eagles elsewhere inflicted significant casualties. "The snowy fields," recalled Fred MacKenzie, "blotched with dead men and ruined armor, by now were aglitter with bright sunlight."[20]

One Panzergrenadier Division, the 15th, was almost destroyed and another German division lost more than eight hundred men. Companies were decimated. Some Germans had gotten to within a mile of the outskirts of Bastogne, but they too were finally stopped by dogged American defenses. Fortunately, the Germans had not concentrated their assaults in one sector. Outnumbering the Americans now by four to one, they would surely have prevailed in one concerted attack but instead had fought piecemeal from several directions.

At 9:15 A.M. that day, McAuliffe was on the radio reporting to General Gaffey, who was commanding the 4th Armored.

"101st Airborne Division in Bastogne," reported McAuliffe, "received a counterattack this morning by enemy tanks and infantry from the West. Some of the enemy broke through into the artillery positions. Situation's sticky but the 101st will handle [it]."[21]

It had been a close-run thing but far more costly for the Germans. The commander of the attacking forces, Kokott, knew that, given the Americans' resistance that morning, he could not now take Bastogne without significant reinforcements. He also learned that south of Bastogne the 5th Fallschirmjäger was in trouble, unable to do much more than lay mines and set tank traps. The plan to take Bastogne had become, he later noted, "a bloody, dubious and costly struggle for what was, in the final analysis, an unimportant village."[22]

Twenty years after the war, McAuliffe would still vividly remember the fighting that day. "It was a terrible attack. . . . You would have thought that the spirit of Christmas had vanished from the world. You could hear the rumble of the artillery, everywhere, incessantly. The dead were all around, frozen to grotesque shapes."

McAuliffe looked at a German "tank-man, stretched half out of his tank, with horror of death stamped on his face. German infantrymen had been snared on barbed wire, then caught in a crossfire until they were left like terrible stiff scarecrows. There was a GI sprawled in a foxhole, trying to stop an agony he could not feel."[23]

The details became seared into the minds of the men who saw them. One of McAuliffe's men, Corporal James L. Evans of the 101st Airborne, came across a German tank: "There was a German . . . burned to a crisp hanging upside down on the right side of the tank. His foot was caught in or near the opening on the top of the tank. There was a brown leather suitcase strapped on the right front of the tank that had not burned."[24]

Evans and his buddies continued toward Bastogne. They spotted McAuliffe in a jeep. He was speaking with a colonel.

A shell flew overhead.

"We all hit the ditches," recalled Evans. "Then another shell came over."

McAuliffe wisely decided to return to Bastogne as fast as possible.

Bastogne was by no means secure; the fighting would only intensify. But in stopping the Germans that morning, McAuliffe's men had achieved greatness in defying the odds. McAuliffe remembered that "there was a great spirit of thankfulness to God. I hadn't planned to go to mass that day, but I happened by this large and imposing home with a steeple-like roof on my way to the command post. I knew the priest and I could see him inside and I felt I should go in. Inside you could hear the guns rumbling in the distance. There was a very large attendance, for the religious feeling was widespread."[25]

RELIGIOUS SERVICES were well attended wherever they were held—in a house, around a jeep, or otherwise. A chaplain with the 12th Infantry Regiment, George Knapp, held six Christmas Day services in a bowling alley in Luxembourg. "Many of those men who had been relieved from the foxholes the night before were there with their gas masks and everything," recalled Knapp."[26]

Meanwhile, at his headquarters in Luxembourg, Patton was increasingly impatient. His tankers had yet to reach Bastogne. Why the delay?

"The [commanding officer] of the Combat Team I ordered sent up isn't sitting on his dead end, is he?" asked Patton. "I want him in the lines."

A staff officer did not know where the team had gotten to.

"Get hold of him," ordered Patton, "and tell him to get the hell up there. I want every man to be fighting. There are to be no reserves. Everybody fights. Tell him I'm coming right out there to see what the hell is going on, and he'd better damned sure be fighting."[27]

Patton left his headquarters, headed once more to visit his commanders in the field. Patton's jeep driver that Christmas Day remembered: "We drove all day long, from one outfit to another. He'd stop and talk to the troops; ask them did they get turkey, how was it, and all that."

Patton moved that afternoon from one command post to another. "As he approached our headquarters from the direction of Arlon a fighter plane (American without markings of any kind) strafed his small convoy of jeeps," remembered Lieutenant Colonel Hal Pattison of the 4th Armored Division. "As any other mortal, General Patton found refuge in the roadside ditch. After his departure and since only his dignity was harmed, we had a good laugh at his expense."[28]

Patton himself recalled it somewhat differently: "When we were with Combat Command 'A' (Brigadier General H. L. Earnest) of the 4th Armored, two German airplanes strafed and bombed us, but without success. This was the only time in the fighting in Germany or France that I was actually picked out on the road and attacked by German Air."[29]

Later that day, Patton arrived at the HQ of the 26th Division. The commanding general, Willard S. Paul, had been worried that Patton was going to dismiss him and was greatly relieved when instead Patton put his arm around his shoulder and asked: "How's my little fighting sonofabitch?"[30]

Paul later told a fellow general: "I was so cheered for not getting relieved, there was nothing I wouldn't do for the man."[31]

When Patton finally returned to Luxembourg, he noted in his

diary that he was impressed by his men's demeanor. "All were very cheerful," he wrote, but "I am not, because we are not going fast enough."[32]

Most men out on the battlefield had received some form of Christmas dinner, including turkey. In some cases, cooks risked their lives to get the hot chow to men in foxholes. And some made the ultimate sacrifice to do so, angering men who thought staying alive was more important than lukewarm turkey. In any case, they would have preferred extra K rations instead.

Other Screaming Eagles spent the day as POWs, vulnerable to friendly fire attacks from the air as they were moved toward the Third Reich. Sergeant Robert Bowen had survived the Normandy invasion and Operation Market Garden only to be captured. As he walked along a road, he was being guarded by a middle-aged German soldier. "He had gotten a ration of fried chicken," recalled Bowen, "and he waved pieces under my nose, saying: 'Das is gut, ya?' Then he would take a bite.".

American planes attacked. "We dove for the ditches, all but [the] taunting guard." Bullets came very close but a brave medic managed to signal by waving his arms and the planes did not return. "The bullets had barely missed my head as they tracked across the road. The taunting guard lay in a widening pool of blood, the chicken leg still grasped in his hand."[33]

THE 37TH TANK Battalion pushed on, slowly closing the gap to Bastogne. The dirty Shermans clanked through four sullen villages in a couple of hours only to have to stop while a bulldozer tank filled a crater in the road. Ahead was a village called Remoiville, some seven miles southeast of Bastogne.

All that morning, as his battalion's progress was on everyone's minds, Creighton Abrams had been tireless. No doubt operating on adrenaline, he'd moved in a jeep from one company to another, issuing instinctual, crisp commands, reading the landscape ahead. But then his jeep drove over a mine and his driver was badly wounded. Abrams was not hit, and after getting the driver medical aid he found another jeep and again returned to action.

Bastogne was tantalizingly close. But Abrams knew the last stretch of road could well be the most dangerous. The Germans blocking the way would surely fight harder than ever, knowing that the relief of Bastogne would herald inevitable defeat.

AT EISENHOWER's headquarters in Versailles, there was precious little Christmas cheer. Ike's assistant and driver, Kay Summersby, recalled: "General Ike, apologetic because the long-awaited Christmas party was impossible, invited some of his intimates to dinner. I thought him more depressed than at any time since I'd met him. He was low, really low."[34]

Nothing had lifted his spirits, not Summersby's graceful presence, nor the delicious dinner of roast turkey, nor the presents from his wife, Mamie—king-sized cigarettes, which he would chain-smoke, and a pair of slippers.

To the north, at his 21st Army Group's headquarters, a confident Montgomery wrote a letter that Christmas Day to the guardian of his son, David, who was at boarding school in England. He explained that he had not been able to get back for Christmas because the Germans had "decreed otherwise. . . . The Americans have taken a 1st class bloody nose; I have taken over command of the First and Ninth American armies and all troops in the northern part of the front, and I am sorting out the mess."[35]

Patton dined that evening with Bradley in Luxembourg and discussed the broader strategic picture and what he regarded as the unforgivably slow response of Montgomery, now indeed commanding Allied forces to the north of the Ardennes.

That same evening, General Hasso von Manteuffel dined on captured American K rations at his headquarters, a Belgian château.

Manteuffel had thoughtfully provided another serving of K rations for a guest, Major Willi Johannmeier, one of Hitler's adjutants.

"The drive to Antwerp must be abandoned at once," said Manteuffel.

There was still time to salvage something from the debacle in the Ardennes, but Hitler's grand scheme had become impossible—and probably always had been.

Johannmeier put a call through to Jodl at Hitler's headquarters and relayed Manteuffel's message.

Manteuffel then spoke to Jodl himself.

"The Führer hasn't made his decision yet," said Jodl.

"But you know a decision has to be made now," insisted Manteuffel, "or it may be too late. What's more, I need immediate replacements."

"I can only give you one more armored division," said Jodl. "And remember the Führer doesn't want you to move back one foot. Go forward! Not back!"[36]

In Bastogne, McAuliffe and his staff also gathered for a Christmas dinner.

A master sergeant named Herman Smith had prepared a meal—lemon meringue pie, K rations, and some tinned salmon.

The dinner table had, according to the journalist MacKenzie, "a centerpiece—a cluster of spruce boughs decorated with a paper star at the top."

McAuliffe ate the rations, but when he and others then started on the pie, the building began to shake from the blasts of bombs dropping close by.

"Let's get out of here," said McAuliffe.

The officers left the room, one of them taking a slice of the pie with him. There was a moment of humor as the pie "splattered in his face as he went out the door, and he was laughing as he dashed into the cellar below."[37]

The humorous moment was but a brief relief. A disappointed McAuliffe contacted Troy Middleton, VIII Corps commander, that evening and told him over the telephone: "We have been let down."[38]

But with the bigger picture at hand, and as Christmas Day drew to a close, George S. Patton was ebullient. The 4th Armored was closing on Bastogne, slower than he'd wanted, yes, but closing. And he was proud of his Quartermaster Corps's success in delivering a modicum of Christmas comfort to his troops. He noted in his diary that "on this Christmas Day every soldier had turkey; those in the front had turkey sandwiches and the rest, hot turkey. I know of no army in the world except the American which could have done such a thing. The men were surprisingly cheerful."[39]

And one German officer sheltering five miles to the northwest of Bastogne, in the village of Champs, was contemplative. In a classroom, the officer found some chalk and left a message on a blackboard:

> May the world never again live through such a Christmas. . . . Nothing is more horrible than meeting one's fate, far from mother, wife, and children.
>
> Is it worthy of man's destiny to bereave a mother of her son, a wife of her husband, or children of their father?
>
> Life was bequeathed to us in order that we might love and be considerate of one another.
>
> From the ruins, out of blood and death shall come forth a brotherly world.[40]

IN FOXHOLES near and around Bastogne, Americans also tried their best to find hope, to get through Christmas night, and to avoid freezing to death.

Then one paratrooper finally learned what Patton had known: that Abrams's forces were approaching from the south.

Relief was at hand.

"[Patton] didn't know the words 'can't do it,'" he recalled. The news was "like manna from heaven."[41]

# PART THREE

---

# Salvation

Sure we want to go home. We want this war over with. The quickest way to get it over with is to go get the bastards who started it. The quicker they are whipped, the quicker we can go home. The shortest way home is through Berlin and Tokyo. And when we get to Berlin, I am personally going to shoot that paper hanging son of a bitch Hitler, just like I'd shoot a snake!

My men don't dig foxholes. I don't want them to. Foxholes only slow up an offensive. Keep moving. And don't give the enemy time to dig one either.[1]

—GEORGE S. PATTON

# CHAPTER 12

## "Let 'er Roll!"

**Remichampagne, Belgium**
**December 26, 1944**

DAWN BROKE on December 26, 1944. Colonel Creighton Abrams climbed up onto a tank, ready to make the final push for Bastogne. He was on a road leading to a hamlet called Remichampagne, six miles from Bastogne. "It had been decided that a special team, mainly consisting of C Company, 37th Tank Battalion, under temporary command of Captain William A. Dwight, would [attack] in order to break the siege of that town and to contact the surrounded American defenders," he recalled.[1]

Creighton's force began to roll. By this stage in the war, one of the greatest menaces was Germans wielding Panzerfausts—single-shot equivalents of the bazooka that could destroy a tank at close range. German teenagers, pumped up on amphetamines, could be lurking behind a tree or a hedgerow or in a ditch and suddenly emerge. And so, unless the infantry had cleared a route, tankers used their most potent weapon, their .50-caliber machine guns, raking roadsides, ripping and shredding trees and fences. Moving at full speed—around twenty-five miles per hour on a road, sixteen miles per hour across open ground— helped reduce the chances of being hit, especially by a German tank or anti-tank vehicle armed with the formidable 88mm gun, the most feared weapon among US forces in Europe, but this was often impossible that day along the icy, winding roads.

IN BASTOGNE, McAuliffe stood beside Captain Parker in a courtyard at the Belgian barracks that served as his head-quarters.

A German plane swooped down and McAuliffe ran for cover.[2]

The plane passed over.

McAuliffe walked back across the courtyard. The journalist MacKenzie watched as he did so. "He seemed much older," he wrote of McAuliffe, "surrendering a little to the weariness."[3]

McAuliffe might have looked drained but his voice was clear and commanding as he spoke to men gathered in the courtyard.

"This is without a doubt the war's most important single en-gagement involving a small force," said McAuliffe. "It has been touch-and-go at times. But the situation definitely is improving, especially now that the clear weather is permitting air opera-tions."[4]

As McAuliffe spoke, Abrams's force closed in. "The Germans had overrun and cut up many American units," recalled Abrams.

"We had orders to pick up the remnants and bring them into our outfit. We found some Americans and we found some Germans. We had to be careful not to shoot the wrong men. We picked up some badly needed American tanks, too, that the Germans had captured, and were using. We didn't have to shoot them up much, so they were all right."[5]

It was around midday on December 26. Abrams had pushed forward in his tank and caught up with his spearhead, B Company, which was commanded by Captain Jimmie Leach.

As Abrams's tank rolled toward Leach's, which was called *Blockbuster*, a German anti-tank gun opened up. Abrams ordered Leach to deal with the German gun. Leach issued an order.

A tank in Leach's company began to position itself for a shot but too slowly for Abrams's liking. His own tank rolled forward. "Abrams fired one round," recalled Leach. It destroyed the German gun. "I [later] recommended him for the [Distinguished Service Cross] . . . A lot of colonels stay back at the goddamn flagpole but not Abrams."[6]

And that seemed the theme of the day. At 2 P.M., the 4th Armored's commander, Major General Hugh Gaffey, contacted Patton.

"Will you authorize a big risk . . . for a breakthrough to Bastogne?" asked Gaffey.

"I sure as hell will!" replied Patton.[7]

Abrams and his tanks reached a hillside that overlooked the villages of Clochimont and Assenois. They were just a few miles from the 101st Airborne's perimeter around Bastogne.

"We're going to get to those people," said Abrams.

One of Abrams's tankers remembered: "The Germans had these two little towns of Clochimont and Assenois on the secondary road we were using to get to Bastogne. Beyond Assenois, the road ran up a ridge through heavy woods. There were a lot of Germans there, too. We were going through fast, all guns firing, straight up that road to bust through before they had time to get set."[8]

As Abrams moved through Clochimont, a German shell exploded, killing a man in a nearby half-track. Then a telephone pole fell on top of a tank. Under sniper fire, Abrams and others crawled out of their tanks and removed the pole so they could advance once more.

It was, according to one account, just after 3 P.M. when Abrams was given a message from Gaffey: "His face was impassive but his eyes glinted. He shoved a big cigar in his mouth. It stuck out aggressively like another gun."

He was standing in the tank turret.

"We're going in to those people now. Let 'er roll."[9]


ASSENOIS WAS fiercely defended. According to tank commander Nat Frankel, the ensuing combat was "a gruesome, last-ditch effort by the Germans . . . these Germans simply refused to fall back; they were a final stonewall in which each block of granite preferred utter demolition to collapse."[10]

Private James R. Hendrix, of the 4th Armored Division, gave his all, displaying extraordinary courage as Abrams's men cleared German positions. "We ran up yelling 'come out,' but they wouldn't," he remembered. "One [German] poked his head out of a foxhole and I shot him through the neck. I got closer and hit another on the head with the butt of my Ml. Others came out with their hands up."

According to his Medal of Honor citation, Hendrix spotted a comrade trapped in a burning half-track and braved "enemy sniper fire and exploding mines and ammunition in the vehicle [and] extricated the wounded man and extinguished his flaming clothing, thereby saving the life of his fellow soldier."[11]

Hendrix didn't receive a scratch. "That's really what made Christmas great for me," he later recalled.[12] In the words of Nat Frankel: "Hendrix was one of the few soldiers who actually did what the Alvin Yorks and Audie Murphys are supposed to have done."[13]

AFTER CLOCHIMONT and Assenois, Abrams's force rolled on toward Bastogne, with less than three miles left. The lead tank, named *Cobra King*, was commanded by Lieutenant Charles Boggess. "I believe it is appointed to each man to have a few minutes of glory in his life," recalled Boggess, who was married and had worked as an undertaker before the war. "Mine lasted four miles and 25 minutes."[14]

Sunset was coming at 4:30 P.M. It would be dark half an hour later. The day was running out. Boggess's tank came to a standstill and then Boggess climbed out and made his way to Abrams's tank. He and Abrams then "studied a well-worn battle map. . . . [Abrams] decided that 'C' Company would take a little-known secondary road leading . . . to Bastogne, a distance of approximately 3½ miles. He explained that there had been no recon work done on the road, but it was known that all this area was held by the enemy. If we could get through on this road, it might work well for a surprise attack."[15]

Abrams then gave a "familiar short and explicit order":

"Get to those men in Bastogne."

Boggess gathered seven tank commanders and briefed them. As the company commander, Boggess would lead the way and set the pace. He would order his gunner to lay fire directly in front of the column. The tank behind him would aim to the right and the one behind that would fire to the left.

Boggess looked over at Abrams's tank.

Abrams gave a hand signal.

Boggess's column moved out. There were forty-five men under his command in C Company.[16]

Ahead, on the outskirts of Bastogne, a 10th Armored technical sergeant, Thaddeus Krasnoborski, heard his radio crackle and then a "steady stream of profanity directed to the Krauts in front of [Boggess's] column [of tanks]." The 4th Armored "was about to punch a hole" through the German line—through the "lousy Kraut bastards."[17]

Abrams arrived at the crest of a hill. In a tank nearby was Abrams's operations officer, Captain William Dwight. There was the sound of planes. "I saw these damn C-47s," recalled Dwight, "coming in to drop their colored parachutes for the 101st. They were taking one hell of a beating. We trembled standing there and watching it. . . . After Abe [Abrams] watched that, he said, 'Well, if those fellows can take that, we're going in right now.' And that was it."[18]

"Concentration Number Nine," said Abrams over the radio. "Play it soft and sweet."

Supporting artillery fired more than four hundred rounds ahead of Abrams's force, blasting an opening toward Bastogne.

Boggess's tank, *Cobra King*, rolled on through a thickly wooded area. Germans fired on the column and Boggess's gunners replied. "We were going through fast," recalled Boggess, "all guns firing, straight up the road to bust through."[19]

Corporal Milton Dickerman was manning the .50-caliber machine gun on Boggess's tank, which was driven by Private Hubert S. Smith.

Smith looked through a periscope. It was dirtied, making seeing ahead harder. "I sorta guessed at the road," he remembered. "Had a little trouble when my left brake locked and the tank turned up a road where we didn't want to go. So I just stopped her, backed her up and went on again."[20]

Two miles beyond Assenois, Boggess looked ahead. There were hundreds of colored parachutes strewn across a field.

Ahead of C Company's column, a Screaming Eagle spotted Boggess's tank and the others following behind and thought they were German.

"Christ, fucked again!"[21]

Boggess's column rolled on, .50-caliber and .30-caliber machine guns blazing. Then Boggess saw a pillbox and ordered Corporal Dickerman to fire, and it was quickly destroyed. Germans were panicking up ahead, on both sides of the road, as they came under fire from the column, taken utterly by surprise, and they "fell like dominoes."

Then Boggess's tank broke out of the woods. Boggess ordered his column to slow down as he neared what appeared to be a line of foxholes. "Out of each hole," he remembered, "a machine gun was leveled at my tank, with a helmeted figure behind each gun."[22]

Americans.

Boggess was worried they would open fire.

"Come on out, this is the 4th Armored!" he shouted.

No one did so.

He shouted again.

An officer climbed out of the foxhole closest to Boggess and approached. Then he was right beside *Cobra King*, smiling and reaching up to shake Boggess's hand.

"I'm Lieutenant Webster of the 326th Engineers, 101st Airborne Division. Glad to see you!"

Boggess shook his hand. He knew that at that moment his men—C Company of the 37th Tank Battalion, 4th Armored, Third Army—"had broken through the bulge and that the siege of Bastogne was over."[23]

Behind Boggess came Abrams. The light was fading fast. A *Yank* magazine reporter spotted Abrams "as dusk started to come down. Col. Abrams rode through—a short stocky man with sharp features—already a legendary figure in this war."[24] Half an hour later, Abrams was talking with Brigadier General Anthony McAuliffe. "The 101st was doing business as usual," Abrams remembered. "Their morale was high. They joined forces with us and we kicked the Germans around some more."[25]

McAuliffe had arrived by jeep so he could welcome Patton's relief force. He had ordered the men with him to look as smart as possible and to be clean-shaven. He did not want Abrams to think that he and his fellow Screaming Eagles had been under extraordinary stress—though of course they had been, doing everything they could to survive.[26]

The arrival of Patton's forces in Bastogne was unforgettable for many who witnessed it. "Our paratroopers were cheering and yelling when they saw us," recalled Sergeant John Beck of the 704th Tank Destroyer Battalion. "There was a fellow from my neighborhood back in Queens, N.Y. in a foxhole at Bastogne with the 101st that saw me as I drove by on the top of my tank destroyer. I didn't recognize him because he was covered with dirt. He told me the story after the war."[27]

Lieutenant Colonel Albin Irzyk, commanding the 8th Tank Battalion, remembered the euphoria of finally breaking through to Bastogne: "The tank radios began buzzing with excitement but surprisingly, after a brief period, things became quiet."

Irzyk's fellow tankers "were completely exhausted, totally wrung out. . . . So there was little celebrating. Their reward was knowing that they had successfully completed a great job."[28]

According to Brigadier General William Roberts, who had served in the 4th Armored Division, Colonel Abrams deserved particular credit for getting Patton's spearhead to Bastogne: "Abrams knew where every tank was. He knew where every piece of equipment was, and he was able to command and move his outfit and always defeated the enemy in front of him. It was just that simple."[29]

Abrams would receive the Distinguished Service Cross for his brilliant leadership.[30] His would be a long and distinguished career. He would notably, according to one report, be "one of the few high-ranking officers to emerge from the Vietnam War with his reputation unscathed."[31]

Abrams became army chief of staff in 1972 but died two years later from cancer. At his funeral in Arlington National Cemetery, President Gerald R. Ford described him as "that rare combination, a man of action who was also a first-class administrator." And: "an American hero in the best tradition."[32]

THE NEWS of the breakthrough to Bastogne delighted Patton. "It was a daring thing and well done," he wrote. "Of course, they may be cut off, but I doubt it. . . . The speed of our movements is amazing, even to me, and must be a constant source of surprise to the Germans."[33]

Once the initial push broke through, there was a corridor for supply of men and matériel. But it was precarious. The Germans were counterattacking. "We have a corridor but it's under fire," Patton wrote that evening. "I'm taking no chances on losing men and supplies that way. There's a big difference between wading in and slugging the enemy and letting him sit off and potshot you."

Patton knew that the enemy expected convoys to follow Abrams's force. The Germans would try their best to destroy any vehicle braving the corridor. "We're not going to play into their hands that way," noted Patton. "Tomorrow, when the corridor has been widened and reinforced, we'll start trucking. Until then we'll continue to supply by air. It's a lot better to be sure than sorry."[34]

Even though Abrams's force had arrived in Bastogne, Patton

knew only too well that the situation was still dire. It was especially the case for the wounded. They needed to be evacuated to hospitals but this would not be possible until the fragile corridor to Bastogne was safer.

Patton's men had succeeded in a considerable feat of arms, pushed and encouraged and exhorted by their flamboyant, mercurial, fire-breathing commander. To reach Bastogne, it had taken five long days and truly massive supporting fire—some fifty-five thousand rounds of artillery.[35]

Not often one for modesty, Patton wrote to his wife, Beatrice, that evening that "the relief of Bastogne is the most brilliant operation we have thus far performed and is in my opinion the outstanding achievement of this war."[36]

Patton was pleased not only by this accomplishment, but that his entreaties to the Almighty had finally yielded results. "My Prayer seems to be working still," he also wrote Beatrice, "as we have had three days of good weather and our air has been very active. Of course, they overstate [their results] at least 50% but they do scare the Huns. . . . I have some [Christmas] boxes from you that I will open after supper."[37]

Long after the war, McAuliffe would pay Patton his due, even if begrudgingly. "Most of us," he remembered, "thought [Patton] never had a very good staff but he certainly accomplished miracles with it."[38]

Much hard fighting remained and the Germans would launch further attacks on Bastogne. But there was no doubting as that historic day, December 26, ended that Patton's warriors and the defenders of Bastogne had written one of the most glorious chapters in all US military history.

# CHAPTER 13

---

# His Finest Hours

**Bastogne, Belgium**
**December 27, 1944**

IT WAS DUSK on December 27 when Maxwell Taylor, the division commander of the 101st Airborne, neared Bastogne in a jeep. He had been stateside when the battle began, and he had arrived in France on Christmas Eve, eager to resume command of his division.

On the way to Bastogne, Taylor stopped at an outpost where he encountered some 4th Armored officers and war correspondents. The corridor into Bastogne was still under attack and fragile indeed.

"You'd better not go into Bastogne yet," said one of the 4th Armored men. "The corridor is so narrow you can spit across it. The Jerries have this road zeroed in good now."

"I have to get in tonight," said Taylor.

He carried on in the jeep. It was less than an hour later when he walked into McAuliffe's headquarters.

The staff was drinking brandy.

"Well, boys," said Taylor, "you're heroes."

"Who, us?" asked McAuliffe.

"Everybody's been worried about you. Just what is the condition of the division?"

"No damned reason to be worried about us," said McAuliffe. "We're ready to attack."[1]


THE GERMAN ARMIES in the Ardennes were in an increasingly precarious situation. It was after dark the next day, December 28, when Hitler held a conference with his senior commanders. Manteuffel and Rundstedt both recommended withdrawal of forces before they became trapped.

Hitler instead ordered them to attack once more.

"The question is whether Germany has the will to remain in existence or whether it will be destroyed," said Hitler. "The loss of this war will destroy the German people. . . . I have never learned to know the word 'capitulation.'"

Hitler then added: "For me the situation today is nothing new. I have been in very much worse situations. . . . As much as I may be tormented by worries and even physically shaken by them, nothing will make the slightest change in my decision to fight on till at last the scales tip to our side."[2]

And so the last great battle on the Western Front continued

unabated, an increasingly bloody slugfest. One soldier in the 82nd Airborne recalled fighting the SS that December 28 and the miserable conditions: "Sometimes you would think, if you were wounded, at least you would be where it was warm and clean, and you would have a good meal, and above all some good sleep and rest, maybe. We continued to lose more men, and half the time we did not even know their names."[3]

Another soldier remembered a GI beside him in a foxhole being hit by machine-gun fire: "We were cut off . . . we were in foxholes by ourselves, so we both knew he was going to die. We had no morphine. We couldn't ease [the pain] so I tried to knock him out. I took off his helmet, held his jaw up, and just whacked it as hard as I could, because he wanted to be put out. That didn't work, so I hit him up by the head with a helmet and that didn't work. Nothing worked. He slowly froze to death, he bled to death."[4]

Harold Lindstrom was an assistant mortar gunner fighting with the 75th Infantry Division on December 29. "I prayed that I be willing to submit myself into His hands," he remembered. "There were too many things happening that I had no control over. From now on I would accept His plans for me."[5]

GIs needed something to hold on to other than a rifle or a buddy in a foxhole at night when sharing body warmth. Many relied on their faith.[6] According to a study done just after the war, conducted by the US Army's Information and Education Division, combatants like Lindstrom were in the majority, especially in terrifying situations, with almost three-quarters relying on prayer as their reason to carry on. In less arduous conditions, less than fifty percent turned to God for help.[7] The closer to death men were, the nearer they felt to the Almighty.

Harold Lindstrom was convinced that only God would spare him. He vowed that if he lived, he would attend church every Sunday. That December 29, his prayers worked: "I felt a calm go over my body. My soul and my body became two different things sharing the same place. My body may become wounded or killed but my soul could not be destroyed or eliminated."

The next day, December 30, a headline appeared in the *Washington Post*: "PATTON OF COURSE." Patton was the man of the hour: "It has become a sort of unwritten rule in this war that when there is a fire to put out, it is Patton who jumps into his boots, slides down the pole, and starts rolling."[8]

That same day, Patton made his way toward Bastogne. Captain Donald N. Martin remembered encountering Patton along the way: "Some people were coming up the hill behind us. I yelled for them to stay down. They paid no heed, just kept walking. Well, this really infuriated me so I started yelling some real Sunday school words at them."

A corporal nudged Martin.

"Sir, you better stop yelling like that—it's General Patton!"

Once Patton joined Martin, they watched as shells began to land on enemy positions. Martin had earlier asked for supporting fire. One shell directly hit the hatch of a German tank, which erupted as the ammunition inside exploded.

"Now by God," said Patton, "that is good firing!"[9]

Sergeant Warren Swanquist of the 10th Armored witnessed Patton's subsequent arrival in shell-ravaged Bastogne itself:

"This jeep came down the alley with flags waving away like crazy, it was General Patton! He had all his guns, his [ivory-handled] pistols. I was right next to him; I could've grabbed him I was so close. He was smiling. I rifle-saluted him and he hand-saluted me."[10]

Patton had many men to congratulate and others to decorate. Screaming Eagle Joseph Pangerl described Patton's visit to the 502nd PIR's regimental HQ to meet with Colonel Steve Chappuis.

Patton pinned a "medal on our Colonel for we were the regiment that finally stopped the last big German effort. I was waiting for him with my camera."

Pangerl snapped away.

Patton noticed him and walked over so Pangerl could get a better shot of his face.

"Now get a good one!"[11]

Charlie Sanderson fought with the 78th Infantry Division. A lieutenant had told him: "We're going to fight until the last man. The first man to turn around, I'll shoot him in the back." And then that day he finally saw "Blood and Guts, General Patton. . . . He saved our ass, you know. We were surrounded."[12]

While visiting Bastogne, Patton stayed in contact with his field commanders. Henry Barnes, a medical evacuation officer, watched that afternoon as Patton barked orders into a field phone. "He had a high-pitched voice and he was bawling out the division commanders of the units on his flanks."

If a commander dared to raise any objection to an order, Patton's response was simple and highly effective.

"I am up here," Patton pointed out. "Why aren't you?"[13]

Earlier that day, Patton had ordered Troy Middleton's 11th Armored Division into action, determined to keep up the pressure on the enemy. There had not been sufficient preparation, let alone reconnaissance, and the division was now struggling to gain traction. Patton met with Middleton later that day at the 11th Armored's command post and expressed his displeasure.

As Patton left, he tripped over the feet of Middleton's jeep driver.

"You dumb fool," said the driver, not realizing it was Patton.

"Well," replied Patton, "you're the first sonofabitch I've seen around this outfit that knows what the hell he's trying to do."[14]

THE FOLLOWING DAY, New Year's Eve 1944, snow fell as darkness descended on Screaming Eagles positioned around Bastogne.

Two men from C Company of the 502nd PIR, Sergeant Layton Black and Corporal Marvin Milligan, manned a machine gun.

"Black, did you see that?" asked Milligan.

"No, where?"

"There!"

"What was it?"

"Something moved!"

"I didn't see anything, can you still see it?"

"No."

Then Black saw something.

"Hey Milligan, what was that?"

"Where?"

"Over there!"

"You mean, right there?"

"No, over more to my left."

"Oh! That's that bush again—I think. Did you hear it, or did you see it, Sergeant?"

"I thought I saw something. It must have been that bush. Yeah, that's what it was. Man, I almost pulled the trigger on this air-cooled baby that time!"[15]

Nerves were frayed. Few men were in the mood to celebrate the New Year. More than eight hundred US tanks and tank destroyers had been lost and almost twenty-five thousand Americans had been captured in just two weeks, since December 16.

But as 1944 drew to a close, there was an eruption of noise as many of the Third Army's 344,935 men—that day's official count—opened fire.[16] As Patton recalled, "At midnight on the night of December 31, all guns in the Third Army fired rapid fire . . . on the Germans as a New Year's greeting."[17]

A German corporal in the 11th Panzer Division, Paul-Arthur Zeihe, remembered that as "the clock struck twelve, the Americans began with their fireworks, sending illuminated rockets in the air." Then he saw GIs climbing out of their foxholes and "jumping, skipping around, shooting their weapons and lighting up the whole valley."

Soon after, Zeihe and his comrades joined in, "firing off illuminated rockets, shooting our weapons."

The impromptu New Year's celebration lasted a few minutes and then it was back to war as both sides returned to their foxholes. "It was one of the most beautiful experiences I had during my service," added Zeihe. "We had allowed our humanity to rise that once."

For mile after mile, one American officer wrote, "the artillery all along the front [fired] everything in the book at the Kraut. . . . It was truly a New Year's greeting that the Krauts out in front will not forget. Too, it is no doubt the loneliest and coldest New Year's Eve that many Americans have ever spent."[18]

When the guns fell silent, recalled Patton, "our forward observers stated they could hear the Germans screaming in the woods."[19]

AT FIVE MINUTES past midnight, Hitler spoke to the German people over the radio from his headquarters at the Adlerhorst.

The war was now a "matter of death and life, to be or not to be, and victory will be ours, because ours it must be."[20]

Hitler sounded confident: "Our people are resolved to fight the war to victory under any and all circumstances. . . . We are going to destroy everybody who does not take part in the common effort for the country or who makes himself a tool of the enemy."

The enemy within would be liquidated.

Then Germany, Hitler concluded, "will rise like a phoenix from its ruined cities and this will go down in history as the miracle of the 20th Century!"[21]

Hitler did not mention the fighting in the Ardennes.

Later that morning of New Year's Day, hundreds of German

fighters from what was left of the Luftwaffe took off from Germany in four formations. Three hours later, more than three hundred Allied aircraft had been destroyed, most of them on the ground at air bases in Belgium and northern France. But the German losses were too high to sustain. More than three hundred German pilots were killed.[22]

On the ground, German casualties mounted ever higher as relentless Allied shelling took its toll. One battalion, the 161st Field Artillery, fired more than twenty-five hundred rounds.[23] Some forward artillery observers inched so close to the enemy that they were killed by friendly fire when they called in strikes.

Private Alan Shapiro of the 87th Division recalled New Year's Day vividly—it was beautiful "as the dazzling brightness of the sun nearly blinded me while reflecting off the snow. It was warm enough walking that we didn't need to wear our overcoats."[24]

Shapiro was one of many men in his division who were suffering because of sore or frostbitten feet. That day, he trudged for six hours, falling behind his platoon.

A captain told Shapiro to catch up.

"My feet hurt," replied Shapiro.

"Our feet hurt too," shot back the captain.

"I don't notice you carrying a pack and, even if you were, I wouldn't give a goddamn. My feet hurt, and I don't give a fuck what you say or think."[25]

That first day of 1945, his third year of leading Americans in combat in World War II, Patton sent a message to the men of his Third Army:

George S. Patton in Bourg, France, in 1918 with a Renault tank.

Major General John J. Pershing, followed by Captain George S. Patton, inspecting the men of Patton's headquarters troop, France, 1917.

Patton with General
Dwight Eisenhower,
Tunisia, 1942.

Patton (*left*) aboard USS *Augusta* with Rear Admiral Henry Kent Hewitt,
November 1942, before Operation Torch, the invasion of North Africa.

Patton pointing the way, Gela, Sicily, July 11, 1943.

Patton with
wounded troops,
Sicily, July 1943.

Patton meeting with a USO group in Sicily, August 1943, including comedian Bob Hope (*second from left*) and singer Frances Langford.

Patton meeting with Field Marshal Bernard Montgomery, July 28, 1943, Sicily.

Patton confers with Lieutenant Colonel Lyle Bernard, 30th Infantry Regiment, August 1943, on the road to Messina.

A determined Patton, summer 1943.

Patton pins the Silver Star on Private Ernest A. Jenkins, October 13, 1944, France. Jenkins belonged to the African American 761st Tank Battalion.

SS soldiers, December 16, 1944.

An SS soldier,
December 16, 1944,
the opening day of the
Battle of the Bulge.

A GI looks at the frozen corpses of victims of the December 17, 1944, Malmedy Massacre.

Belgian civilians massacred by German troops, December 1944.

GIs from B Company, 101st Engineers, at the height of the fighting in the Battle of the Bulge.

Tankers in action near Bastogne, December 1944.

C-47s drop supplies to troops in Bastogne, December 1944.

*(Opposite page, top)*
Situation map, Bastogne, December 21, 1944.

*(Opposite page, bottom)*
Situation map, Bastogne, December 25, 1944.

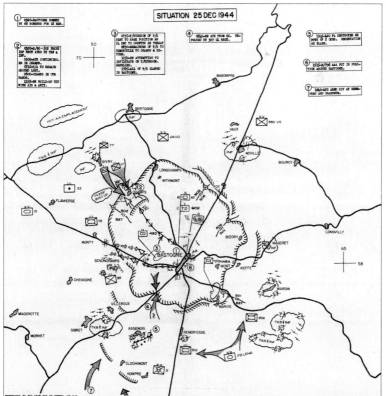

A grim Christmas dinner at the 101st Airborne headquarters in Bastogne, December 25, 1944. Brigadier General Anthony McAuliffe, commander of the 101st Airborne during the siege of Bastogne, sits with his arms folded at the rear of the table.

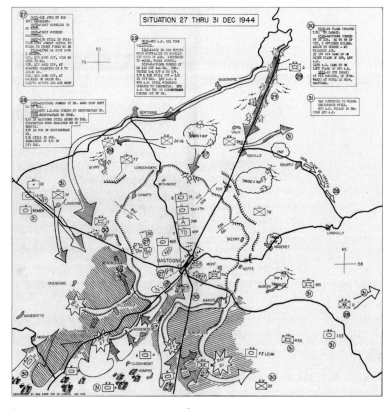

Situation map, Bastogne, December 27–31, 1944.

US troops from the 89th Infantry Division crossing the Rhine under fire, March 1945.

US troops in action, spring 1945.

Hammelburg POW camp, liberated April 6, 1945.

On April 12, 1945, the top brass visits Ohrdruf, the first concentration camp to be liberated by US troops. General Eisenhower stands third from left with General Omar Bradley to his right and Patton on the far right.

The final straight. US tanks roll down an autobahn in Germany, spring 1945.

The victors. The senior American commanders in Europe in WWII. Seated (*left to right*): Generals William H. Simpson, George S. Patton, Carl A. Spaatz, Dwight D. Eisenhower, Omar N. Bradley, Courtney H. Hodges, and Leonard T. Gerow. Standing (*left to right*): Generals Ralph F. Stearley, Hoyt S. Vandenberg, Walter B. Smith, Otto P. Weyland, and Richard E. Nugent.

Patton during a welcome home parade, Los Angeles, June 9, 1945.

Willie, Patton's ever-faithful dog, beside his dead master's belongings, January 1946.

*My New Year wish and sure conviction for you is that
under the protection of Almighty God and the
inspired leadership of our President and the High
Command, you will continue your victorious course
to the end that tyranny and vice shall be eliminated,
our dead comrades avenged, and peace restored to a
war-weary world. . . . I can find no fitter expression of
my feelings than to apply to you the immortal words
spoken by General Scott at Chapultepec when he said,
"Brave soldiers, veterans, you have been baptized in
fire and blood and have come out steel."*[26]

Patton also held a press conference in Luxembourg that day. He explained that his Third Army had "hit this son-of-a-bitch—pardon me—in the flank . . . with the result that he is damn well stopped and going back."

Patton then added with a flourish: "If you got a monkey in a jungle hanging by his tail, it is easier to get him by cutting his tail than kicking him in the face. The same thing is true here. I am very pleased with the situation. . . . To me it is a never-ending marvel what our soldiers can do."[27]

Patton was asked what he planned to do next.

"We want to catch as many Germans as possible, but he is pulling out."

"If you pinch off a lot of Germans," a reporter asked, "is there any chance of the front collapsing?"

"What do you think I went to church for yesterday . . . ?"

"What about the [enemy] concentration of armor?"

"They got damn little armor left—unless they have reproductive tanks."

"Just how important was Bastogne?"

"It was as important as the Battle of Gettysburg was to the Civil War."[28]

# CHAPTER 14

## Bloodred Snow

**The Ardennes, Belgium**
**Early January 1945**

THE GERMAN onslaught in the Ardennes had been stopped, at great cost. Now, on January 3, the Allies launched a massive counterattack. Field Marshal Bernard Montgomery, whose hesitancy had irked Patton repeatedly since the Sicilian campaign in 1943, went on the offensive with his First Army, pushing through the northern Ardennes, as elements of Patton's Third Army to the south aimed for Hitler's remaining forces to the east of Bastogne. Eisenhower later wrote: "From that moment on it was merely a question of whether we could make sufficient progress through the defenses and through the snowbanks of the Ardennes to capture or destroy significant portions of [the enemy's] forces."[1]

Eisenhower's dry analysis belied the reality—a deadly slog in one of the worst winters of the twentieth century. As Montgomery finally attacked to the north, Patton's forces headed toward the town of Houffalize, which lay to the northeast of Bastogne. But the maps Patton looked at showed that four divisions in his VIII Corps were making agonizingly slow progress, much to Eisenhower's displeasure. Indeed, the Allied supreme commander believed Patton's advance was "slow and laborious," as he reported to his boss, Army Chief of Staff George Marshall.[2] If Eisenhower had visited the front and seen conditions and studied the topography, he would have understood why.

Seventy-ton King Tiger tanks and determined Waffen SS troops were blocking Patton's path, yes. But snow most years arrived late in the region, and early 1945 was no exception, with a foot or more falling in just a few hours some days. Wading through drifting snow was often deadly—it was impossible to sprint to cover when shells began screaming overhead. And the Germans fought ferociously east of Bastogne, inflicting hundreds of casualties each day. More American troops were in fact killed in that first week of 1945 than had been lost trying to break through to Bastogne.

The human cost was on grisly display in the many quickly erected aid stations set up to cope with the flood of badly injured men. The horror would be etched in memories long after the war. "I can still smell the ether, the bitter coffee, cigarette smoke," remembered one member of the 81st Medical Battalion attached to the 11th Armored Division, "and the persistent stench of putrefying flesh and the small heap of amputated arms and legs that had been tossed carelessly into a corner. . . . No one had the time or opportunity to dispose of the pitiful mound."[3]

Patton was troubled by the high losses and slow progress. "We can still lose this war," he confided in his diary. "The Germans are colder and hungrier than we are, but they fight better. I can never get over the stupidity of our green troops."[4]

Among the green troops thrust into the maw on January 4 was the 17th Airborne Division, which had arrived from Britain just a few weeks before. Colonel James Pierce's 194th Glider Infantry Regiment and Colonel James Coutts's 513th Parachute Infantry Regiment attacked German positions northeast of Bastogne.

They were up against two combat-hardened units, the 3rd Panzergrenadier Division and the Führer Begleit.

The Germans responded savagely to the attack, and soon, along high ground, in snow several feet deep, the 17th suffered terrible casualties on what became known as "Dead Man's Ridge."[5] The 17th Airborne was indeed cut to shreds. Patton later noted in his diary that it had received "a very bloody nose [with] the loss of 40% in some of its battalions."[6]

Some men, in combat for the first time, panicked. "We have had replacements who would flop down with the first burst of enemy fire," complained one officer, "and would not shoot even to protect others advancing."[7]

German-born Jew Private Kurt Gabel belonged to the 513th PIR and vividly recalled the ferocity of combat that day. He was crossing a snow-covered field when German rockets, Nebelwerfer, screamed through the sky and then exploded.

"Hit it!" shouted Gabel's platoon leader.

Gabel and others dived to the ground as more rockets screeched overhead.

"Move!"

An officer was running toward Gabel and shouting.

"Get up!"

The officer looked furious.

"Get up, you stupid bastards. You'll die here. There's no cover. Move! Move!"

The officer kicked one of Gabel's platoon members.

"Get 'em up, goddamn it!" the officer yelled.

Gabel did as he was told and managed to make it across the field in one piece. He and others dropped into a drainage ditch for cover.

"Fix bayonets!" ordered Gabel's platoon leader.

Gabel had never imagined having to do so. That tactic belonged, surely, to an earlier war. Not this one. He listened to fourteen men fix their bayonets.

"Let's go," said the platoon leader.

Gabel and others charged the German lines.

"Geronimo!" screamed one paratrooper.

Others yelled too.

Gabel joined in.

It was kill or be killed. Some Germans were trying to put their hands up. Bayonets thrusting, stabbing. The German position fell. Then Gabel and others moved on and took a small village.[8] Amid the carnage, some men went above and beyond the call of duty, proving that the 17th Airborne, however green, could still get the job done, whatever the price.

Sergeant Isadore Seigfreid Jachman, like Gabel a German-born Jew in the 17th Airborne, earned the Medal of Honor that January 4. Jachman's company was pinned down by intense

German fire and being attacked by two tanks. Jachman sprinted across open ground, grabbed a bazooka from a wounded man, and then closed on the tanks before firing at both. Even though he was fatally wounded, he hit one and forced the other to withdraw.[9] Jachman was one of the thousand casualties suffered by the division in just three days.[10]

The following day, January 5, Patton wrote to his wife, Beatrice: "The whole country is covered with snow and ice. How men live, much less fight, is a marvel to me. . . . A 280 shell just hit near here. . . . Those Germans are vicious fighters. . . . Sometimes even I get skeptical about the end of this show."[11]

It seemed that the Germans were dead set on defending every yard as Patton's troops fought eastward of Bastogne, trying to regain the ground that had been lost in the early days of the Battle of the Bulge. "Resistance never let up," recalled an officer in the 83rd Division, "and the brutality for which the SS troops were notorious was brought home to us."

On one occasion, a platoon in the 83rd Division was pinned down by heavy German fire as it crossed a snow-covered field. The soldiers dug down into the snow for cover, but most were nevertheless killed or wounded. The Germans then drew near and kicked each American body. If a soldier cried out in pain, he was executed. Only one man of twenty-seven survived—he had pretended to be dead.[12]

Many casualties were patched up, given a few days of rest and hot meals, and returned to combat. Only those who received a "million-dollar wound" got to go home.

Captain Ben Kimmelman of the 28th Infantry would forever be haunted by the expressions of those who were sent back into action: "Men who were wounded and were redeemable were in a very bad position. . . . It's very hard to forget the expressions on their faces . . . a kind of hollow-eyed, lifeless, slack-jawed expression. . . . It's almost as though they're going to a hopeless doom."[13]

Notably, the counterattack by US forces that early January included the 761st Tank Battalion, known as the "Black Panthers" because it comprised African Americans. Before they had first entered combat, Patton made a point of addressing the men from the unit assigned to his Third Army.

"Men, you're the first Negro tankers to ever fight in the American Army," Patton said on November 2, 1944, standing on the hood of a half-track. "I would never have asked for you if you weren't good. I have nothing but the best in my Army. I don't care what color you are as long as you go up there and kill those Kraut sonsofbitches."[14]

The Black Panthers did not disappoint. They earned plaudits but they too suffered mightily that early January to support the 87th Infantry Division, one unit losing nine of eleven tanks over forty-eight hours.[15]


THERE WAS ONE last chance for glory—a final prize for Patton and his Third Army in the Ardennes. On January 8, Patton was back in his jeep, visiting his commanders in the field. The key objective would now be the town of Houffalize, around ten miles to the northeast of Bastogne. Once Allied troops reached Houffalize, the "bulge" caused by the German offensive would be erased. The battle would be as good as won.

Patton knew that Field Marshal Montgomery's forces to the north were pushing toward the town. Understandably eager to be viewed as the clear winner, Patton wanted his troops to get to Houffalize first.

The weather that January 8 was brutal once more, minus six degrees Fahrenheit, and the roads were jammed with trucks. Trails in some areas were so iced that they became "regular toboggan slides" in the words of 2nd Armored Division commander Ernest Harmon.[16] "It is the coldest weather I've ever experienced," one officer noted in his diary that day. "The wind was just like a knife to the face. . . . The roads are full of ditched vehicles with freezing drivers alongside them, waiting for whatever help can come."[17]

Patton passed ambulances full of men from the 90th Division as he moved toward the front. He recalled that he "passed through the last combat team of the 90th Division moving up for battle. These men had been in trucks for a great many hours with the temperature at six degrees below zero, and were thoroughly chilled."

Patton looked at a long line of ambulances. They were full of wounded. Some of them spotted Patton and "stood up and cheered. It was the most moving experience of my life, and the knowledge of what the ambulances contained made it still more poignant."[18]

Patton reached the city of Arlon, some thirty-five miles south of Houffalize, and met with the highly capable James Van Fleet, commander of the 90th Infantry Division and a member of the famous West Point class of 1915, "the class the stars fell on," which had also included Eisenhower and Bradley. Patton's faith in Van Fleet, a standout fullback on the undefeated 1914 Army football team, would prove well-founded. He would go on to command the US Eighth Army during the Korean War.

Patton and Van Fleet discussed what was going to happen when the 90th went into action the following day.

Patton patted Van Fleet on the back.

"Van Fleet," said Patton, "you've never failed me. I know you can do it."[19]

Van Fleet appreciated Patton's faith in him. "When you praise somebody," he remembered, "damn it! You have to go out and succeed, and that's in football. That's in anything. You capture the art of leadership there, and that was one of Patton's prime qualities."[20]

That same day, January 8, Hitler finally decided to withdraw some of his forces in the Ardennes. Above all, he could not risk the destruction of what tanks remained. But that did not mean that the fighting became any easier for Patton's troops. When Van Fleet's 90th Division attacked north, toward Houffalize, on January 9, the Germans inflicted heavy casualties.

Following Patton's example, Van Fleet was determined to lead from the front and almost lost his life when mortar fire killed several officers close by.

Van Fleet's division moved barely a mile that day. It would suffer more than a thousand casualties before the fighting in the Ardennes was finally over.[21]

THE GERMANS were still a formidable foe but they could not sustain their losses for much longer. Finally accepting that his last gamble, in the Ardennes, had not paid off, Hitler decided to save what remained of his most dedicated fighters—the SS. The next day, January 10, Field Marshal Walther Model notified his commanders: "The Führer has ordered that I and II Panzer Corps, with the 1st, 2nd, 9th and 12th SS Panzer-Divisions, with immediate effect, are to assemble for rapid refitting behind Army Group B and placed at the disposal of Commander-in-chief West in such a way that they no longer become involved in combat."[22]

The following day, January 11, Third Army staff received reports that the SS was indeed starting to withdraw.[23] There was even better news just a day later: The Russians had launched a massive offensive in the east, as Stalin had promised. It comprised one hundred eighty divisions, many of them armored. Within two weeks, the Red Army would be only a hundred miles from Berlin.

The Red Army soon seized Germany's Silesian area with its heavy industry, a critical loss. The mines there had produced over fifty percent of Germany's coal, without which rail lines and factories could not operate.

As the Russian advance gathered momentum, Patton visited a hospital in Luxembourg. In Sicily, he had notoriously slapped a soldier, thinking he was a malingerer. The incident had caused outrage when it became public back in America and led to him being sidelined for a year. Patton's reputation as a hotheaded bully was forever set, but in fact Patton most often showed his deep compassion and concern for his men when he encountered them in hospitals.

Lieutenant Roger Boas, a forward artillery observer who had

fought from Normandy with the 4th Armored Division, had bronchial inflammation. Patton saw him lying in a bed.

"What's the matter with you, boy?" asked Patton.

"I have bronchitis, sir."

"What outfit are you in, boy?"

"4th Armored Division, sir."

Patton put his hand on Boas's shoulder.

"Lieutenant, you had your share of hard work. You stay here as long as you have to."

Patton carried on through the ward and came across a lieutenant who was about to have a limb amputated. He decided the young man should be awarded the Silver Star and asked an aide to provide one.

"Sir, I don't have one," replied the aide.

Boas remembered that Patton "again went into one of his profane periods of dressing this chap down, went on for quite a while. I'm sure this man never forgot it. An hour later, a full colonel came with a Silver Star for the lieutenant and ice cream for all of us . . . The next day the lieutenant was dead."[24]

# CHAPTER 15

---

# Houffalize

**Third Army Headquarters, Luxembourg**
**January 13, 1945**

VICTORY WAS finally within grasp. On January 13, Patton wrote
in his diary: "There is a distinct difference in the mental attitude
of the officers and men today. . . . They all feel that they are on
the winning side, pursuing a beaten enemy; while yesterday . . .
they were dubious as to whether we could stop the German
attack. It is an interesting psychological situation. Now that all
feel the enemy is licked, they are sure of themselves."

Patton continued: "Until today, I was the only one sure of
victory. The fighting today has been bitter, but it is just what one
would expect, as it is to the northeast of Bastogne where the enemy must hold in order to extricate what he has left east of the
town. We will get them."[1]

To the men tasked with "getting them," the challenges of combat remained colossal, as the weather worsened again and temperatures dropped to well below freezing, some nights hovering around minus eighteen degrees Fahrenheit.[2]

The drive toward Houffalize continued. Patton had hoped to reach the town, seventeen miles from his front line, in twenty-four hours, but his Third Army was now confronting nine German divisions—three times the number it had faced during the drive to Bastogne. Patton was nevertheless encouraged by the "mental attitude" of his troops—they were now "chasing a sinking fox and babbling for the kill."[3]

These men had learned many hard lessons, and the new men had to learn from them quickly. They had been forced to adapt and become ingenious and creative to stay alive.[4] They used blankets and paper to insulate their thin field jackets, wore two woolen shirts if they could, and tried their best to stay dry if at all possible. They knew to put blankets over their heads in foxholes to maintain their body warmth, and sometimes woke up with the blankets frozen as stiff as wood.

They painted tanks white and wore ghoulish white sheets. Rubber tracks on tanks were replaced by metal cleats. Old-timers left their weapons and ammunition outdoors rather than carry them into buildings because once warm the firing mechanisms would freeze when men stepped outside.

There were other ways to defy the bone-numbing conditions. One soldier remembered: "It was so cold that we crawled under tanks, to absorb some of the heat emitted from the engines."[5]

On January 14, in the War Diary of the German High Command, it was noted that the Germans had now been pushed onto the defensive. Crucially, even as Patton noted the bitter fighting, the Allies now enjoyed great superiority in artillery fire and had control of the skies over the battlefield.

The constant shelling of German positions was particularly demoralizing. One SS officer, Karl Leitner, remembered jumping into a ditch and then a shell hitting a tree nearby. "My sergeant must have been badly wounded in the lung—he just gasped, and after a short time died."[6]

Another shell exploded and Leitner was hit in several parts of his body by shrapnel. He had to use the dead fellow's body for protection from flying shards before being rescued several hours later.

DEATH WAS everywhere. On January 15, Patton was again in his jeep, driving his men on toward Houffalize, concerned that Montgomery's forces to the north now might actually beat him to the town. "The weather still remained hideously cold," Patton noted in his diary. "At one point we came across a German machine-gunner who had been killed and apparently instantly frozen, as he was in a half-sitting position with his arms extended, holding a loaded belt of ammunition."

Patton also spotted "a lot of black objects sticking out of the snow." A closer look revealed they were the toes of corpses. "Another phenomenon resulting from the quick-freezing of men killed in battle," he wrote, "is that they turn a sort of claret color—nasty sight."[7]

By then, Patton's troops, attacking from the south of Houffalize, were just ten miles from the medieval town, lately headquarters for what remained of the once formidable 116th Panzer
Division.[8] It was 5:15 P.M. when a half-track arrived in a village
called Bertogne. Major Michael Greene of the 41st Cavalry Reconnaissance Squadron of the 11th Armored Division got out of
the half-track and waited.

A jeep pulled up. It carried two men: Brigadier General Willard "Hunk" Holbrook of Combat Command A, and Colonel
J. J. B. Williams, the division chief of staff.

Greene stepped toward the men.

"Colonel Foy is up forward with Troop C," said Greene.

Holbrook shook hands with Greene.[9]

"Mike," said Holbrook, "we have a mission—an extremely
important mission—a *must*, directed by General Patton. Someone must get up to Houffalize tonight and contact the First
Army as it comes down from the north."[10]

"This is a delicate, difficult assignment," stressed Williams.
"But someone has to get through to establish contact with
the 2nd Armored Division as it comes down from Achouffe. They
may already be there. General Patton wants this mission accomplished without delay. And he wants this division to do it."[11]

Greene was young for a major, in his mid-twenties.

Holbrook knew Greene's father. He was a good man, reliable.
The son would hopefully be made of the same stuff.

"Mike, I want you to lead the mission," said Holbrook. "This
is your chance to get a good medal."

"Yes, sir," said Greene, who could not have cared less about
medals. He just wanted to see action.

———

IT WAS AFTER dark in a nearby village called Rastate. Seventeen light tanks were gathered. Their crews had been ordered to await Major Greene. He was running late because his half-track had been put out of action by a mine.

A burly lieutenant called "Big Gene" Ellenson, who had been a college football star, surveyed a narrow road leading through dark woods.

GIs suddenly emerged from the woods, terrified.

"The Krauts are all over the place!" cried a soldier as he fled the woods.

An officer appeared, equally distraught.

"You can't go fifty yards up that road without being blown to hell," he declared.

Ellenson turned to a soldier at his side.

"The hell with the deal," he said. "I'm going back and tell them they'll need a lot more than a few light tanks and armored cars to get to Houffalize. I'm going to tell Major Greene to blow it out his barracks bag. I'll be damned if I go up that trail tonight."

"We are all going up that trail tonight."

Ellenson turned around and found himself facing Major Greene.

"And *you* are going to lead the way," added Greene. "We're moving out immediately. Nothing will impede our progress. If any vehicle is knocked out, push it off the trail. If any man is wounded, he'll have to take care of himself."[12]

Ellenson kept his counsel and began to carry out his orders.

The force under Greene moved out and through the woods. Ellenson led the way.

Greene followed close behind Ellenson. There were no Germans fifty yards ahead, as had been warned. The pair "proceeded slowly," Greene recalled, tanks and other vehicles following hundreds of yards behind, moving "nervously and anxiously through the long dark night hoping that the next minute would bring daylight and the objective."[13]

At 6:30 A.M. on January 16, the two men passed a water mill and then saw buildings "some six hundred yards to the east," recalled Greene.[14]

Ellenson moved ahead on foot, expecting Germans to open fire any second.

Greene's force followed. It was dawn as light tanks and half-tracks moved down toward the Ourthe River.

Greene and Ellenson's advance party  finally reached a road.

A sign read: HOUFFALIZE.

"Well," said Greene, "we're in Houffalize."

He shook hands with Ellenson.

They turned and began to make their way toward the vehicles in the task force.

Ellenson spotted movement.

"Hey, Major, there's someone up there."

Ellenson could see a figure, camouflaged in white, with an automatic gun.

Ellenson cried out but the soldier did not appear to hear him.

"Let's get up there," said Ellenson. "It's probably a 2nd Armored patrol."

Greene carried only a .45 pistol. He followed Ellenson.

They were soon several yards from a foxhole.

"Hey, are you Armored?" asked Ellenson.

The camouflaged figure turned and aimed a gun at Greene and Ellenson.

Thankfully, one of the GIs in the advance party opened fire.

The camouflaged German took off and then alerted other Germans.[15]

A fierce firefight ensued.

Finally, the bullets stopped flying.

"Major, look," said Ellenson.

Greene saw men walking on high ground across the Ourthe River.

Were they Germans?

"Send a patrol over there," said Greene. "Tell them to proceed cautiously."

The figures in the distance if not German probably belonged to the First Army. Greene's men were eager to link up with them if they indeed were Americans.

In the midst of this tense moment, a jeep pulled up.

Two men got out of the jeep.

"We're correspondents."

"This is a hell of a place to be," said Greene.

"We wanted to be in at the closing of the Bulge."

"Well, this is the right place."

"Is this Houffalize?"

Greene pointed into the distance.

"That's the town signpost over there."

"Major, is it okay with you if we walk up to the sign? Then we can dateline our story Houffalize."

Greene agreed.

"It's pretty quiet now," he said. "Come on."

Greene and the reporters walked over to the sign.

The reporters jotted down Greene's name and noted that he came from Philadelphia.

There was the sound of mortar fire.

"We'd better get out of here," said Greene.

As they took cover, men from the patrol sent by Ellenson returned.

The leader of the patrol was ecstatic.

"That's the 41st Infantry of the 2nd Armored up there. We made contact at 0905!"[16]

The linkup between Patton's Third Army and the First Army had happened at last, recalled Greene, "thereby eliminating the Ardennes salient that the Germans had created in the Allied lines a month before."[17]

Ellenson grinned.

"All right," said Greene. "Let's not stand around doing nothing. Let's move into Houffalize."[18]

Patton noted in his diary that day: "At 0905, 41st Cavalry of the 11th Armored Division made contact with 41st Infantry of the 2nd Armored Division in Houffalize, thus terminating the Bastogne operation as far as Third Army is concerned."[19]


IT WAS something of a Pyrrhic victory. Eisenhower later recalled that the push to reach Houffalize had been so painfully slow, given the stiff German resistance, that, as so often before in the war, "most of the enemy troops to the westward of the closing gap had succeeded in withdrawing."[20]

The Germans had occupied Houffalize since December 20, and as a result, it had been so heavily bombed that some two hundred civilians had been killed.[21]

Patton would soon compose a poem—inspired by the famous Christmas carol "O Little Town of Bethlehem"—to describe the utter destruction he passed by:

> *Oh little town of Houffalize,*
> *How still we see thee lie;*
> *Above the steep and battered streets*
> *The aeroplanes sail by.*
> *Yet in the dark streets shineth*
> *Not any goddamned light;*
> *The hopes and fears of all my years,*
> *Were blown to hell last night.*[22]

Patton wrote to his son, George, later that day: "Leadership . . . is the thing that wins battles. I have it—but I'll be damned if I can define it. Probably it consists in knowing what you want to do and then doing it and getting mad if anyone steps in the way."[23]

# CHAPTER 16

---

# Battered Bastards

**Bastogne, Belgium**
**January 18, 1945**

FIVE HUNDRED "BATTERED BASTARDS" from what remained of the 101st Airborne Division stood before General Troy Middleton, VIII Corps commander, as a bitter wind whipped across the central marketplace in Bastogne, much of which had been rendered uninhabitable because of shelling and bombing.

The Screaming Eagles had lost 2,370 comrades in desperate combat while holding the town in December, and more than two thousand more men that cruelest of Januarys. Their dead buddies had been stacked by the dozen in frozen piles to await burial.

"I think," said Middleton, "you're the best bunch of fighting men in the United States or any other army in the world."[1]

That same day, January 18, in London, Winston Churchill ad-

dressed the House of Commons. He did not refer to the Screaming Eagles but he made a point of emphasizing the sacrifice of so
many Americans during the battle.

"The United States troops have done almost all the fighting,"
said Churchill, "and have suffered almost all the losses. We must
not forget that it is to American homes that the telegrams of personal losses and anxiety have been going during the past
month. . . . Care must be taken not to claim for the British Army
an undue share of what is undoubtedly the greatest American
battle of the war, and will, I believe, be regarded as an ever-
famous American victory."[2]

Back in the US, the newspapers were still catching up and full
of stories about the fighting at Bastogne. Patton now felt that his
Third Army, if not he himself, had been somewhat overlooked.
On January 20, he complained: "The 101st Air Borne [sic] call
themselves the triple B's—'Battered Bastards of Bastogne.' They
did well but like Marines of the last war, they get more credit
than they deserve."

Patton added in a letter to his wife: "The weather could not be
worse. It is snowing like hell again now. But we are still going
forward about a mile a day. . . . I doubt Willie [Patton's pet dog]
needs a sweater. . . . When I am reading in bed, he gets in with
me. But as I start to open the window he hurries into the bath
room where it is warm."[3]

Temperatures had reached new lows. The Screaming Eagles
left Bastogne as they had arrived—in open trucks, in terrible
conditions, bound for Alsace. They did not get far. The next day,
January 19, recalled Patton: "The condition of the roads, due to

sleet and ice, was so bad we could not move either the 101st or the 76th Division."[4]

But their accomplishments were massive. As the battle had neared its end, Patton had spoken with reporter Leland Stowe of the *Chicago Daily News*. Stowe was no eager-to-flatter hack. He had been one of the first American journalists to warn about Nazi militarism in the 1930s, and he had received the Pulitzer Prize in 1940 for his war reporting. He would end the war having worked in forty-four countries on four continents.

Stowe recalled that Patton had a pistol nearby.

"You see that pistol," said Patton in his high-pitched voice. "Take a good look. By God, it's ivory-handled—not pearl. All this cockeyed nonsense about me wearing a pearl-handled revolver . . . ! Just a bunch of ignoramuses. . . . Why, no real gunman would carry a pearl-handled pistol. . . . It's bad luck. . . . Besides, I wear that particular gun because I killed my first man with it."

Patton had a broad grin, clearly enjoying playing to type. As Stowe watched, he picked up a telephone and contacted one of his corps commanders.

"The Germans are preparing to attack at daybreak," said Patton. "Stop the bastards where they are!"

Patton put the phone down. He then began to talk about the Third Army during its drive to Bastogne.

"Yes," said Patton, "we broke all records moving up here. It was all done by three of us . . . me, my chauffeur, and my chief of staff. All I did was to tell my division commanders where they'd got to be tomorrow. Then I let the others do it. . . . To tell you the truth, I didn't have anything much to do with it."

Patton was in fine form.

"The Americans are sons of bitches of soldiers—thanks to their grandmothers! All you've got to do is to show them the value of discipline . . . give them the habit of obeying in a tight place. Yes. The American is a hell of a fine soldier."

Patton then said he did not care what people said about him. "I've studied military history all my life. Georgie Patton knows more about military history than any living person in the United States Army today. With due conceit—and I've got no end of that—I can say that's true."[5]

PATTON WAS as boastful and relentless as ever, seemingly invigorated after his troops had reached Houffalize, eager to stay on the attack. On January 21, he was back in his jeep, egging on his men yet again. With one of his staff, Major Alexander Stiller,[6] he came across a line of trucks carrying replacement soldiers. The trucks had stopped on an icy road running up a hill.

Patton saw several officers, clearly inexperienced, and took matters into his own hands, ordering the replacements to get out of the trucks and push them past the iced section of the road. Before long, the convoy of trucks was moving again and at speed.

After the war, a soldier remembered a similar incident: "We were stuck in snow and he [Patton] came by in a jeep. His face was awful red, and he must have been about froze, riding in that open jeep. He yelled to us to get out and push. And first I knew there was General Patton pushing right alongside of me."[7]

Few commanders, if any, of Patton's rank spent as much time outside as he did that winter, when temperatures were markedly lower than normal in the Ardennes. He described in a letter to his wife how being driven around "in a jeep is not so hot, not in zero weather. . . . I have a woolen scarf that I find makes a lot of difference—if you keep your neck warm. I also have a lap robe made of a shelter half lined with a blanket and I have plastic glass doors on the side of the jeep."[8]

It was around this time, in late January, that Patton met in Luxembourg with Father James O'Neill, some six weeks after O'Neill had written Patton's famous prayer for the Third Army.

Patton smiled at O'Neill.

"Well, Padre, our prayers worked," said Patton.

"I knew they would."

O'Neill recalled that Patton then "cracked me on the side of my steel helmet with his riding crop. That was his way of saying, 'Well done.'"[9]

Well done but not over. On January 30, the Germans attacked with two divisions—a final, belated thrust that inevitably failed but reminded the Americans that the enemy had not forgotten how to inflict casualties even as the rump of its forces pulled back to defend the Fatherland.

Patton again visited Bastogne, passing along the road that his 4th Armored had opened up. He came "quite close" to the enemy. "Luckily they were not firing."

In Bastogne, Patton also recalled, he then gave the "Distinguished Service Cross [to] Brigadier General McAuliffe, who commanded the 101st during the fight. . . . We then drove around so the soldiers could see us, and they were quite delighted."[10]

The decoration ceremony marked Patton's final formal act of the Battle of the Bulge. His Third Army had, he boasted, "moved farther and faster and engaged more divisions in less time than any other army in the history of the United States—possibly in the history of the world."[11]

Patton had pushed his men, in his words, "beyond endurance" to gain victory.[12] His Third Army had paid a high price with more than forty-four hundred men killed and more than twenty thousand wounded. In all, the US Army suffered seventy-five thousand casualties with nineteen thousand men lost in the fighting in the Ardennes, making the battle the deadliest for the US in World War II.[13]

Patton had enjoyed his finest hours as a combat commander during the Battle of the Bulge, overshadowing his peers. No other episode in the war, other than D Day, had been so closely followed back home, no other accomplishment so celebrated. Victory in the battle had doomed the Third Reich. The loss of German men and matériel meant the war in Europe had effectively been won.

Patton was the only senior general whose reputation was enhanced. "Patton, he is your best," said Field Marshal von Rundstedt after the war.[14]

One captured German officer, Lieutenant Colonel Freiherr von Wangenheim, remembered how Patton had been the one American general to unnerve some of Hitler's field commanders: "General Patton was always the main topic of military discussion. Where is he? When will he attack? Where? . . . How? With what?"

Indeed, the Third Army's volatile, ever-aggressive leader had been the "most feared general on all fronts"; his tactics had been "daring and unpredictable." He had been the most advanced in his thinking, "the best commander of armored and infantry troops combined."[15]

Patton had indeed performed magnificently. But he rightly stressed that the greatest credit should lie with US troops. Captain Charles MacDonald, who fought in the Battle of the Bulge as a company commander in the 23rd Infantry Regiment before being wounded on January 17, recalled that the American soldier had answered Patton's prayers for victory by remaining stalwart, by standing his ground and putting the lie to Hitler's assertions that US troops were inferior. "Surprised, stunned, unbelieving, incredulous, not understanding what was hitting him," Mac-Donald later wrote, "he nevertheless held fast until his commanders ordered withdrawal or until he was overwhelmed. . . . His was a story to be told to the sound of trumpets."[16]

IN LUXEMBOURG, shortly after the Battle of the Bulge ended, a prominent clergyman, Daniel A. Poling, received Monsignor O'Neill's "personal copy," he recalled, of "Patton's much-discussed prayer . . . for battle weather." Poling was working as a correspondent for several newspapers. He believed the words of the prayer were "typically Patton . . . from the Old Testament rather than the New and had the ring of Joshua and David at their militant best. They were not written for a soft time but for their occasion; they were words to make men strong—and they did."

Poling reported from Luxembourg that back in the United States, people no longer believed that God changed the weather in response to any invocation, let alone one from a general famous for his often less-than-Christian cussing and outbursts. Exhortations to the gods of war were for the ancient Greeks and Romans, warriors of yore before Christ's birth.

But soldiers showed Poling their prayer cards, issued just in time before Hitler's final great onslaught in the west. Poling added that "the only doubters seemed to be among the officers, especially a few chaplains; but there were no doubters at Patton's headquarters."[17] Everywhere he went, Poling noted, he found men in Patton's Third Army who "believed—firmly believed—that God" had answered Patton's prayer.

# PART FOUR

## Victory in Europe

Lead me, follow me, or get out of my way.[1]

—GEORGE S. PATTON

# CHAPTER 17

---

# To the Rhine

**Houffalize, Belgium**
**February 1, 1945**

BARELY A single building had been left standing. The full fury of American artillery had left piles of bricks and mortar, so much devastation that bulldozers had to clear paths through the rubble so that the top brass could visit the towns' centers.

Patton visited St. Vith and Houffalize on February 1 with his aide Codman, who described the two towns as the most "liberated" he had seen: "In both the destruction is appalling. Perhaps the sense of desolation is heightened by the intense cold, the temperature being well below zero—*our* zero, not the sissy Centigrade variety."[1]

Patton was eager to push on and attack once more, this time toward the fabled Siegfried Line, with its more than eighteen thousand bunkers, tank traps, and tunnels stretching from

Holland to Switzerland. Once the Westwall, as the Germans called it, had been crossed, there remained the mighty Rhine, the last natural obstacle between the Allies and Berlin, more than a hundred fifty miles to the east of Houffalize.

As one of his staff members, Colonel Paul Harkins, remembered, thirteen divisions from the Third Army were poised to go on the offensive that early February, positioned "abreast of the Moselle, Sauer and Our Rivers, ready to crack the Siegfried Line from Saarlautern, north to St. Vith."

Codman noted that Patton's "every waking hour is concentrated on our next forward move to the Rhine. He and General Bradley see eye to eye on the question. Both are convinced the Germans have finally shot their bolt and that it is folly to slow down now. The difficulty, as heretofore, is to get the green light from Topside."

And to that point, the following day, February 2, Patton received an after-dinner message that made him explode with fury. Just as he was about to go on the offensive, he was being asked to send forces to help Field Marshal Montgomery to the north.

"If they continue to rob us of our troops to save the face of Monty," fumed Patton, "both Bradley and I will turn in our uniforms."[2]

The strike toward the Rhine had been set for February 6, when Major General Manton Eddy, commanding Patton's XII Corps, would begin the attack.

But Patton was impatient.

He wanted to go earlier.

"Make it the Fourth," he told Eddy.

"Goddamnit, General," replied Eddy, "you never give me time to get ready. The trouble is you have no appreciation of the time and space factor in this war."

"Is that so?" Patton said. "If I had any appreciation of it, we'd still be sitting on the Seine."

It was to be the fourth.

When Patton then contacted army group headquarters, he was told by General Lev Allen, the chief of staff:

"No dice, George. You are to commit nothing—pending further orders."[3]

Patton called his staff together.

"This doesn't sound good to me," he told them. "I'm afraid we're going to be halted again in the middle of a going attack in order to start another one you know where, that has little promise of success. I have the sneaking suspicion that SHAEF is out as usual to exalt the Field Marshal."

He soon learned from Bradley what was really going on: "Monty did it again, George."

Bradley told Patton that he was to "go on the defensive while Montgomery will resume the offensive in the north. It wasn't Ike this time. Orders from Combined Chiefs."

"What are we supposed to accomplish?" asked an exasperated Patton.

"Montgomery wants to secure a wide stretch of the Rhine as quickly as possible so that we would have a quick entry if Germany collapsed suddenly."

"I'm convinced we have a much better chance to get to the

Rhine first with our present attack," insisted Patton. "When are the British supposed to jump off?"

"Probably on the 10th."

"I doubt if Monty will be ready by the 10th. But what are *we* supposed to be doing in the meantime?"

Bradley wasn't about to make Patton wait around.

"You can continue your attack until February 10th and maybe even after that, provided your casualties aren't excessive and you have enough ammunition left."

Patton soon called a meeting of his staff.

"It would be a foolish and ignoble way," he said, "for the Americans to end the war by sitting on our butts. And, gentleman, we aren't going to do anything foolish or ignoble."

The Third Army would continue to attack.

"Let the gentlemen up north learn what we are doing when they see it on their maps."[4]

Patton could once again practice his favorite form of war— American Blitzkrieg. Before the Third Army had become operational under Patton's command, he had laid out his combat credo in no uncertain terms: "Forget this goddamn business of worrying about our flanks. . . . Flanks are something for the enemy to worry about, not us. I don't want to get any messages saying that, 'We are holding our position.' . . . We're not interested in holding on to anything except the enemy. We're going to hold on to him by the nose and we're going to kick him in the ass."[5]

Patton was delighted to be back waging war early that February. And he was as impatient as ever with commanders and units that did not move as fast as he wanted. After learning that the 94th Infantry Division had made disappointing progress, Patton called a meeting of all its officers.

Lieutenant Walter Unrath remembered Patton arriving at a large meeting hall.

"Attention!"

Everyone jumped to his feet.

Patton strode down a center aisle and then walked onto a stage. He pushed an officer aside and grabbed ahold of a microphone. Patton then told the officers before him that they had lost too many men, had had too many taken prisoner, and had not reached their objectives.

They should start leading from the front, setting an example.

Patton cursed profusely, remembered Unrath, using "choice words normally associated with the colorful language of the stables of a cavalry troop."

This went on for twenty minutes and then Patton walked slowly to the edge of the stage and looked at the front row— senior officers, among them generals as well as battalion and regimental commanders.

Patton stared at these leaders icily. Then he told them they'd get new objectives within a few days, and if these were not met, the "entire front row will be empty the next time I meet up with this division."

Patton stood still, glaring at the front row for what "seemed like an eternity."

The men before him felt intensely uncomfortable.

Patton then bounded out of the meeting hall.

He'd made his point. And his showmanship worked. "I must observe," recalled Unrath, "it was a changed division after Patton's lecture. I suspect they moved twice as fast, took hills from the rear and the regimental commanders and generals were seen more frequently at the front lines."[6]

Still, there was only so much even the most disciplined and energetic could accomplish, given the continuing winter conditions, which affected roads badly. Patton apparently became so frustrated that he called for sled dogs to be shipped from the States. Early that month, some of his forces started to use pack-horses to get supplies to the front lines.

There was also the constant worry that his Third Army would be ever more depleted, with divisions sent to the north to aid Montgomery. Patton felt that he was fighting three wars—against the weather, against his higher-ups, and against the Germans. He was reading Caesar's *Gallic Wars* in the evenings, aware that he was following the path of ancient warlords, with destiny calling him, and he was "mad" that he had to "beg for opportunities to win battles."[7]

If only he had an emperor for a boss rather than Omar Bradley, the "tent maker," as Patton had nicknamed him.[8] He could "smell the sweat of the Legions" as he followed one road used by Caesar.[9]

"You know," Patton would tell a reporter, "that old bald-headed Roman [Caesar] was one of the greatest students of terrain this world has ever seen. So all I had to do when I was chasing those Krauts across France and we came to a river or a ridge of hills was say, 'Where did that old Roman so-and-so cross or get through?' And then I'd say, 'If it was good enough for Julius it's good enough for George,' and we'd go over."[10]

PATTON PUSHED his Third Army hard, but on February 10, as he had been warned, he came under pressure to halt his offensive. "Bradley called up to ask me how soon I could go on the defensive," recalled Patton. "I told him I was the oldest leader in age and in combat experience in Europe, and that if I had to go on the defensive I would ask to be relieved. He stated I owed too much to the troops and would have to stay on. I replied that a great deal was owed to me, and unless I could continue attacking I would have to be relieved. I further suggested that it would be a good thing if some of his staff visited the front to find out how the other half lived."[11]

Patton still had plenty of ammunition. Casualties were no more than might have been expected and so Bradley allowed Patton to press on.

Patton still didn't shy away from that front himself, often spending six hours each day in his jeep, believing the "acid test of battle brings out the metal."[12]

According to his aide Codman, Patton "took a spectacular trip" on February 13. The 5th Infantry Division had just crossed the Sauer River and entered Germany. Patton and Codman dashed across "a narrow smoke-screened pontoon bridge, under and over which the current [was] running fast . . . a little nerve-racking, especially under fire."

They got across and the GIs on the other side were "surprised to see the General, and he in turn, in spite of graphic reports, was astounded by the elaborateness and ingenuity" of the abandoned German pillboxes.[13]

Patton could see American shells exploding in the distance—in Germany. It was quite a moment.

Patton examined the German defenses. A barn door opened and behind it was the muzzle of an 88mm gun jutting through six feet of concrete.

"Now I *know* the Germans are crazy," said Patton. "No more crazy, however, than our directive from on high to maintain an 'active defense.' There are times when I'm sorry the word 'defense' was ever invented."[14]

IT WAS high time to take a short break from the war. No general was superhuman and Patton badly needed a rest. And so, on February 14, 1945, he left for Paris, where he stayed in the elegant George V hotel. A visit to the Folies Bergère had been arranged by Lieutenant General Walter Bedell Smith, Eisenhower's chief of staff. In between acts, Patton and his entourage went backstage, and, according to Patton's aide Codman, "all the little naked girls blink[ed] their mascara in awe as the General brush[ed] by."

There were raucous toasts. Champagne corks popped.

The female director of the Folies put her hand on Patton's arm as he was about to return to his seat.

"Please remember, General," she said, "from now on, whenever you are in Paris, should you feel the need of a little repose . . ."

"Jesus!" said Patton. "I am not that old!"[15]

The next morning, Patton went to Versailles to meet with Eisenhower and was then scheduled to attend a duck shoot that had been arranged with other generals.

Patton fell ill with food poisoning at lunch before the shoot and was soon laid up in bed at the George V hotel, having been persuaded to rest for a few hours at least, old or not. Then it was back to war.[16]

When Patton returned to the front, he presented the Medal of Honor to Lieutenant James H. Fields of the 4th Armored Division. Fields was one of 472 recipients of the medal for actions in WWII.[17]

Patton told the 4th Armored Division's commander, Major General Hugh Gaffey, that Fields should see no more action. He later noted that he'd said so "because it has been my unfortunate observation, that whenever a man gets the Medal of Honor or even the Distinguished Service Cross, he usually attempts to outdo himself and gets killed, whereas, in order to produce a virile race, such men should be kept alive."[18]

That same day, February 22, Patton also visited the 94th Infantry Division, whose senior officers he had admonished so angrily a few weeks before. An infantryman in the 94th, Alvin H. Kruse, remembered standing guard at a door when Patton arrived to check on the division's progress as it fought toward the Siegfried Line.

Kruse heard the sound of a German machine gun.

A dozen or so bullets hit the door, missing Patton by inches.

Patton looked at the door and then walked over to Kruse.

"That was a close one, wasn't it?"

"Sir, it's been close here all morning."[19]

A few days later, Patton visited Brigadier General William Morris, the talented leader of the 10th Armored Division. Morris had requested demotion in order to be sent to Europe with the 10th Armored, which had performed so effectively during the relief of Bastogne.

Morris was not in the town where Patton was due to meet him, and an MP led Patton and his party to another location—a fortuitous move, as the town was then shelled heavily. Returning to his headquarters, Patton visited what he'd been told was a medieval château but actually turned out to be a "modern winery with some very bad wine."

As he explored the place, he recalled that "a shell came about as close to our heads as it could without hitting us."[20]

Patton's luck was holding. But for how long? Sooner rather than later, if he continued to visit troops so close to the front, it would surely run out.

NOT SINCE the previous August, during the breakout from Normandy, had Patton's Third Army enjoyed such momentum, sometimes racing ahead of designated objectives. On March 1, Patton's forces seized the ancient city of Trier. Ironically, that same day Patton received a message from SHAEF instructing him to bypass the city because it would no doubt require four divisions to liberate it.

Patton was delighted to be able to reply: "HAVE TAKEN TRIER WITH TWO DIVISIONS. WHAT DO YOU WANT ME TO DO? GIVE IT BACK?"[21]

The next day, Patton traveled due north of Trier and visited the fabled Siegfried Line. Near Bitburg, he inspected a pillbox, one of thousands of defensive installations and bunkers built along the Westwall. Some four hundred miles long, the defensive line was replete with its "dragon's teeth," concrete tank traps, and heavily mined.

The edifice Patton visited was an elaborate three-story installation, complete with kitchen, laundry, and showers. It had been seized by US troops, who had blown a rear exit with dynamite.

Patton examined the ten-inch-thick cupolas and saw marks in them where, as he remembered, "our 90mm shells, fired at a range of two hundred yards, had simply bounced."

Formidable though the Siegfried Line defenses had been in the Bitburg area, Patton's forces overcame them in a few days without excessive casualties.

"Pacifists would do well," wrote Patton, "to study the Siegfried and Maginot Lines, remembering that these defenses were forced; that Troy fell; that the walls of Hadrian succumbed; that the Great Wall of China was futile. . . . In war, the only sure defense is offense, and the efficiency of offense depends on the warlike souls of those conducting it."[22]

The Third Army's fifth campaign of the war gained momentum. Maximum force was used whenever necessary. One sergeant, Harry Fisher, who had fought with the Third Army from Normandy into Germany, recalled: "Patton's philosophy was simple. 'Attack, attack and keep attacking.' Never give your enemy a chance."

Fisher remembered advancing on a German village one day that late winter of 1945: "They put out white flags to surrender.

When our boys walked in and came close to the village buildings, they started shooting at them—an ambush. They retreated quickly. Patton gave the order to bring up the artillery and told them to level the whole damn village. . . . He leveled it and left it as a lesson to them if they were going to pull the same trick again what to expect."[23]

Patton still pushed his Third Army relentlessly. One day, he came across some of his men who had stalled. There was a problem. A self-propelled gun was stuck beneath a railway bridge.

Patton gave the commander of an artillery unit three choices.

"Colonel, you can blow up the goddamn gun. You can blow up the goddamn bridge. Or you can blow out your goddamn brains, I don't care which."[24]

On another occasion, a corps commander outlined a proposed attack to Patton.

Patton wanted to know when it would begin.

"Wednesday."

"That's too late."

Wednesday, said the commander, was the earliest date possible.

Patton was not having that.

"But general," said the commander, "you must remember that it takes time to do these things."

"Then what the hell are you wasting your time here for?"[25]

Progress was swift, and General Eisenhower was delighted. On March 7, Patton's 4th Armored finally reached the Rhine, having covered more than fifty miles in less than two days.

For publicity purposes, it was announced that the "two

hundred thousandth German prisoner" had been taken by the Third Army.[26] A photograph was taken of a German soldier with a sign stating that he was number two hundred thousand, but it was never released to the press—such labeling was "contrary to the Geneva Convention."[27]

The Third Army was on a roll. Patton's forces were soon seizing hundreds of square miles of enemy territory each day and swarming southward along the Rhine. At a Third Army HQ briefing the morning of March 17, Eisenhower stood up and proclaimed in front of Patton and his staff: "The trouble with you people in the Third Army is that you do not appreciate your own greatness; you are not cocky enough. Let the world know what you are doing, otherwise the American soldier will not be appreciated at his full value."

Patton accompanied Eisenhower to an airfield from where Eisenhower was to fly to another meeting, this time with the Seventh Army.

"George," said Eisenhower, "you are not only a good General, you are a *lucky* General, and, as you will remember, in a General, Napoleon prized luck above skill."

"Well," replied Patton, laughing, "that is the first compliment you have paid me since we served together."[28]

Patton's chief of staff, Hap Gay, later asked Patton during a staff meeting why Eisenhower had been so complimentary about the Third Army.

"That's easy," said Patton. "Before long, Ike will be running for President. The Third Army represents a lot of votes."

Some of Patton's staff smiled.

"You think I'm joking? I'm not. Just you wait and see."[29]

Eisenhower would indeed go on to run for and be elected president. If he had failed throughout the war to flatter Patton or bolster his ego sufficiently, Ike was nevertheless appreciative of his old friend's achievements and would soon recommend that Patton receive a fourth star.

# CHAPTER 18

# The Crossing

**Berlin**
**March 18, 1945**

THE THIRD REICH, predicted by Hitler to last a thousand years, was falling apart. On the evening of March 18, German armaments minister Albert Speer attended a "situation conference" with Hitler and others. These meetings now took place deep in the Führer's bunker beneath the city streets of Berlin.

Speer recalled that the subject of that day's conference was the "defense of the Saar, now hard pressed by Patton's army."

Hitler addressed Speer.

"Tell the gentlemen yourself what a loss of the Saar coal will mean to you!"

"That would only speed up the collapse," blurted Speer.

Hitler stared at Speer, upset by his honesty.

The conference ended, and later, after midnight, early on

March 19, Speer's fortieth birthday, Speer met with Hitler once more.

Hitler presented Speer with signed photographs of himself.

He apologized for his handwriting.

"Lately," said Hitler, "it's been hard for me to write even a few words in my own hand. You know how it shakes. Often, I can hardly complete my signature. What I've written for you came out almost illegible."

Speer presented Hitler with a memorandum in which he had laid out how dire the situation for Germany was.

"This time you will receive a written reply to your memorandum!" said Hitler icily.

"If the war is lost," added Hitler, "the people will be lost also. It is not necessary to worry about what the German people will need for elemental survival."

The German people had failed Hitler. To him, they too were now expendable.

Hitler believed that the "nation has proved to be the weaker, and the future belongs solely to the stronger eastern nation. In any case only those who are inferior will remain after this struggle, for the good have already been killed."[1]

THE PACE of the Third Army's advance that March took an exacting toll on many of Patton's men. But there would be no letup, however close to the limit many soldiers were. Patton was now obsessed with beating Montgomery across the Rhine—a great prize indeed for an army commander who understood its symbolism perhaps better than any of his peers. Patton knew

Montgomery was going to try to cross on March 24, only days away.

Time was of the essence.

On March 20, Patton visited General Manton Eddy's XII Corps.

He paced up and down.

"I want you to cross the river at Oppenheim tomorrow!" Patton told Eddy.

"Just give us another day," replied Eddy.

"No!" shouted Patton.

Eddy wasn't going to be bullied by Patton, who stomped off, furious.

Eddy was soon on the telephone to Major General S. Leroy "Red" Irwin of the 5th Division.

"You've got to get across, Red. Georgie's been tramping up and down and yelling at us."[2]

Irwin did as he was told. His men reached the banks of the Rhine at Oppenheim on the afternoon of March 22. That night, at 10 P.M., they clambered into boats and began to cross the river. The Germans were taken by surprise as six battalions got over under cover of darkness. There was no artillery or air support.

It was the first successful attack across the Rhine by boat since Napoleon, and Patton knew it of course.[3]

Private Al Elliot belonged to a mortar company of the 5th Infantry Division. "Explosions were happening all around us," he remembered. "You felt the bump in the boat and through the concussion in the air."

Water splashed against Elliot and the others in his boat.

"It was a moment when you thought you might breathe your last with every breath."

He could hear screams as men were hit in other boats, but he could not "even tell if they were in front or behind or to the side, because of the acoustics on the water. Through it all, you knew you couldn't do but one thing: Paddle!"[4]

The next day, Bradley received a call from Patton.

"Brad," said Patton, "don't tell anyone but I'm across."

"Well, I'll be damned. You mean across the Rhine?"

"Sure am," Patton said. "I sneaked a division over last night. But there are so few Krauts around there they don't know it yet. So don't make any announcement—we'll keep it a secret until we see how it goes."

By that afternoon, Patton's 4th Armored Division and the entire 90th Division were across the river—"without benefit of aerial bombing, ground smoke, artillery preparation, and airborne assistance," a Third Army report noted.[5]

That evening, Patton contacted Bradley again, shouting into the telephone: "Brad, for God's sake, tell the world we're across! I want the world to know Third Army made it before Monty starts across."[6]

When Eisenhower learned of the crossing that same day, he wrote to congratulate Patton:

> I have frequently had occasion to state, publicly, my appreciation of the great accomplishments of this Allied force during the past nine months. The purpose of this note is to express to you personally my deep appreciation of the splendid way in which you have conducted Third

*Army operations from the moment it entered battle last
August 1. You have made your Army a fighting force
that is not excelled in effectiveness by any other of equal
size in the world, and I am very proud of the fact that
you, as one of the fighting commanders who has been
with me from the beginning of the African campaign,
have performed so brilliantly throughout.*[7]

It was more of that rare praise, music to Patton's ears. In his
diary that day, Patton wrote: "I am very grateful to the Lord for
the great blessings he has heaped on me and the Third Army, not
only in the success which He had granted us, but in the weather
which He is now providing."[8]

It was a day to always be remembered. His men's crossing
"was most remarkable in that the total casualties in killed and
wounded were only 28," he noted. "This does not mean it was no
fight. It means the 5th Division, making its 23rd river crossing,
was very skillful, and the operation was very daringly performed."[9]

Perhaps the most affecting acclaim for Patton's achievement
in crossing the Rhine came from his son, George, who wrote
from West Point, where he was a cadet, to congratulate his father: "Tonight I guess is one of the greatest moments in history
and to think that you're the guy that did it. Well, I can't express
myself. The Rhine bridged—God damn! . . . I know you took a
calculated risk, and won again."

Patton's son added: "I'll die happy, so help me God, if I can
serve under you in combat for one lonely month. I called up
mother last night and she was right-square-out-of-this-world

with enthusiasm. . . . Damn I don't know how you do it, I really don't. Well just stay healthy so both of us can go to Asia. Hot damn."[10]

Patton himself had arrived that day in Nierstein, south of Mainz. Midway across a pontoon bridge over the Rhine, he had stopped.

"Time out for a short halt," said Patton.

Patton walked to the edge of the bridge and looked down into the waters.

"I've been looking forward to this for a long time," said Patton, who then proceeded to urinate into the river.

"I didn't even piss this morning when I got up," added Patton, "so I would have a really full load. Yes, sir, the pause that refreshes."[11]

Patton carried on across the bridge. Once across the river, he knelt down and scooped earth from the ground.

He stood up and let the soil fall through his fingers.

"Thus, William the Conqueror."[12]

# CHAPTER 19

## Hubris

**East of the Rhine**
**Late March 1945**

GERMANY HAD BEEN DEVASTATED. Hundreds of thousands had been made homeless by day and night bombing. Countless civilians were also fleeing ahead of the Red Army, whose advance had proved unstoppable.

Patton wrote to his wife, describing streams of refugees clogging roads. "The displaced persons," noted Patton, were "utterly forlorn. I saw one woman with a perambulator full of her worldly goods sitting by it on a hill crying, an old man with a wheelbarrow, a woman and five children with a tin cup crying."

Once the Third Army was across the Rhine, nothing now stood in its way for long. "In hundreds of villages," wrote Patton, "there is not a living thing. . . . Most often houses are heaps of stone. They brought it on themselves, but these poor peasants are not responsible. Am I getting soft?"[1]

Harry Feinberg served with the 4th Armored Division. It was often his job to interrogate prisoners. "They were happy to give up," he recalled. "I mentioned Patton, and they'd stand up. The name would freeze the blood in their veins. . . . After attacks, General Patton would come by, drive in his jeep . . . and call us all over to say, 'Good job, boys.'"

On one occasion, Feinberg got a close-up look at the by now legendary commander. "I was interested not in looking at him or listening to him, but in [seeing] the two ivory-handled guns on his belt. He was big. Tall. His eyes were always blood-shot. I think he drank a lot of booze. And he shortened the war for us."[2]

Patton was in his pomp. The celebrated *Life* magazine photographer Margaret Bourke-White visited Patton's head-quarters on March 24 and watched as the warrior chose which uniform to wear for her portrait. Also present was Major General Otto Weyland, head of XIX Tactical Air Command, which was providing superb air support for Patton's Third Army.

"Things have been going too smoothly," Patton said. "It makes me jittery when things go too well."

Patton donned a steel helmet.

"Don't show my jowls," ordered Patton. "And don't show the creases in my neck. Stop taking pictures of my teeth. Why are photographers always taking pictures of my teeth?"

When Bourke-White was finished, Patton celebrated by handing out glasses of bourbon.

"If I ran out of bourbon and cigars," said Patton, "I'd be a healthier man."

Someone wanted to know what Patton was going to do when the war was over.

"Go back to my yacht." His sailboat was "a lovely boat."

The conversation returned to the war.

Patton wanted to fly in a P-47 the very next day.

"You can't go on any mission, General," said Weyland. "That's one thing we won't let you do."[3]

ON LAND, by that evening of March 24, the 4th Armored had reached the Main River, more than twenty miles east of the Rhine.

That evening, Major General Manton Eddy, commander of Patton's XII Corps, called General William Hoge, who led the 4th Armored.

Eddy said that Patton had asked him to send a force more than fifty miles behind enemy lines to free "nine hundred American prisoners" near a town called Hammelburg.

Patton also contacted Hoge.

"This is going to make MacArthur's raid on Cabanatuan [look like] peanuts."[4]

Patton was referring to the prison camp recently liberated by MacArthur's forces in the Philippines. Some five hundred men had been set free in one of the war's most daring raids, which had brought MacArthur glowing publicity.

Hoge was concerned.

"We'd be encroaching on the Seventh Army zone," he told Patton.

"Bill," replied Patton, "I want you to put a little task force together. Now get on with it."

Hoge again questioned the mission.

"I've cleared this with Bradley," said Patton.

"My people are exhausted. The division is only at half strength as it is."

"Bill, I promise I'll replace anything you lose—every man, every tank, every half-track. I promise."

Hoge had no choice but to do as instructed.

"I'll get Abrams of Combat Command B right on it, sir."[5]

Hoge contacted Creighton Abrams, who had led the spearhead of the 4th Armored into Bastogne.

Abrams was briefed on the proposed mission.

"Fifty miles is a long way," said Abrams. "If we have to go that far, I want my whole command to go."

That would involve as many as four thousand men.

"No, it has to be a small force," replied Hoge. "And Army says it has to go tonight."

That was clearly not possible.

"I'd like to talk to Army, sir."

"Don't worry, you'll get your chance. Patton is planning to come down to your command post."[6]

The next day, March 25, Patton arrived at Abrams's command post in Aschaffenburg. It was 10 A.M. when the general met with Abrams, who offered to lead the mission, employing his entire armored command with supporting artillery and two battalions of tanks.

That was too large a force for Patton's liking. It was decided that Abrams would not be involved. The officer chosen to lead the rescue mission instead was twenty-four-year-old Major Abraham Baum, a Jew from the Bronx who before the war had been a pattern cutter in the garment industry.[7]

Baum later recalled that Patton spoke with him out of earshot of others.

"Listen, Abe—it is Abe, isn't it?"

Baum nodded.

"I thought so. You pull this off and I'll see to it that you get the Congressional Medal of Honor."

"I have my orders, sir. You don't have to bribe me."[8]

It was 5 P.M. on March 25 when Baum briefed the officers in his rescue force. They had barely enough fuel to get to the camp and back.

Baum's men had hardly slept since crossing the Rhine four days before. Wearily, they began to prepare for Patton's special operation. Among the prisoners at Hammelburg, Baum would learn, was none other than Patton's son-in-law, West Point graduate Lieutenant Colonel John Waters, who had been captured in North Africa in early 1943. Waters had married Patton's daughter Beatrice in 1934.

That same day, Patton wrote to his wife: "Hope to send an expedition tomorrow to get John." Two days later, Patton noted in his diary: "I am quite nervous all morning over the task force I sent to rescue the prisoners, as we could get no information concerning them. I do not believe there is anything in that part of Germany heavy enough to hurt them, but for some reason I was nervous—probably I had indigestion."[9]

He had every reason to be nervous. The whole affair proved to be an inexcusable waste of lives. Having fought its way to Hammelburg, Baum's force would free many prisoners only to be surrounded by the Germans as the rescued and their liberators tried to return to American lines. Of the eleven officers and 303 men, thirty-two would be killed and 256 would be wounded, captured, or missing by March 28.

Allied Supreme Commander Dwight Eisenhower would soon make a report to US Army Chief of Staff George Marshall on April 15, 1945: "[Patton] sent off a little expedition on a wild goose chase in an effort to liberate some American prisoners. The upshot was that he got 25 prisoners back and lost a full company of medium tanks and a platoon of light tanks."[10]

Eisenhower added: "Foolishly, [Patton] then imposed censorship on the movement, meaning to lift it later, which he forgot to do. The story has now been released, and I hope the newspapers do not make too much of it. . . . Patton is a problem child, but he is a great fighting leader in pursuit and exploration."[11]

The decision to send such a small force was indeed a serious error, an enduring major stain on Patton's reputation. "It was a story that began as a wild goose chase and ended in tragedy," Bradley later wrote. "I did not rebuke him for it. Failure itself was George's own worst reprimand."[12]

Luckily for Patton at the time, the failed rescue attempt was not discovered by the press for ten days, by which time other momentous events were crowding the headlines. Patton was

fortunate indeed that what would be referred to as the "Hammelburg Affair" did not become a career-ending scandal. He
would concede that "throughout the campaign in Europe I know
of no error I made except that of failing to send a Combat Command to take Hammelburg."[13]

# CHAPTER 20

## The Final Straight

**Frankfurt, Germany**
**April 3, 1945**

THE END WAS NIGH. German resistance was collapsing all along the Western Front. In some cities and towns, fighting was fierce, but the Allied advance continued inexorably. On April 3, Patton's command post was set up in a German barracks on the outskirts of Frankfurt—so heavily bombed that it looked like a "brick and stone wilderness."[1]

Patton stopped in a town called Bad Kreuznach and came across "American prisoners of war."

Among the men were several who were guilty of wounding themselves to avoid combat. One of them was an officer, which Patton found particularly contemptible.

Patton later recalled talking to them.

"Did you get the man who shot you?"

"No, sir, I done it myself."

"Oh, you did! What time did it happen, in the daytime?"

"No, sir, it was at night."

"Did you suffer much?"

"No, sir, my buddy fixed me up right away."

"Do you know what you are?"

"No, sir, I don't."

Patton addressed other men nearby.

"Now, all of you other soldiers listen."

Patton swore at one of the men and gave the officer a dressing down, describing him and the others as cowards who had "added to the labor and risk of brave men who did not use this means of getting out of battle."[2]

A week later, on April 11, Patton's anger rose again. He was with his aide Codman when they arrived in Hersfeld after passing through Wiesbaden, where Patton had had lunch with Bradley. Patton got angry when he spotted many abandoned gas cans that had not been salvaged. Then he passed two GIs who were with two "not un-decorative young ladies," remembered Codman.

"Stop," shouted Patton.

The jeep pulled up at the grass verge of the autobahn.

Codman later recalled that Patton said: "What the so-and-so do you mean by fraternizing with those so-and-so German so-and-sos?"

"Sir," said one of the soldiers, "these are two Russian ladies who have lost their way. We are trying to learn their language so as to direct them properly."

Patton looked angry but then he saw the humor in the reply.

"O.K.," said Patton, "you win."

Patton told his driver, John Mims: "Go ahead."

They pulled away.

"That," said Patton, "is really a new one."[3]

BY THE SECOND week of April, the Third Army was rolling ever faster into Nazi Germany, covering dozens of miles some days. As time ran out for Hitler and his forces, Patton had mixed feelings, sensing that his glory hours were now behind him. He admitted as much on April 12 in a letter to his wife: "I love war and responsibility and excitement. Peace is going to be Hell on me."[4]

But horror and astonishment, as impossible as it might have seemed given all that had occurred, still lay ahead. Amid the ashes of the Third Reich, Patton would discover the full evil and moral corruption of Nazism and Hitler's gangster regime. On the morning of the twelfth, the day he wrote to his wife, Patton joined Bradley and Eisenhower on an inspection of a salt mine at Merkers where a massive German gold reserve had been hidden.

Two generals, bespectacled Manton Eddy and Otto Weyland, accompanied Patton as well as Bradley and Eisenhower. They stepped onto a freight hoist and were then lowered two thousand feet into a dark mine shaft.

"If that clothesline should part," said Patton, referring to the cable, "promotions in the United States Army would be considerably stimulated."

"O.K., George, that's enough," said Eisenhower. "No more cracks until we are above ground again."

At the bottom of the shaft, the generals found a tunnel that they followed until they came across a large cavern where, remembered Charles Codman, they found many "boxes, cases, crates . . . [full of] jewels, paintings, dental bridgework and fillings."[5]

Before them were piles of Nazi loot. Eisenhower remembered "a hoard of gold, tentatively estimated by our experts to be worth $250,000,000, most of it in gold bars. These were in sacks, two 25-pound bars to each sack. There was also a great amount of minted gold from different countries of Europe and even a few millions of gold coins from the United States."[6]

There was also a great deal of German currency in bales.

"What are those?" asked Eisenhower.

"They are earmarked to meet future German Army payrolls," said an interpreter.

"I doubt if they will be needed," said Eisenhower.[7]

They left the mine, emerging into daylight, then had lunch before flying to Gotha, from where they were driven to the concentration camp at Ohrdruf. It was the first camp in the Nazis' vast archipelago of suffering and evil to be liberated by the US Army, just eight days before on April 4 by the 89th Infantry Division and the 4th Armored Division.

Most of the camp's inmates, numbering more than ten thousand in late March, had been murdered in the camp, had died of exhaustion and disease, or had been shot to death on forced marches to other camps.

The Americans had arrived before the SS could destroy all the evidence of their atrocities. There were piles of bodies and pits and pyres with partly burned bodies.

An officer approached Patton and his fellow generals once they had entered the camp.

"They tried to eliminate the evidence before we arrived," said the officer, "but as you can see, they were not very successful."

The generals were given a tour of the camp. One building was crammed with corpses. An Austrian Jewish survivor showed the visitors the camp's gallows. Photographers accompanied Patton's party, and Eisenhower, Bradley, Patton, and others were shown looking at a pyre covered with burned corpses.

Patton looked down at singed bones and ash, his hands behind his back, pistol at his hip. Eisenhower stood, one hand partially in his trouser pocket, beside Bradley as a *Stars and Stripes* reporter, a couple of feet from Eisenhower, took notes.

At another stop on the tour of the camp, Eisenhower stood with hands on hips as he watched a survivor demonstrate torture methods used by the SS. Patton and Bradley were close by, grim-faced as an interpreter pointed and spoke.

Eisenhower would soon cable his boss, George Marshall, US Army chief of staff:

> The things I saw beggar description. While I was touring the camp, I encountered three men who had been inmates and by one ruse or another had made their escape. I interviewed them through an interpreter. The visual evidence and the verbal testimony of starvation, cruelty and bestiality were so overpowering as to leave me a bit sick. In one room, where [there] were piled up twenty or thirty naked men, killed by starva-

tion, George Patton would not even enter. He said that he would get sick if he did so. I made the visit deliberately, in order to be in a position to give first-hand evidence of these things if ever, in the future, there develops a tendency to charge these allegations merely to "propaganda."[8]

Patton was indeed so disgusted by the inhumanity that he left the party, went behind a building, and then vomited. He described the scenes in a vivid account in his diary:

In a shed . . . was a pile of about 40 completely naked human bodies in the last stages of emaciation. These bodies were lightly sprinkled with lime, not for the purposes of destroying them, but for the purpose of removing the stench.

When the shed was full—I presume its capacity to be about 200, the bodies were taken to a pit a mile from the camp where they were buried. The inmates claimed that 3,000 men, who had been either shot in the head or who had died of starvation, had been so buried since the 1st of January.

When we began to approach with our troops, the Germans thought it expedient to remove the evidence of their crime. Therefore, they had some of the slaves exhume the bodies and place them on a mammoth griddle composed of 60-centimeter railway tracks laid on brick foundations. They poured pitch on the bodies and then built a fire of pinewood and coal under them. They were not very successful in their operations because there was a pile of human bones, skulls, charred torsos on or under the griddle which must have accounted for many hundreds.[9]

The generals left, shaken, and waited for cars to arrive to take them back to Gotha.

A GI was nearby.

He "accidentally bumped into [a] Nazi ex-guard," recalled Codman, "and from sheer nerves began to giggle."

Eisenhower was not amused and stared at the GI icily.

"Still having trouble hating them?" said Eisenhower.

Eisenhower turned to his fellow generals.

"I want every American unit not actually in the front lines to see this place," he said. "We are told that the American soldier does not know what he is fighting for. Now, at least, he will know what he is fighting *against*."[10]

Eisenhower was deeply disturbed by what he had seen. It was "beyond the human mind to comprehend." That evening, he still looked "sick" and "very angry" according to one of his staff.

Noting his distress, Patton poured Eisenhower a drink.

Eisenhower said he couldn't "understand the mentality that would compel these German people to do a thing like that."

Other matters were discussed. That same evening, Eisenhower told Patton that he was going to order the advance of the First and Ninth Armies at the Elbe River. They would not push on to Berlin. Instead, Patton's Third Army would attack southeast toward Czechoslovakia.

"From a tactical point of view, it is highly inadvisable for the American Army to take Berlin," said Eisenhower, "and I hope political influence won't cause me to take the city. It has no tactical or strategic value and would place upon American forces the burden of caring for thousands and thousands of Germans, displaced persons and Allied prisoners of war."[11]

Patton couldn't believe what he was hearing.

"Ike, I don't see how you figure that out," said Patton. "We had better take Berlin, and quick—and on to the Oder!"[12]

Later that evening, Patton insisted that the Ninth Army could be in Berlin in just two days.

"Well, who would want it?" said Eisenhower.

"I think history," replied Patton, "will answer that question for you."[13]

The following day, Patton and Eisenhower would witness even more atrocity, visiting Buchenwald concentration camp, liberated by the Americans on April 11, 1945. One eyewitness recalled: "The inmates liberated by our forces were skeletons . . . many of the captives were professional soldiers . . . and they pulled their wasted bodies into gallant salutes as Eisenhower, Patton and their staffs passed them. It was enough to make strong men weep—and some American officers did unabashedly."

Patton walked into a barracks at Buchenwald. "On each side were four tiers of bunks," he later wrote, "in which the inmates lay at right angles to the wall. They looked like animated dummies. . . . When we went through, they attempted to cheer but were too feeble."

Patton's chief of staff, Hap Gay, accompanied Patton. "The

scenes witnessed there are beyond the normal mind to believe," he noted. "No race except a people dominated by an ideology of sadism could have committed such gruesome crimes . . . inmates, all in a bad stage of starvation . . . Even those who lived, in my opinion, will never recover mentally."[14]

IT WAS just after midnight when Eisenhower and Bradley retired to their quarters in the Third Army headquarters. Patton went to check the time on his wristwatch. It wasn't working, so he turned on the radio and then heard a BBC news report. President Roosevelt was dead.

Before going to war in November 1942, Patton had met at the White House with Roosevelt, whom he admired. He had assured his commander that he would be "either a conqueror or a corpse."[15] That April 12, the president had died of a cerebral hemorrhage at his Warm Springs retreat in Georgia.[16]

Patton rushed from his caravan and went to break the news to Eisenhower and Bradley.

The three generals sat in their bathrobes and discussed Roosevelt and his successor, Harry Truman, until 2 A.M. Bradley was skeptical about Truman, who surely would not be able to "fill Roosevelt's large shoes."[17]

Patton believed it was "very unfortunate that in order to secure political preference, people are made Vice Presidents who were never intended, neither by Party nor by the Lord to be Presidents."[18]

The three generals turned in to get some sleep, "depressed and sad," remembered Eisenhower.[19]

# THE FINAL STRAIGHT

The next day, duties called and Patton appeared at a ribbon cutting for a pontoon bridge that had been built across the Rhine at Mainz.

Major General Ewart G. Plank handed Patton a pair of scissors.

"What are you taking me for, a tailor?" said Patton. "Goddamnit, give me a bayonet."[20]

And recognition from his seniors came at last. On April 17, during a brief visit to Paris, Patton was at breakfast reading his least favorite newspaper, *Stars and Stripes*. He discovered that he had received a fourth star. Charles Codman found him the only set of four stars in Paris before he left.[21]

"It's nice," said Patton, ever Patton, "but I'd have enjoyed it more if it had come with the first batch."[22]

BACK IN Germany, three days later, on April 20, it was a sunny afternoon as the four-starred general was being flown in a Piper Cub to visit one of his units. Suddenly, a German aircraft appeared and fired on Patton's plane.

Charles Codman was in another Piper Cub and saw the German attack Patton's plane again but thankfully miss. There was Patton, pointing something at the German plane, which looked uncannily like a British Spitfire.

Was Patton brandishing his pistol? Then Codman saw Patton was actually holding a camera. "What a man. Rat, tat, tat, tat. Over and past, another miss, another zoom. Both Cubs are down low now, contouring the fences, the hollows, and the treetops. A terrific whining scream, guns chattering. Another miss?

Yes, thank God. Pull-up? No, too fast, too low. The fighter hits a knoll in the field ahead, ricochets like a flat stone on the surface of a still pond. Hits again, slews, disintegrates. Finis."[23]

Patton was as courageous and pugnacious as ever, even in the last days of a war that had already been won. So too were many of his men. One evening that spring, Patton met with his nephew, twenty-nine-year-old Fred Ayer, an FBI agent serving as an agency liaison with the US military in Europe.

"You know, Freddy, the psychology of the fighting man is a strange thing," Patton told Ayer. "Early, well before dawn, I watched men of an almost green division, soaking wet and cold, cross a swollen river in the face of steep hills packed deep with concrete gun emplacements, machine guns, mines and barbed wire. They crossed without hesitation and walked right through that concentration of fire."[24]

On another evening, while drinking bourbon and smoking cigars late into the night, Ayer listened as Patton talked about how he was perceived by the press and others.

"Yes, I know, people ask why I swagger and swear, wear flashy uniforms and sometimes two pistols. Well, I'm not sure whether some of it isn't my own damned fault but, however that may be, the press and others have built a picture of me."

He now had to act out his public persona.

"So now, no matter how tired, or discouraged, or even really ill I may be, if I don't live up to that picture my men are going to say, 'The old man's sick, the old son-of-a-bitch has had it.' Then their own confidence, their own morale, will take a big drop."[25]

Patton also discussed the risks he had taken by being close to the front so often: "I get criticized, every day, for taking needless risks by being too often right up front. What good is a dead general? they ask. I say, what damn good is a general who won't take the same risks as his troops?"[26]

To that end, Patton kept a carbine within reach of his cot at night after hearing rumors that German airborne teams of assassins were preparing to strike American targets. Patton's Third Army was by now almost across Bavaria, approaching Czechoslovakia. "By April 22nd," wrote Patton, "it was obvious to me that the end of the war was very close."[27]

In that last week of April, Patton's Third Army was joined by the 13th Armored Division. Lieutenant Phillip Foraker, a tank platoon leader, remembered Patton taking time to make sure the division knew how he expected it to fight, even with just days left before the war would surely be over.

Foraker claimed, "Patton was the only Army commander who personally met with all the officers and noncoms of our division. He told us how to fight. . . . We would pull up outside of a German town and if the white flags aren't out, we put a round of white phosphorous into the roof of one house."

If the Germans did not surrender—if white flags did not show in the windows—then the artillery was to be called in "to destroy the town before proceeding. . . . We were to attack at night. He said we would get good results with fewer casualties."[28]

Patton was right. But not about everything, as some of his troops had long known only too well.[29] He still insisted that all officers be clearly identified, but in combat, snipers would pick them off first. That left units leaderless, and so the wise—those who wanted to survive—covered their insignia "with mud, or took them off," recalled one officer.[30]

Another soldier, Staff Sergeant Al Neuharth of the 86th Infantry Division, remembered Patton turning up as he and others rounded up prisoners—some of the more than a million taken by Patton's Third Army during the war. More and more Germans were surrendering, often in droves.

Patton pulled up in a jeep.

Prisoners were sitting down nearby.

Patton was furious.

"Get those fucking Krauts on their feet and moving, or I'll put you behind the same barbed wire they're headed for!"

Neuharth saluted and did as he was told.

A soldier moaned about Patton being a son of a bitch.

Neuharth laughed.

Patton was indeed a "borderline S.O.B.," remembered Neuharth. "But he was a winner. He knew how to move men and win wars. I would have followed him nonstop all the way to Berlin on foot."[31]

The prisoners now were indeed everywhere. It had been estimated by American planners that some million German soldiers would need to be placed by June in huge camps—"cages." But as April drew to a close, there were already almost 1.5 million in Germany alone. From the air they appeared as forlorn, field gray masses packed together behind barbed wire.

Germany was teeming with the traumatized and the defeated. Allied POWs also had to be dealt with—deloused, nursed back to health in many cases, and repatriated. On April 29, 1945, near the town of Moosburg in southern Bavaria, Patton visited Stalag VII-A, which had been liberated just hours before. Some hundred fifty thousand prisoners had at some point spent time in the camp, and it was now crowded with an extraordinary seventy-six thousand–odd inmates, many of them malnourished.[32]

Patton made quite an entrance, arriving in an American-flag-waving jeep and passing through the main gates of the camp.

Patton stood up in the jeep.

It stopped just inside the gates.

A mass of emaciated American POWs, many in tears, rushed toward Patton, having recognized him.

An officer from among the POWs was soon standing before Patton. He saluted Patton.

Patton returned the salute.

"It is we who salute you and all these brave men," said Patton.[33]

Men cried with relief and joy and there were screams and yells.

Patton noticed a German flag atop a flagpole.

"I want that son-of-a-bitch cut down, and the man that cuts it down, I want him to wipe his ass with it!"[34]

An American prisoner took the flag from Patton's jeep and replaced the German flag with it and then a "thunderous cheer erupted that could be heard as far west as New York City. Thousands of young men looked up at the American flag as tears streamed unashamedly down their grimy youthful faces."[35]

Patton inspected the camp. He shook countless men's hands. He told one man that he would "whip the bastards all the way to Berlin."[36]

Those soldiers tasked with doing so were increasingly jittery, as they sensed the war was almost over. No one wanted to be the last man to lose his life to defeat Hitler, however much they admired Patton.[37] "How I want the war to end," wrote one man. "The danger now begins to frighten me. To die at this stage—with the door at the end of the passage, the door into the rose garden, already in sight, ajar—would be awful."[38]

# CHAPTER 21

---

# The End

**Berlin**
**April 30, 1945**

IN BERLIN, Adolf Hitler could hear the Russians fighting close to the Reichstag. On April 30, around 3:30 in the afternoon, he died by suicide in Berlin as the Red Army approached his bunker. In the last words of a final testament, the leader of the Third Reich remained as virulently anti-Semitic as throughout his thirteen years in power: "Above all I charge the leaders of the nation and those under them to scrupulous observance of the laws of race and to merciless opposition to the universal poisoner of all peoples, International Jewry."[1]

The news of the Führer's death spread fast, but Patton at first did not believe it: "There was a rumor . . . that Hitler was dead and that Himmler was about to surrender. Personally, I do not put any credence in it, but I believe that most German troops will surrender because they had nothing but defeat since the initial landing in Normandy."[2]

That same day, Patton was present during an interrogation of Brigadier General Boelsen of the 18th Panzergrenadier Division.

"Tell the general," said Patton, "that he does not have to answer any questions that I ask."

But Patton did want to know "how long this unnecessary killing will have to go on. . . . Are they [the Germans] going to keep on getting killed to no purpose?"

"The ordinary fighting man," replied Boelsen, "and the professional soldier have long seen the unnecessary continuance of fighting and recognize this, but the honor to which they are bound as soldiers makes them continue to fight, especially the professional soldier. As long as the country is at war, they are honor-bound to fight. . . ."

"How is the war going to end," asked Patton, "and do we have to kill them all?"

"I believe that the speedy advances of your forces will end it. Large groups will be captured as you go on. . . ."

"Do you think that there will be any underground movement, fighting from ambushes, etc.?"

"The population in general, no . . . The average run of the population . . . wants to be spared any further war. . . ."

"It seems foolish," replied Patton, "[for the Germans] to [continue to] fight."[3]

By this time, Patton was determined to reach Prague before the Russians, eager to claim the city as his final prize. Ironically, so close to the end of hostilities, he had his closest brush yet with death during the entire war. On May 3, he was with Charles

Codman in a jeep, moving at speed, when an ox-drawn cart pulled out into the road.

The jeep driver, John Mims, reacted fast enough to avoid a crash—by just a few inches as Patton remembered.[4]

Codman claimed it was closer: a "heavy wagon pole which protruded ahead of the team grazed the General's head."

Patton knew he'd come close to death.

"After all I've been through," he later told Codman, "think of being killed on the road by a team of oxen."[5]

Patton wanted to seize as much territory as possible before he was told to stop, which could happen any day now. Every town liberated was one the Russians would not occupy. Already, he distrusted Stalin's forces, regarding them as uncivilized hordes, enemies of democracy, communist conquerors, not liberators. On May 5, V Corps commander Major General Clarence Huebner was at dinner when one of his staff handed him orders that assigned his force to the Third Army.

"Well, I'll give us just about twelve hours before General Patton calls up and tells us to attack something."

Huebner and his staff were served soup.

Huebner's chief of staff was called to the telephone.

The soup was still hot when he returned to the dinner table.

"General, it's General Patton. He wants to talk to you."

"Hello, Huebner?" asked Patton.

"Hello, General. How are you?"

"Fine. Where in the hell have you been since Sicily?"

"Oh, we've been around making a nuisance of ourselves."

"I'm sure glad you're back with me again."

"Glad to be back, General."

"I want you to attack Pilsen in the morning."

"Yes, sir!"

"Can you do it?"

"Yes, sir."

"Fine, move fast now. We haven't got much time left in this war. I'll be up to see you. Good-bye."

"Good-bye."

Huebner went back to the dinner table.

"Instead of twelve hours," he said, "it was twelve minutes. We attack Pilsen at daybreak."[6]

It was around this time that Bradley contacted Patton and asked him why "everyone in the Third Army" wanted to "liberate the Czechs?"

Patton wanted to save the Czechs from communism but did not say that.

"Oh, Brad," he replied, "can't you see? The Czechs are our allies and consequently their women aren't off limits. On to Czechoslovakia and fraternization!"[7]

Patton shouted into the telephone for good effect: "How in the hell can you stop an army with a battle cry like that?"

But the next day, May 6, Bradley called Patton with news.

Prague was off-limits. It would not be Patton's final prize of the war.

"Ike does not want any international complications at this late date," explained Bradley.

"For God's sake, Brad," Patton retorted, "it seems to me that a great nation like America should let others worry about complications."

The following day, May 7, Patton was sleeping in his trailer.

There was a green telephone beside his bed. It rang. Bradley was on the line.

"It's all over, George," said Bradley. "Ike has just telephoned from Reims. The German Army has surrendered, effective midnight tomorrow, 8 May. As of now, everyone is to stay put in line."[8]

Bradley had not slept and was in no mood to celebrate. Deeply affected by the loss of so many young Americans under his command during the war, Bradley "thanked God for victory."[9] Patton felt bone-weary, like so many of his men, and lonely.

Early that morning, both men's boss, Dwight Eisenhower, had sent a simple message to Washington after General Alfred Jodl had signed the formal surrender in Reims: "The mission of this Allied force was fulfilled at 0241, local time, May 7, 1945. Eisenhower."[10]

ONLY DECADES later would many of the soldiers who had survived the liberation of Europe be able to look back and make some sense of the ordeal. Forty years after the war ended, one GI, Bruce Egger of the 26th Infantry Division, would echo the sentiments of so many others who had returned home after the horrors of the Ardennes and other battlefields.

"We were miserable and cold," wrote Egger, "and exhausted most of the time [and] scared to death. . . . But we were young and strong then, possessed of the marvelous resilience of youth, and for all the misery and fear and the hating every moment of it the war was a great, if always terrifying adventure. Not a man among us would want to go through it again, but we were all proud of having been severely tested and found adequate. The only regret is for those of our friends who never returned."[11]

There had been more than five hundred eighty thousand US casualties in the campaign to liberate Europe, and more than a hundred thirty-five thousand Americans had died. By contrast, a third of German males born from 1915 to 1924 had lost their lives. Nineteen million civilians had died in a Europe that had in many areas been reduced to rubble. More than two-thirds of the continent's industrial base had been destroyed. Firestorms and relentless bombing had left only the walls of buildings standing for mile after mile in many of Germany's major cities and beyond.

Patton's Third Army had been in action for nine months and ninety-eight days, suffering some hundred sixty thousand casualties with more than twenty-seven thousand killed. Almost twenty thousand men were missing in action at war's end. The Third Army had liberated thousands of cities, towns, and villages.

"I can say this," Patton later wrote, "that throughout the campaign in Europe . . . I was under wraps from Higher Command. This may have been a good thing, as perhaps I am too impetuous. However, I do not believe I was, and feel that had I been permitted to go all out, the war would have ended sooner and more lives would have been saved."[12]

HIS JOB was done. On May 8, the morning following the surrender, Colonel Robert S. Allen, one of Patton's staff, watched as Patton arrived for his final briefing of the war at the Third

Army's headquarters in Regensburg. Some five hundred thousand men were now under Patton's command.

Patton entered the briefing room.

"Good morning."

Colonel Allen later recalled that Patton's dog, Willie, was at his master's side. Patton slapped Willie "on the rump and pointed to the floor. Willie eyed Patton for a moment, then lay down obediently."[13]

Patton's staff knew they were witnessing the end of an extraordinary chapter in US military history.

"This will be our last operation briefing in Europe," said Patton. "I hope and pray that it will be our privilege to resume these briefings in another theater that still is unfinished business in this war. I know you are as eager to get there as I am. But you know the situation. However, one thing I can promise you. If I go, you will go."[14]

Patton continued: "I say that because the unsurpassed record of this headquarters is your work. It has been a magnificent and historic job from start to finish. You made history in a manner that is a glory to you and to our country."

Patton wanted his staff to appreciate just how much he had relied on them.

"There probably is no Army commander who did less work than I did," he said. "You did it all, and the imperishable record of Third Army is due largely to your unstinting and outstanding efforts. I thank you from the depths of my heart for all you have done."

Patton then became emotional.

"Well, as the Church says, 'Here endeth the Second Lesson.'"[15]

Allen later remembered that Patton "stood silent for a few minutes looking at the staff, and they at him. Then he nodded to the chief of staff, and snapped his fingers at Willie, and started for the door at the end of the long room."

Patton's staff began to stand up.

"Keep your seats," said Patton.

Patton was heard to say to an aide: "Wonder what the rivers in Japan are like? See if you can get some terrain maps of Japan."[16]

As Patton left the room, he spoke to another aide.

"The best end for an old campaigner," said Patton, "is a bullet at the last minute of the last battle."[17]

Patton's chief of staff, Hap Gay, announced that from the next morning, the staff would wear helmet liners, not the steel helmets required for combat.

Patton reacted with one last order before he exited.

"And make damn sure those liners are painted and smart-looking," he commanded. "I don't want any damn sloppy headgear around here."[18]

It was hard to believe it was all over. Many soldiers in his Third Army were too tired to celebrate, too numb to feel much except relief.

Patton's final casualty report listed 21,441 men killed among 248,427 casualties. "The eighth of May marked exactly two and one-half years since we landed in Africa," Patton noted. "During all that time until midnight of 8-9, we had been in practically continuous battle, and, when not in battle, had been under the strain of continuous criticism, which I believe is harder to bear."[19]

That evening, Patton was to host guests, including Judge Robert Patterson, the undersecretary of war.

"See that everything is done to make the Secretary happy," Patton told his aide Codman. "I want to obtain his promise that we shall all be sent immediately to the Far East."[20]

It was not to be.

Patton walked to his spartan trailer, where he had already prepared a message for his troops belonging to an extraordinary thirty-nine divisions. He had led hundreds of thousands of Americans in the European Theater from November 1942 until the very end of the fighting in Europe.[21]

The message—delivered to his men that day—read:

SOLDIERS OF THE THIRD ARMY, PAST AND PRESENT

During the 281 days of incessant and victorious combat, your penetrations have advanced farther in less time than any other army in history. You have fought your way across 24 major rivers and innumerable lesser streams. You have liberated or conquered more than 82,000 square miles of territory, including 1500 cities and towns, and some 12,000 inhabited places. . . .

During the course of this war I have received promotions and decorations far above and beyond my individual merit. You won them; I as your representative wear them. The one honor which is mine and mine alone is that of having commanded such an incomparable group of Americans, the record of whose fortitude, audacity, and valor will endure as long as history lasts.[22]

Patton addressed correspondents attached to the Third Army at 11:30 A.M. that May 8. He again walked into a briefing room, with Willie once more plodding behind him, and then announced that the war was officially at an end.

Patton pointed to a map showing Central Europe. He looked somber.

"This [war] was stopped right where it started," said Patton. "Right in the Hun's backyard which is now Hitler's graveyard. But that's not the end of the business by any means. What the tin-soldier politicians in Washington and Paris have managed to do today is another story you'll be writing for a long while if you live."

Patton couldn't help himself. He was being rash in his use of words. They were ill-advised indeed.

"They have allowed us to kick hell out of one bastard," added Patton, "and at the same time forced us to help establish a second one as evil or more evil than the first. We have won a series of battles, not a war for peace. . . . This day we have missed another date with our destiny, and this time we'll need Almighty God's constant help if we're to live in the same world with Stalin and his murdering cutthroats."[23]

Patton was not done.

"I wonder how the dead will speak today," he said, "when they know that for the first time in centuries we have opened Central and Western Europe to the forces of Genghis Khan. I wonder how they will feel now that they know there will be no peace in our times and that Americans, some not yet born, will have to fight the Russians tomorrow, or ten, 15 or 20 years from tomorrow."[24]

Omar Bradley would arrive for lunch, and that evening Patton would dine with his closest aides and staff. Beneath Teutonic portraits, the men sat in total silence. There was the "clink of silver knives and forks on gold plates."

One of his staff recalled: "No popping of corks, no paper caps, confetti, or tin horns." These men had been together for more than two years of war, from Africa to the Czechoslovakian border.

At the end of the meal, Patton folded his napkin.

"No more fighting until we get to China," he said. "I don't know how I am going to stand it."

He left and his closest staff followed him to a marble staircase leading to a garden.

Patton turned and faced his staff.

"Good night. I shall be in my trailer."

He began to step down the marble staircase.

Then he looked back at his men.

"There is a species of whale," he said, "which is said to spend much of its time lying on the bottom of the deepest part of the ocean. I don't mind saying at the present moment I feel lower than that whale's arse."[25]

# PART FIVE

# A Warlord No More

Death must not be feared. Death, in time, comes to all men. Yes, every man is scared in his first battle. If he says he's not, he's a liar. Some men are cowards but they fight the same as the brave men or they get the hell slammed out of them watching other men fight who are just as scared as they are. The real hero is the man who fights even though he is scared. . . . Remember that the enemy is just as frightened as you are, and probably more so.[1]

—GEORGE S. PATTON

# CHAPTER 22

---

# Peace Breaks Out

**Third Army Headquarters, Bad Tölz, Germany**
**May 1945**

PATTON'S MOOD DARKENED. Peace had broken out, and he didn't like it one bit. The end of the war in Europe unbalanced Patton, set him off kilter. Because he didn't have the constant pressure of combat command, his passions became prejudices. He became increasingly outspoken and impolitic, as if he no longer cared what he said or whom he offended.

Patton's aide Colonel Paul Harkins recalled Patton sitting at his desk at his headquarters at Bad Tölz in southern Germany, around twenty miles from Munich, a few days after the end of the war.

Patton was enjoying a good cigar, taking notes.

General Hobart Gay entered Patton's office in what had been a Waffen SS barracks during the war.

"General, there's a Russian brigadier general out in my office who says he has instructions to speak to you personally."

"What the hell does the son-of-a-bitch want?"

"Well, I only have part of the story, but it's about river craft on the Danube."

"Bring the bastard in, and you and Harkins come with him."

The Russian was shown into Patton's office. He explained that German boat owners had moved their craft to the American zone of occupation rather than have to deal with the Russians. Then the Russian demanded that Patton make sure the boats were handed over to "Russian control."

Patton was incensed. He pulled out a pistol from a drawer and slammed it on the top of the desk.

"Gay, goddammit!" he cried. "Get this son-of-a-bitch out of here! Who in the hell let him in? Don't let any more of the Russian bastards into this headquarters. Harkins! Alert the 4th and 11th Armored and 65th Division for an attack to the east."

Gay showed the Russian out.

The Russian was stunned by Patton's attack, "white as a sheet."

Gay returned a few minutes later and found Patton casually smoking his cigar. His pistol was back in his desk's drawer.

Patton was smiling.

"How was that?" asked Patton. "Sometimes you have to put on an act, and I'm not going to let any Russian marshal, general, or private tell me what I have to do. . . . [C]all off the alert of the divisions. That's the last we'll hear from those bastards."[1]

Patton didn't hear from any Russian about the boats again.

His contempt for the Russians did not abate.

In Berlin, later that month, Patton was a guest at a review of ebullient Russian troops.

The Russians dispatched an interpreter to ask Patton to join them for a celebratory drink.

When the interpreter told Patton of the invite, he shot back: "Tell that Russian sonuvabitch that from the way they're acting here I regard them as enemies and I'd rather cut my throat than have a drink with one of my enemies."

The interpreter was shocked.

"I am sorry, sir, but I cannot tell the general *that*."

Patton insisted, telling the interpreter that he was to tell his bosses exactly what Patton had just said. The nervous interpreter did so. A Russian general standing nearby merely smiled and said something to the interpreter, who walked back over to Patton.

"The general says that he feels exactly like that about you, sir. So why, he asks, couldn't you and he have a drink after all?"[2]

Patton calmed down and did so.

The encounter did nothing to soften his views about the Russians.

One day, Patton spoke on the telephone with General Joseph T. McNarney, Eisenhower's deputy in Europe.

"Hell," Patton exclaimed, "why do we care what those Goddamn Russians think? We are going to have to fight them sooner or later; within the next generation."

There was no time to lose.

"Why not do it now while our Army is intact and the damn Russians can have their hind end kicked back into Russia in three months?" asked Patton. "We can do it ourselves easily with the help of the German troops we have, if we just arm them and take them with us; they hate the bastards."

Patton had gone too far.

"Shut up, Georgie, you fool!" said McNarney. "This line may be tapped and you will be starting a war with those Russians with your talking!"

Patton ignored him.

"I would like to get it started some way," he continued. "That is the best thing we can do now. *You* don't have to get mixed up in it at all if you are so damn soft about it and scared of your rank—just let me handle it down here. In ten days I can have enough incidents happen to have us at war with those sons of bitches and make it look like their fault. So much so that we will be completely justified in attacking them and running them out."

McNarney was dumbfounded. He hung up. The conversation was proof to him that Patton was not in the least fit for his post-war role as military governor of Bavaria. He was dangerously unhinged. He should be replaced.

Patton continued to rant to his aide Paul Harkins about the Russians: "I really believe that we are going to fight them, and if this country does not do it now, it will be taking them on years later when the Russians are ready for it and we will have an awful time whipping them. We will need these Germans and I don't think we ought to mistreat people whom we will need so badly."[3]

Patton's views could not have been more different from those of Eisenhower, who believed in keeping to agreements reached with Stalin on how postwar Europe should be divided. Cooperation with the Russians was essential to maintaining some kind of stability.

———

FINALLY, for the first time in three years, Patton was headed home. He was to be part of a monthlong "goddamn bond-raising tour," as he put it.[4] It was June 7 when his C-54, escorted by fighters, touched down at Bedford in Massachusetts.

The plane came to a standstill before a group of welcoming officials and Patton's wife and two of his children, and he stepped down. One of Patton's aides recalled: "The morning sun glinted from [his] polished boots, gold-buckled belt, the pistol thrust into it, the handle of his riding crop, the varnished helmet with its four stars and three insignia—1 Armored, the Seventh and the Third Armies."[5]

There was a cheer from onlookers as Patton appeared, followed by a seventeen-gun salute.

Patton approached his wife, Beatrice, and then took off his helmet and kissed her. They had not seen each other since 1942.

She stroked his cheek.

"Oh, I'm so glad you're back."[6]

Reporters watched the reunion.

"When he left me . . . he told me he expected to die fighting," said Beatrice. "It seems like a miracle that he has come back." Patton had told her that he expected to be killed in the war and she had tried to accept she might not see him again.

Patton told the same reporters: "I sincerely hope I fight the Japanese."

Patton and his wife and daughters were then driven twenty-five miles to Boston. It was an extraordinary journey capped by a welcome in the city itself by around a million people who shouted his name and filled the streets. Women threw flowers. Many wept openly.

A crowd of twenty thousand gathered at the Hatch Shell on the Charles River Esplanade.

Among those waiting for Patton were four hundred wounded veterans of his beloved Third Army.

"With your blood and your bones we crushed the Germans before they got here," Patton told the men. "This ovation is not for me, George S. Patton—George S. Patton is simply a hook on which to hang the Third Army."

Patton saluted the wounded, standing at attention.

A state dinner followed at the Copley Plaza Hotel. Again, he was lionized. According to one report: "Patton lost his composure in the face of all the tributes. He bowed his head and tears streamed down his cheeks. It was some time before he dared to trust his own voice, and even then it shook with feeling. Three times as he spoke of the men of the Third Army in terms of glowing praise he choked up and stopped to regain his composure."[7]

Patton finally sat down and wiped tears from his eyes with his handkerchief. The next stop was Denver, and yet more massive crowds, yet more hurrahs. Then it was on to his native California. At the Coliseum in Los Angeles, a hundred thousand people watched as he wept and then cursed as he railed against Japan.

A mock battle involving tanks was staged at the Coliseum. Aware of Patton's propensity to make off-color remarks, the army public relations officers with Patton had come up with a simple method of avoiding possible embarrassment—an off switch to silence his microphone. But before the vast crowd, which included much Hollywood royalty, someone forgot to turn the microphone off after Patton had finished his prepared remarks.

"Magnificent," Patton was heard to say.

The mock battle was "almost as good as the real thing. And God help me, I love it [combat]."[8]

No other general would have so publicly declared his affection for war. Patton's comments were broadcast live on radio nationwide.

Patton also appeared before an adoring crowd at the Hollywood Bowl, with the film star Humphrey Bogart making a speech in his honor.

"It is foolish and wrong," Patton told one audience, "to mourn the men who died. Rather we should thank God that such men lived."[9]

In San Marino, Patton's hometown, Patton again addressed a crowd after being handed a bouquet of flowers.

"I know I've made a lot of widows during my life," he announced, "but this is the first time I've had to stand around looking like a damned bride."[10]

In Pasadena, Patton laid a wreath at his parents' graves—they had died a year apart in the twenties—and then flew back east, where, on June 13, he visited President Truman in the White House. The two had little in common other than their service in World War I when, in 1918 during the Meuse–Argonne offensive, Truman's unit had supported Patton's tank brigade.

Patton was later quoted as saying they were "a couple of soldiers" who had reminisced "about the artillery."[11] For him, it was a fruitless meeting. Patton had hoped that Truman would help him get assigned to the Pacific, but Truman did not want to intervene.

At the Pentagon, Patton learned that he would definitely not be sent to the Pacific.[12] He also paid a visit to Walter Reed Hospital, where his daughter Ellen was caring for double amputees—who had asked her if they could meet her father.

Reporters followed him to Walter Reed, much to Patton's irritation.

"I'll bet you goddam buzzards are just following me to see if I'll slap another soldier, aren't you?" he snapped. "You're all hoping I will!"[13]

Patton wept openly when he saw the double amputees.

Finally, he wiped away his tears.

"God damn it," he said, "if I had been a better general, most of you wouldn't be here."

Late that June, Patton spent a last day with his daughters before returning to Europe.

"Well, goodbye girls," he told them in all seriousness, "I won't be seeing you again. Take care of George. I'll be seeing your mother, but I won't be seeing you."

The war was over, said one daughter. He was being foolish.[14]

Before he left, there was also time that June for Patton to relax with his wife at their country home in Massachusetts. According to Patton's aide Codman, the couple would "simply sit on the sofa hand in hand and together look out over the rolling fields—silently, timelessly. When there is so much to go into, where does one begin?"[15]

———

THERE WAS still a war on. Hundreds of thousands of Americans were massing for an invasion of Japan. And Patton was undoubtedly still at the peak of his powers, a fact recognized in a report written that June 30, 1945, by none other than Omar Bradley, who was positively gushing in his praise, describing Patton as "colorful, courageous, energetic, [with a] pleasing personality, impetuous. Possesses high degree of leadership, bold in operations, has a fine sense of both enemy and own capabilities. An outstanding combat leader."

Bradley added: "Of the 10 general officers of this grade known to me, I would list him Number One as a combat commander. Renders willing and generous support to the plans of his superiors, regardless of his personal views on the matter."[16]

Patton's name was on a list of potential generals submitted by the War Department to General Douglas MacArthur, who was commanding US Army forces in the Pacific, but MacArthur wanted nothing to do with Patton, however highly he was rated. MacArthur's ego was too great. Patton would not be permitted to serve under him and possibly steal his glory.

As for the battleground he'd left behind, Patton flew back on July 3 toward the stark reality of a postwar continent where crime was rampant and more than ten million were displaced, hunger was common, and communism was fast gaining in popularity.

Patton's spirits lifted as his plane neared Germany. Three fighter groups of P-51s—which "played around our nose like porpoises," he recalled—escorted his plane to Holzkirchen Field, from where he was driven toward his headquarters in Bad Tölz.

Fifty planes then provided "continuous and nerve-wracking protection—nerve-wracking in that they seldom missed the tops of the pine trees along the road by more than ten feet." It was a glorious reception. He was glad to have returned: "It gave me a warm feeling in my heart to be back among soldiers."[17]

Patton flew to Berlin to attend the nearby Potsdam Conference on July 16. He was present when President Truman and other attendees watched the American flag raised in the American-controlled sector of the ruined city.

There was little love lost between the outspoken general, born into the American aristocracy, and the dour Truman, who had previously noted in his diary: "Don't see how a country can produce such men as Robert E. Lee, John J. Pershing, Eisenhower and Bradley and at the same time produce Custers, Pattons and MacArthurs."[18]

Patton was utterly unsuited and mostly uninterested in his new job as the peacetime governor of Bavaria. It had been a mistake to give him such a role. Both Eisenhower and Marshall should have better used his talents. He found distractions: hunting with General Ernest Harmon; riding for hours on end in the Bavarian countryside with his chief of staff, Hap Gay. He read a great deal, mostly military history such as Julius Caesar's *Commentaries*, and smoked too many cigars—so many that he had a sore on a lip, which caused him to complain loudly to Colonel Harkins.

"Goddamnit, Paul," he growled, "I'm stopping smo-*goddamn*-king for good. You keep these ci-*fuckin'*-gars."[19]

ON AUGUST 10, having learned about the Japanese surrender, Patton wrote to his wife: "Well the war is over. We just heard that Japan had quit. Now the horrors of peace, pacafism [*sic*], and unions will have unlimited sway. I wish I were young enough to fight the next one. It would be . . . [great] killing Mongols."[20]

Patton's bellicose views were at odds too with the priorities of the soldiers who had served under him. All they wanted was to go home. While America celebrated victory in a war—and the *end* of a war—that had cost more than four hundred thousand US lives, Patton became ever more downcast. His "usefulness" to the world had ended, he believed.[21]

That same August 10, Patton wrote in his diary: "Now all that is left to do is to sit around and await the arrival of the undertaker and posthumous immortality. Fortunately, I also have to occupy myself with the de-Nazification and government of Bavaria, and the recruiting of the industries of the German people so that they can be more self-supporting."[22]

The Germans were no longer to be despised for atrocities such as those he'd witnessed at Ohrdruf. They were potential allies against the communists. He believed the Germans "could have been a good race and we are about to replace them with the Mongolian savages and all Europe with Communism."

Eisenhower warned Patton twice about his views, in late August and then in a letter on September 12, in which he demanded Patton conduct rigorous denazification as he had been instructed. On September 22, Patton finally sealed his own fate. He held a press conference and said that the military government he led in Bavaria would "get better results if it employed more former members of the Nazi party in administrative jobs and as skilled workmen."

An American reporter asked: "After all, General, didn't most ordinary Nazis join their party in about the same way that Americans become Republicans or Democrats?"

"Yes," said Patton, "that's about it."

The resulting headline caused outrage: "AMERICAN GENERAL SAYS NAZIS ARE JUST LIKE REPUBLICANS AND DEMOCRATS."[23]

Eisenhower had finally had enough and erupted in fury. Patton had gone far too far. Eisenhower cabled him on September 25, asking him to "please take the first opportunity to fly up here on a good weather day and see me for an hour."[24]

On September 28, Patton was instead driven for more than seven hours in heavy rain to Eisenhower's office in the IG Farben Building in Frankfurt.

According to Kay Summersby, Eisenhower had "aged ten years" in deciding Patton's fate. Also present was Eisenhower's chief of staff, Walter Bedell Smith, no admirer of Patton.

The conversation between the three was "long and acid . . . one of the stormiest sessions ever staged in our headquarters," added Summersby. "It was the first time I ever heard General Eisenhower really raise his voice."[25]

Patton spoke with his old friend for two hours. Eisenhower was, remembered Patton, "more excited than I have ever seen him."[26]

"The war's over," said Eisenhower, "and I don't want to hurt you—but I can't let you be making such ridiculous statements. I'm going to give you a new job."[27]

Patton said he should "be simply relieved."

Eisenhower was having none of that.

Patton replied that in that case he "should be allowed to continue the command of the Third Army and the government of Bavaria."[28]

Eisenhower offered Patton a new position.

Patton could lead the Fifteenth Army, whose task it would be to prepare an official history of the war in the European Theater.

It was an astonishing demotion, but, Eisenhower stated, Patton would have to resign if he did not accept it.[29]

Patton did not want to resign and so he agreed to Eisenhower's proposal.[30] The sad, fraught meeting ended with Eisenhower telling Patton that a train was available to take him back to Third Army headquarters at 7 P.M.

"If you are spending the night of course you will stay with me," said Eisenhower, "but since I feel you should get back to Bad Tölz as rapidly as possible, I have my train set up to take you and it leaves at 7 o'clock."

Eisenhower looked at his watch.

"It's leaving in half an hour."[31]

The old friends would not be dining together as was their custom. Those days were done.

Patton was not wearing his pistol as he emerged from the meeting. He looked pale, stunned by Eisenhower's decision, betrayed. They'd known each other twenty-five years.

"I took the train," noted Patton in his diary.[32]

Later that evening, Patton did not appear too angry or

wounded. An aide who accompanied Patton back to his head-quarters, Major Van Merle-Smith, recalled him being "very calm and very humble."[33]

Over dinner, Patton considered his future.

"I've obeyed orders," he said, "and done my best; and now there's nothing left."[34]

"I had to relieve George Patton from [the] Third Army," Eisenhower told his son John on September 28. "I'm not moving George for what he's done—just for what he's going to do next."[35]

Patton had told Eisenhower several times during the war: "I hope you know, Ike, that I'm keeping my mouth shut. I'm a clam."[36]

Finally, Eisenhower had been forced to act to make sure Patton could no longer be anything but a clam. According to Eisenhower's son, Patton's "bitterness remained cloaked." His father "never grasped the terrible hurt he had done Patton in relieving him of his beloved Third Army."[37]

The legendary General James Doolittle, a close friend of Patton who had led the famous first air strike on Japan in 1942, later noted: "To Ike, Patton was one of those rare, indispensable leaders who won wars; unfortunately, men like Georgie were too often unfit for peacetime assignments. I have often thought Ike used Georgie . . . to 'sic 'em.' But when the fight was won, he would have to put him in isolation somewhere until the next scrap."[38]

When the press learned of Patton's switch in command, many headlines made for painful reading.

The military's own *Stars and Stripes* bluntly announced: "PATTON FIRED."[39]

Patton later wrote: "This [press] conference [on September 22] cost me command of the Third Army, or rather, of a group of soldiers, mostly recruits, who then rejoiced in that historic name.... It is rather sad to me to think that my last opportunity for earning my pay has passed. At least, I have done my best as God gave me the chance."[40]

Perhaps no other man in the Third Army knew Patton better than his driver, Master Sergeant John Mims, who had served the general faithfully and with humor and grace for four long years.

When Patton learned that Mims had taken the opportunity to finally return to the United States, Patton burst into anger in front of one of his aides, Major Alexander Stiller.

"Hell, no, he isn't going home."

"General, I want to tell you ... ," replied Stiller, "there isn't a God damn thing you can do about it.... He has performed his duty over here and he's entitled to go. He has a young wife back home."[41]

Patton calmed down.

"You're right. Tell him to get ready to go."[42]

Before Mims left for the United States, Patton decorated him with the Silver Star.

Other aides and staff had already departed and very soon he would lose his entire army. It was deeply depressing.

Patton reassured his wife in a letter on October 5 that he had quickly recovered from the humiliation of losing his command of the Third Army: "My head is bloody but unbowed. All that I regret is that I have again worried you.... I was terribly hurt for a few days but I am normal again."[43]

It was not true. He was a superb actor. "Nothing in his dress or bearing," remembered one of his staff, "reflected the torture of his soul."[44]

Patton met with his successor as Third Army commander, the brilliant Lucian Truscott, also a cavalryman to the core, on October 5, the same day he wrote to Beatrice about being "normal again."

"Lucian, if you have no objection," said Patton, "I want to have a big formal ceremony and turn over command to you with considerable fanfare and publicity. I don't want Ike or anyone else to get the idea that I am leaving [here] with my tail between my legs."[45]

Two days later, the staff of the Third Army gathered before their commander for the last time, on a rainy morning. Patton stood before them in a gymnasium where the change-of-command ceremony was to be held.

Many on his staff were deeply saddened.[46]

"All good things must come to an end," said Patton. "The best thing that has ever come to me thus far is the honor and privilege of having commanded the Third Army. . . . Good-bye—and God bless you."

He had tears in his eyes.

A band played "Auld Lang Syne," followed, as Patton left, by the Third Army marching song, "He's a Jolly Good Fellow."

Patton arrived at his new command headquarters in Bad Nauheim on October 8.

A senior officer greeted him.

"Well," said Patton, "you know damn well I didn't ask for this job, don't you?"

When Patton appeared in a mess hall, he was welcomed by his new staff of some hundred officers.

"There are occasions," announced Patton, "when I can truthfully say that I am not as much of a son-of-a-bitch as I may think I am. This is one of them."

The officers "roared with surprised delight."[47]

LATER THAT FALL of 1945, Patton held a luncheon in Nuremberg for twenty senior officers who had served with him in Europe. Among them was Major General William E. Kepner, commander of 8th Air Force Fighter Command before leading the 8th Air Force's 2nd Bomb Division.

Kepner had already met Patton several times. He recalled Patton being "a striking looking fellow" who "had a high voice." He had "seen [Patton] and watched him play polo in World War I when I was executive officer of Headquarters Troops, Occupation Forces in Koblenz."

Kepner and others ate lunch without Patton, who was late: "He was to come in on a plane and the weather was too bad." After lunch, Kepner went to watch a polo match. There were more than a hundred senior officers attending. "Every one of them was spic and span except me," remembered Kepner. "I had a flat Air Force hat and yellow trench coat."

Kepner had provided air support for Patton. He wasn't "particularly awed" by the legendary Third Army commander.

Then Patton suddenly appeared among the throng of senior officers.

Patton tapped a riding whip against his polished boots.

"Keep on talking," he said, "don't stop for me. I'm just looking you over to see how many [of you] look like officers and there's damn few of you."

Patton spotted Kepner and smiled.

"You're a hell of a host," said Kepner. "You invite me over here, I furnish you air support, and you don't even show up for lunch."

"Well, this pilot of mine said the weather was too bad and didn't want to fly. Too risky."

"That's right! You listen to that pilot and you'll live longer. Don't tell him when to fly."

"I won't."

Kepner and Patton chatted pleasantly for a few minutes.

"I'd like to know," asked Kepner, "how you get away with this idea of not complying with orders."

"Oh, I comply with orders."

"Well, there's an order here that soldiers will not associate— fraternize—with the Germans. And you got all kinds of it down the road from my headquarters."

"Oh, I don't have any of that."

"I'll find you 20 witnesses within two hours that will swear they've seen your men in these places."

"I didn't say anything about it except I put out an order that 'no man of the Third Army will appear in the presence of Germans at any time, at any place, unless he has on his boots, has a belt, has on a helmet, and everything will be shined up spic and span and stay that way.' Now you know damned well you can't do any fraternizing dressed like that."

"You win," replied Kepner.

They both laughed.

Kepner later remembered Patton with great fondness: "I liked the guy. He was a great guy. Just phenomenal, really, but he created a lot of trouble." Kepner respected Patton because he got things done. He took risks. He was aggressive. He had pushed through holes in enemy lines after Kepner's forces had bombed. Yes, he was a "wonderful tactician."

Patton had caused Eisenhower many a headache because of his impetuousness and impolitic statements. But "Patton was the guy," concluded Kepner, "that broke out . . . and opened things up. That kind of guy is hard to find . . . he was an extraordinary man."[48]


ON NOVEMBER 11, 1945, Patton reached sixty. In February 1909, he had written to his future wife, Beatrice: "I don't expect ever to be sixty not that it is old but simply that I would prefer to wear out from hard work before then."[49] Thirty-six years on, he was maudlin, nostalgic.

It should all have ended in a more glorious manner, as it had for Patton's paternal grandfather, who had died of his wounds, wearing a Confederate uniform during the Civil War. There was that old quote he often gave: "The proper end for the professional soldier," he had said, "is a quick death inflicted by the *last* bullet of the *last* battle."[50]

It was with great sadness that Patton finally decided to retire from the US Army. "My present plan is to finish this job, which is a purely academic one, about the first of the year," he informed Charles Codman, "and then submit my resignation after which

I can do all the talking I feel like and may write the book you suggest, 'War and Peace as I Knew It.'"

Patton had not made the decision lightly. He'd been mulling over his future for two months.

But he ultimately told Gay that his choice to leave the army was "the only honorable and proper course to take."

Gay urged Patton to talk to others and to his wife, Beatrice: "These people are part of your life and you don't want to make a decision as momentous as this and which will affect them as much as it will you, without discussing it with them."

Patton had made up his mind.

He would rather be "outside the tent pissing in, than inside the tent pissing out."[51]

On December 3, Patton wrote in his diary for the last time. He had attended lunch with Eisenhower's replacement in Europe, General Joseph McNarney, and others: "I have rarely seen assembled a greater bunch of sons-of-bitches." The luncheon had reminded him of "a meeting of the Rotary Club in Hawaii where everyone slaps every-one else's back while looking for an appropriate place to thrust the knife."[52]

He wrote to Beatrice on December 5. He would be home for Christmas. "I have a month's leave but don't intend to go back to Europe. . . . I hate to think of leaving the Army but what is there?"

Hap Gay was increasingly worried by Patton's despondency.

His boss needed some distraction.

On the evening of December 8, Gay suggested Patton might enjoy some pheasant shooting.

"You haven't done any hunting for quite a while," Gay said.

"You could stand a little relaxation before you take off for home. . . . I know exactly where to go for some good hunting."

Gay had chosen an area not far from Speyer, to the southwest of Heidelberg.

Patton was indeed interested.

"You've got something there, Hap. Doing a little bird-shooting would be good. . . . Yes, let's do it. You arrange to have the car and guns on hand early tomorrow and we'll see how many birds we can bag."[53]

# CHAPTER 23

## The Last Days

**Bad Nauheim, Germany**
**December 9, 1945**

IT WAS YET again a bitterly cold morning in Germany—Patton's last before he was due to leave the next day, December 10, bound for the United States. He was to take Eisenhower's plane to Southampton, then cross to New York aboard the USS *New York*.

At 7 A.M., Patton's orderly, Master Sergeant William George Meeks, gave orders for Pfc. Horace Woodring to ready Patton's car, a 1938 Model 75 Cadillac, a four-star pennant attached to the front bumper.

Woodring had impressed Patton, who had boasted the driver was "better than the best Piper Cub to get you there *ahead* of time."[1] Woodring himself recalled: "I was with [Patton] seven days a week for those last months. . . . I drove like I *thought* Patton would want me to drive. . . . I was coming over a hill one day at high speed. A dog ran out in the street—a German shepherd— and I ran over that dog. I didn't bat an eye. Patton just said, 'You ruthless son of a bitch.' And he grinned. . . . I guess that impressed him, because after that I could do no wrong."[2]

Woodring had fond memories indeed: "We always traveled at a high rate of speed [because] he never had time for travel. Most of the time we took the 1938 Cadillac limo. It could go close to a hundred miles per hour wide open. And we did that whenever we [were] on the autobahn. Whenever we were on the open road, he'd say 'Let's go!' And that meant go wide open."[3]

Patton was accompanied by Hap Gay that morning as they left Bad Nauheim at 9 A.M. A jeep carrying a hunting dog followed the Cadillac as it headed south and sped toward the town of Speyer along an autobahn.

The Cadillac was acting up and Woodring stopped twice to fix it.

"This is a very careful driver," said Patton. "He seems to sense when there is something wrong with the car."

Around 11 A.M. Patton's party approached a checkpoint. An MP asked for identities.

The MP was shivering from the cold.

Patton got out of the Cadillac and patted the young MP on the back.

"You are a good soldier, son," said Patton. "I'll see to it that your C.O. is told what a fine MP you make."[4]

It was 11:45 as Patton's party passed through the outskirts of Mannheim, which had been heavily bombed.

Gay and Patton chatted away happily.

Patton looked around.

There were piles of debris.

Patton pointed to the right side of the road.

"How awful war is! Look at all those derelict vehicles, Hap!"[5]

Gay recalled the car pulling up at a railroad crossing and then having to wait for a train to pass. "We went on. We hadn't gone 100 yards when a truck was coming down facing towards us—the driver happened to look up to see where he was supposed to turn off, and he turned off in front of us. We weren't going, in my opinion, over 15 miles an hour."

The truck collided with the Cadillac.

Patton was jolted forward, his head striking the steel frame of the partition separating the front and rear seats of the Cadillac.

"Are you hurt?" Patton asked Gay.

"No, not a bit."

"Are you hurt?" Patton asked the driver.

"No, not a bit."

"I believe I am paralyzed," Patton told Gay. "Take and rub my arms and shoulders and rub them hard."

Gay did.

"Damn it, *rub* them."[6]

"I don't think it's advisable to move you, General," said Gay.[7]

Woodring recalled that the crash "took all the skin from the General's forehead for approximately three inches above his eyebrows and three inches across, partially scalping him and completely separating his spinal column."[8]

An ambulance arrived from the 130th Station Hospital near Heidelberg. Tape was placed across Patton's head to keep the scalp in place. He entered a hospital some twenty-five miles away just before 1 P.M. that day. He was awake and knew how badly he was injured, because he could not move his limbs.

There was a medical report after X-rays had been done: "Fracture simple, third cervical vertebra with posterior dislocation of fourth cervical. Complete paralysis below level of third cervical. Condition critical, prognosis guarded."[9]

Patton was paralyzed, having broken his neck.

A doctor named Frank Yordy tended to Patton and asked if he could do anything for him.

"Relax. . . . I'm in no condition to be a terror now."

Patton then "chuckled."

Not long after, Patton spoke again: "Jesus Christ, what a way to start a leave."

The hospital's chaplain arrived in Patton's room.

"Well, let him get started," said Patton, "I guess I need it."[10]

Several other chaplains met with Patton over subsequent days. One day, Chaplain Andrew J. White informed Patton: "Incidentally, General, your own chaplain has just arrived and will soon be in to see you."

"You mean Father O'Neill?" asked Patton.

That was whom he wanted to see, the man who'd created his famous prayer. But the newly arrived chaplain was Reverend William Price—still, an Episcopalian like Patton.

"Well, send him in and let him go to work."[11]

The chaplain got to work. He said a few prayers.

Patton said thank you.

Everything possible was done to try to save Patton's life. A specialist, Colonel R. Glen Spurling, even flew to Germany with

Patton's wife, Beatrice. On December 10, Spurling had stepped off a train in Cincinnati and then been handed a telegram: "You will . . . proceed to the airport . . . where an army plane will fly you to Washington, thence Germany."[12]

Spurling entered Patton's room and talked to Patton alone because, as Spurling recalled, "the General wanted the truth."

"Now, Colonel," said Patton, "we've known each other during the fighting, and I want you to talk to me as man to man. What chance have I to recover?"

Spurling said he could not give a definite answer.

"What chance have I to ride a horse again?" asked Patton.

"None."

"In other words," Patton said, "the best that I could hope for would be semi-invalidism."

"Yes."

"Thank you, Colonel, for being honest."

Patton put on a brave face.

"Colonel," he added, "you're surrounded by an awful lot of brass around here. There are more generals than privates, so far as I can gather from the nurses and the doctors. I just want you to know that you're the boss. Whatever you say goes."

Spurling went into further detail about Patton's physical state.

"I'll try to be a good patient," said Patton.

Patton fell asleep. He awoke around midnight. A nurse read him a message from President Truman.

"That was nice, wasn't it?" said Patton.[13]

Beatrice spent as much time as she could with her husband.

Messages arrived from all over the world. Beatrice read a letter from Eisenhower out loud, no doubt knowing how much it
would mean to her husband:

> *You can imagine what a shock it was to me to hear of*
> *your serious accident. . . . By coincidence, only the day*
> *before yesterday, I had directed that you be contacted*
> *to determine whether you wanted a particular job*
> *that appeared to be opening up here in the States. . . .*
> *It is always difficult for me to express my true*
> *sentiments when I am deeply moved. . . . You are*
> *never out of my thoughts and . . . my hopes and*
> *prayers are tied up in your speedy recovery.*

Spurling believed that Beatrice had "lived her life" for Patton.
At 1:30 A.M. on December 14, Patton woke and then told a
nurse he wanted to "forget it all."[14]

Patton's condition did not improve. Eight days later, on the
afternoon of December 21, Beatrice spent several hours reading
to her husband. She was taking a break in the hospital's dining
room with Spurling when both were asked to go to Patton's bed-
side quickly.

It was too late. There was no final goodbye. Patton had died
at 5:55 P.M. from "pulmonary edema and congestive heart
failure."[15]

It was exactly a year since he had enjoyed his finest hours—
leading his Third Army in the Battle of the Bulge, among the
greatest battles ever fought by the US Army. Just a few days

before he died, Patton had written: "Anyone in any walk of life who is content with mediocrity is untrue to himself and to American tradition."[16]

"Patton died as he had lived—bravely," recalled Spurling. "Throughout his illness there was never one word of complaint regarding a nurse or doctor or orderly. Each and every one was treated with the kindest consideration. He took orders without question—in fact, he was a model patient."[17]

A soldier who had served under Patton in his Third Army wrote to his parents from Germany the next day: "Last night one of the greatest men that ever lived died. That was Patton. The rest of the world thinks of him as just another guy with stars on his shoulders. . . . All the flags are at half-mast. We are making every Heinie that passes stop and take off his hat. They can't understand our feelings for him."[18]

PATTON WAS to be buried on December 24 in the American cemetery in Luxembourg. His grave site was beside that of a Third Army soldier who had died in the Battle of the Bulge. Some six thousand other fallen Americans lay beside him.

Thousands of soldiers visited while he lay in state for two days.[19]

December 24 was a foggy, rainy day.

Winter's grip had broken. Patton's favorite psalm was sung:

My soul followeth hard after thee . . . but those that seek my soul, to destroy it, shall go into the lower parts of the earth. They shall fall by the sword: they

shall be a portion for foxes. But the king shall rejoice
in God; every one that sweareth by him shall glory; but
the mouth of them that speak lies shall be stopped.

Reporters watched the deeply moving ceremony. According
to one account: "In the final moments of the ceremony, Master
Sergeant Meeks . . . who had served the General faithfully as his
orderly for years, presented to Beatrice the flag that had draped
the casket."

Forty-nine-year-old William G. Meeks, an African American
World War I veteran who had served with the Buffalo Soldiers
while Patton had pioneered tank warfare, was crying and his face
was screwed up in grief. "He bowed slowly," the report continued, "and handed the flag to Mrs. Patton. Then he saluted stiffly
to her. For an instant their eyes met and held. Sergeant Meeks
turned away. . . . A 12-man firing squad raised its rifles and a
three-round volley of salutes echoed into the Luxembourg hills."[20]

The United Press mentioned that Patton was buried "in what
he himself called 'damned poor tank country and damned bad
weather.' But he was buried in a precision-like military ceremony, touched by pomp and tendered by grief. Big generals and
little soldiers were there, as were the royalty and the commoners
of this tiny country from which Patton drove the Germans in
that last crucial battle last Christmastide."[21]

The New York Times carried perhaps the finest obituary for
one of the US Army's greatest of all generals:

Long before the war ended, Patton was a legend. Spectacular, swaggering, pistol-packing, deeply religious

and violently profane, easily moved to anger because he was first of all a fighting man, easily moved to tears, because underneath all his mannered irascibility he had a kind heart, he was a strange combination of fire and ice. Hot in battle and ruthless too, he was icy in his inflexibility of purpose. He was no mere hell-for-leather tank commander but a profound and thoughtful military student.

He has been compared with Jeb Stuart, Nathan Bedford Forrest and Phil Sheridan, but he fought his battles in a bigger field than any of them. He was not a man of peace. Perhaps he would have preferred to die at the height of his fame, when his men, whom he loved, were following him with devotion. His nation will accord his memory a full measure of that devotion.[22]

Jim Gavin, who had led the 82nd Airborne during the Battle of the Bulge, remembered: "His spirit and enthusiasm had seemed unquenchable. When I learned that he was to be buried among the soldiers who had been killed in battle, it reminded me of a refrain from an old West Point song, 'Benny Havens, Oh!'—'May we find a soldier's resting place beneath a soldier's blow.'"[23]

Omar Bradley, who had worked with Patton so closely, would later recall: "It was better for Patton and his professional reputation that he died when he did. The war was won; there were no more wars left for him to fight. . . . In time he probably would have become a boring parody of himself—a decrepit, bitter, pitiful figure, unwittingly debasing the legend."[24]

Three weeks after her husband's death, Beatrice wrote in her journal: "The star is gone . . . the accompanist is left behind. There must be a reason, but I pray for understanding."

Her journal's next entry read:

> I have just stripped your ribbons from your uniforms to be refitted for George. He will be proud to wear them. Why is it that a beloved one's clothes mean so much? The creases of his body in a coat—and where his legs bend at the groin—it always seems that I must write you what is passing. Both girls have played Ouija and it always says "Take care of B—Big B." I could never work it. They may be psychic, being of your blood—I am only your lover—I don't even dream of you at night, and how I wish I could. Perhaps someday.[25]

Beatrice would die in 1953, at the age of sixty-seven. Her body was cremated and the ashes spread over her husband's grave in the Luxembourg American Cemetery.[26]

No man had known Patton better than his aide throughout most of the war, Colonel Charles Codman. "To [Patton]," he wrote, "the concepts of duty, patriotism, fame, honor, glory are not mere abstractions, nor the shopworn ingredients of Memorial Day speeches. They are basic realities—self-evident, controlling. . . . In the time of Roger the Norman or in ancient Rome, General Patton would have felt completely at home."[27]

Patton's had been a life defined by courage, victory, and faith. As for Patton's "favorite prayer," his grandson Robert Patton would later note that it could be found in the writings of Socrates, not in the Bible: "All knowing Zeus; give me what is best for me. Avert evil from me though it be the thing I prayed for; and give me the good, for which, from ignorance, I did not ask."

Patton had played a vital part in destroying "one of history's most profane regimes." In doing so, "he was given what was best for him, was given, indeed, the good. His prayer was answered."[28]

# ACKNOWLEDGMENTS

Thanks to guide/historians Joris Nieuwint and Reg Jans for a brilliant on-the-ground tour of the Ardennes. My research was also helped by the Battle of the Bulge Association, Melissa Davis at the George C. Marshall Foundation, and Melissa Crawford and Lara Szypszak at the Library of Congress. Kady Ashley, Daphne Larkin, David Robbins, Nigel Gilbert, and Kristian Baehre kept me going in difficult times, as did amazing traveling companions and dear friends John Snowdon, Lisa Pucillo, and Bob Fryer, and Jim and Kathleen Kennedy. Holly Rotondi at Friends of the National World War II Memorial, Tim Frank at Arlington National Cemetery, and Tim Gray at the WWII Foundation were helpful beyond words. And a big thanks also to veterans George Arnstein, Harry Miller, and Harold Billow. The late Jim Hornfischer, my agent, helped get this book off the ground and David Vigliano stepped in kindly in his absence. My editors, Brent Howard and John Parsley, were as supportive as ever, as indeed was the whole team at Dutton.

# SELECTED BIBLIOGRAPHY

Abdul-Jabbar, Kareem, and Anthony Walton. *Brothers in Arms*. New York: Broadway Books, 2004.

Allen, Robert S. *Lucky Forward*. New York: Vanguard Press, 1947.

Ambrose, Stephen E. *Band of Brothers*. New York: Simon & Schuster, 2001.

———. *Citizen Soldiers*. New York: Simon & Schuster, 1997.

Anderson, Robert. *A Soldier's Tale, Bastogne, December 1944: 150th Signal Company, 10th Armored Division*. Ransom Canyon, TX: privately published, 2000.

Astor, Gerald. *A Blood-Dimmed Tide: The Battle of the Bulge by the Men Who Fought It*. New York: Dell, 1994.

———. *The Mighty Eighth*. New York: Dutton Caliber, 2018.

Atkinson, Rick. *The Guns at Last Light*. New York: Picador, 2014.

Ayer, Fred. *Before the Colors Fade*. Boston: Houghton Mifflin, 1964.

Bando, Mark. *101st Airborne: The Screaming Eagles in World War II*. Minneapolis, MN: Zenith Press, 2007.

Baron, Richard, Major Abe Baum, and Richard Goldhurst. *Raid! The Untold Story of Patton's Secret Mission*. New York: G. P. Putnam's Sons, 1981.

Barron, Leo. *Patton at the Battle of the Bulge*. New York: NAL Caliber, 2015.

Bartov, Omer. *The Eastern Front, 1941–45: German Troops and the Barbarisation of Warfare*. Houndmills, UK: Palgrave Macmillan, 2001.

Beck, Alfred, Abe Bortz, Charles W. Lynch, Lida Mayo, and Ralph F. Weld. *The Corps of Engineers: The War Against Germany*. Washington, DC: Center of Military History, 1985.

Beevor, Antony. *Ardennes 1944: The Battle of the Bulge*. New York: Viking Penguin, 2015.

Blumenson, Martin. *The Patton Papers, 1940–1945*. Cambridge, MA: Da Capo Press, 1996.

Bourke-White, Margaret. *"Dear Fatherland, Rest Quietly."* New York: Simon & Schuster, 1946.

Bowen, Robert. *Fighting with the Screaming Eagles: With the 101st Airborne from Normandy to Bastogne.* Havertown, PA: Casemate, 2010.

Bradley, Omar N. *A Soldier's Story.* New York: Henry Holt and Company, 1951.

———, and Clay Blair. *A General's Life: An Autobiography.* New York: Simon & Schuster, 1983.

Brotherton, Marcus. *A Company of Heroes.* New York: Berkley Caliber, 2010.

———. *We Who Are Alive and Remain.* New York: Berkley Caliber, 2009.

Burgett, Donald R. *Seven Roads to Hell: A Screaming Eagle at Bastogne.* New York: Dell, 2000.

Caddick-Adams, Peter. *Snow & Steel: The Battle of the Bulge, 1944–45.* New York: Oxford University Press, 2015.

Chernitsky, Dorothy, ed. *Voices from the Foxholes: Men of the 110th Infantry During World War II.* Uniontown, PA: privately published, 1991.

Codman, Colonel Charles R. *Drive.* Boston: Little, Brown and Company, 1957.

Cole, Hugh M. *The Ardennes: Battle of the Bulge.* Washington, DC: Office of the Chief of Military History, 1965.

Collins, Michael, and Martin King. *The Tigers of Bastogne.* Havertown, PA: Casemate, 2013.

———. *Voices of the Bulge: Untold Stories from Veterans of the Battle of the Bulge.* Minneapolis, MN: Zenith Press, 2011.

Compton, Lynn, with Marcus Brotherton. *Call of Duty: My Life Before, During, and After the Band of Brothers.* New York: Berkley Caliber, 2008.

Corsi, Jerome. *No Greater Valor.* Nashville, TN: Nelson Books, 2014.

Craig, Berry. *11th Armored Division Thunderbolt,* vol. II. Paducah, KY: Turner Publishing, 1992.

Critchell, Laurence. *Four Stars of Hell.* Nashville, TN: Battery Press, 1982.

De Lee, Nigel. *Voices from the Battle of the Bulge.* Newton Abbot, UK: David & Charles, 2004.

D'Este, Carlo. *Eisenhower: A Soldier's Life.* New York: Henry Holt and Company, 2002.

———. *Patton: A Genius for War.* New York: HarperCollins, 1995.

Doolittle, General James H., with Carroll V. Glines. *I Could Never Be So Lucky Again.* New York: Bantam, 1991.

Doubler, Michael D. *Closing with the Enemy: How GIs Fought the War in Europe, 1944–1945.* Lawrence: University Press of Kansas, 1994.

Dupuy, Trevor N., David L. Bongard, and Richard C. Anderson Jr. *Hitler's Last Gamble: The Battle of the Bulge.* New York: HarperCollins, 1994.

Egger, Bruce E., and Lee MacMillan Otts. *G Company's War: Two Personal Accounts of the Campaigns in Europe, 1944–1945.* Tuscaloosa: University of Alabama Press, 1992.

Eisenhower, Dwight D. *At Ease: Stories I Tell to Friends.* New York: Doubleday, 1967.

———. *Crusade in Europe: A Personal Account of World War II.* New York: Doubleday, 1948.

Eisenhower, John S. D. *The Bitter Woods: The Battle of the Bulge*. Cambridge, MA: Da Capo Press, 1995.
———. *Strictly Personal*. New York: Doubleday, 1974.
Ellis, John. *The Sharp End*. New York: Charles Scribner's Sons, 1980.
Elstob, Peter. *Bastogne: The Road Block*. London: Macdonald, 1968.
———. *Hitler's Last Offensive*. London: Secker and Warburg, 1971.
Farago, Ladislas. *The Last Days of Patton*. New York: McGraw-Hill, 1981.
———. *Patton: Ordeal and Triumph*. New York: Ivan Obolensky, 1963.
Fox, Don. *Patton's Vanguard: The United States Army Fourth Armored Division*. Jefferson, NC: McFarland, 2003.
Frankel, Nat, and Larry Smith. *Patton's Best*. New York: Hawthorn Books, 1978.
Freeman, Roger A. *The Mighty Eighth*. London: Arms & Armour Press, 1986.
Gabel, Kurt. *The Making of a Paratrooper: Airborne Training and Combat in WWII*. Lawrence: University Press of Kansas, 1990.
Gavin, James M. *On to Berlin*. New York: Viking, 1978.
Graham, Don. *No Name on the Bullet*. New York: Viking, 1989.
Green, Michael, and Gladys Green. *Patton and the Battle of the Bulge*. Osceola, WI: MBI Publishing, 1999.
Green, Michael, and James Brown. *War Stories of the Battle of the Bulge*. Minneapolis, MN: Zenith Press, 2010.
Guarnere, William, and Edward Heffron. *Brothers in Battle, Best of Friends*. New York: Berkley Caliber, 2007.
Harkins, Paul D. *When the Third Cracked Europe*. Harrisburg, PA: Stackpole Books, 1969.
Hartman, J. Ted. *Tank Driver: With the 11th Armored from the Battle of the Bulge to VE Day*. Bloomington and Indianapolis: Indiana University Press, 2003.
Hastings, Max. *Armageddon: The Battle for Germany, 1944–1945*. New York: Vintage, 2012.
———. *Inferno: The World at War, 1939–1945*. New York: Vintage, 2011.
Hirshson, Stanley P. *General Patton: A Soldier's Life*. New York: Harper Perennial, 2002.
Hofmann, George F. *The Super Sixth: History of the 6th Armored Division in World War II*. Louisville, KY: Sixth Armored Division Association, 1975.
Houston, Robert J. *D-Day to Bastogne: A Paratrooper Recalls World War II*. Smithtown, NY: Exposition Press, 1980.
Irzyk, Albin F. *He Rode Up Front for Patton*. Raleigh, NC: Pentland Press, 1996.
———. *Patton's Juggernaut: The Rolling 8-Ball*. Oakland, OR: Elderberry Press, 2017.
Keane, Michael. *Patton: Blood, Guts, and Prayer*. Washington, DC: Regnery Publishing, 2012.
Kershaw, Alex. *The Longest Winter*. Cambridge, MA: Da Capo Press, 2004.
Killblane, Richard, and Jack McNiece. *The Filthy Thirteen*. Havertown, PA: Casemate, 2003.
Koch, Oscar W., with Robert G. Hays. *G-2: Intelligence for Patton*. Philadelphia: Army Times Publishing Company / Whitmore Publishing Company, 1971.

Koskimaki, George E. *The Battered Bastards of Bastogne: The 101st Airborne in the Battle of the Bulge*. New York: Ballantine Books, 2007.

Lande, D. A. *I Was with Patton*. St. Paul, MN: MBI Publishing, 2002.

Lovoi, Joseph W. *Listen . . . My Children and Stay Free*. New York: Vantage Press, 2000.

MacDonald, Charles B. *The Last Offensive*. Washington, DC: Center of Military History, 1990.

———. *A Time for Trumpets: The Untold Story of the Battle of the Bulge*. New York: Quill / William Morrow, 1985.

MacKenzie, Fred. *The Men of Bastogne*. New York: David McKay Company, Inc., 1968.

Malarkey, Don, with Bob Welch. *Easy Company Soldier*. New York: St. Martin's Press, 2008.

Mansoor, Peter R. *The GI Offensive in Europe: The Triumph of American Infantry Divisions, 1941–1945*. Lawrence: University Press of Kansas, 1999.

Marshall, S. L. A. *Bastogne: The Story of the First Eight Days*. Washington, DC: Center of Military History, 1946.

McDonald, Frederick A. *Remembered Light: Glass Fragments from World War II*. San Francisco: Frederick A. McDonald Trust, 2007.

McDonough, James, and Richard Gardner. *Skyriders: History of the 327/401 Glider Infantry*. Nashville, TN: Battery Press, 1980.

McManus, John C. *Alamo in the Ardennes*. Hoboken, NJ: John Wiley & Sons, Inc., 2007.

McMorrow, Merle W. *From Rome to Berlin via Bastogne*. Charleston, SC: Book-Surge, 2009.

Mitchell, Ralph M. *The 101st Airborne Division's Defense of Bastogne*. Fort Leaven-worth, KS: Combat Studies Institute, 1986.

Moorehead, Alan. *Eclipse*. New York: Coward-McCann, 1945.

Morelock, J. D. *Generals of the Ardennes: American Leadership in the Battle of the Bulge*. Washington, DC: National Defense University Press, 1994.

Munch, Paul G. "Patton's Staff and the Battle of the Bulge." *Military Review* 70, no. 5 (May 1990): 46–54.

Murray, Williamson, and Allan R. Millett. *A War to Be Won: Fighting the Second World War*. Cambridge, MA, and London: Belknap Press of Harvard University Press, 2000.

Neill, George W. *Infantry Soldier: Holding the Line at the Battle of the Bulge*. Norman: University of Oklahoma Press, 2002.

Nichol, John, and Tony Rennell. *The Last Escape*. New York: Viking, 2002.

Odom, Charles B. *General George S. Patton and Eisenhower*. New Orleans: Word Picture Productions, 1985.

Parker, Danny S. *Battle of the Bulge: Hitler's Ardennes Offensive, 1944–1945*. Cambridge, MA: Da Capo Press, 2004.

———. *Fatal Crossroads*. Cambridge, MA: Da Capo Press, 2012.

———. *To Win the Winter Sky: The Air War over the Ardennes, 1944–1945*. Conshohocken, PA: Combined Books, 1994.

Patton, George S. *War as I Knew It*. London: W. H. Allen, 1947.

Patton, Robert H. *The Pattons: The Personal History of an American Family*. New York: Crown, 1994.

Pay, Don. *Thunder from Heaven: Story of the 17th Airborne Division, 1943–1945*. Nashville, TN: Battery Press, 1980.

Poling, Daniel A. *Faith Is Power for You*. New York: Greenberg, 1950.

Price, Frank James. *Troy H. Middleton: A Biography*. Baton Rouge: Louisiana State University Press, 1974.

Province, Charles M. *Patton's Third Army: A Daily Combat Diary*. New York: Hippocrene Books, 1992.

Rapport, Leonard, and Arthur Northwood. *Rendezvous with Destiny: A History of the 101st Airborne Division*. Old Saybrook, CT: Konecky & Konecky, 1965.

Reynolds, Michael. *Men of Steel*. Havertown, PA: Casemate, 2006.

Rickard, John Nelson. *Advance and Destroy: Patton as Commander in the Bulge*. Lexington: University Press of Kentucky, 2011.

Sampson, Francis L. *Look Out Below! A Story of the Airborne by a Paratrooper Padre*. Washington, DC: Catholic University of America Press, 1958.

Schrijvers, Peter. *Those Who Hold Bastogne: The True Story of the Soldiers and Civilians Who Fought in the Biggest Battle of the Bulge*. New Haven, CT: Yale University Press, 2014.

Shirer, William L. *The Rise and Fall of the Third Reich*. New York: Simon & Schuster, 2011.

Simms, James B. *A Soldier's Armageddon*. Manhattan, KS: Sunflower University Press, 1999.

Simpson, Louis. *Selected Prose*. New York: Paragon House, 1989.

Sorley, Lewis. *Thunderbolt: General Creighton Abrams and the Army of His Times*. New York: Simon & Schuster, 1992.

Speer, Albert. *Inside the Third Reich*. Translated by Richard and Clara Winston. New York: Macmillan, 1970.

Stargardt, Nicholas. *The German War*. New York: Basic Books, 2015.

Summersby, Kay. *Eisenhower Was My Boss*. New York: Dell, 1948.

Toland, John. *Battle: The Story of the Bulge*. Lincoln: University of Nebraska Press, 1999.

———. *The Last 100 Days*. New York: Modern Library, 2003.

Tolhurst, Michael. *Bastogne*. Barnsley, UK: Leo Cooper, 2001.

True, William, and Deryck Tufts True. *The Cow Spoke French: The Story of Sgt. William True, American Paratrooper in World War II*. Bennington, VT: Merriam Press, 2002.

Truscott, Lucian K. *Command Missions*. New York: E. P. Dutton, 1954.

Valera, Charley. *My Father's War*. Bloomington, IN: iUniverse, 2017.

Ward, Geoffrey C., and Ken Burns. *The War*. New York: Alfred A. Knopf, 2007.

Weaver, Michael E. *Guard Wars: The 28th Infantry Division in World War II*. Bloomington and Indianapolis: Indiana University Press, 2010.

Weigley, Russell F. *Eisenhower's Lieutenants: The Campaign of France and Germany, 1944–1945*. Bloomington: Indiana University Press, 1981.

Weintraub, Stanley. *11 Days in December.* New York: NAL Caliber, 2007.

Whiting, Charles. *Patton.* New York: Ballantine, 1970.

Wilson, Charles E. *Frail Children of Dust: From Bastogne to Bavaria with the Fighting Fourth Armored Division, 1944–1945.* San Francisco: Austin and Winfield, 1993.

Wilson, Joe. *The 761st "Black Panther" Tank Battalion in World War II.* Jefferson, NC: McFarland, 1999.

Winters, Dick, with Cole C. Kingseed. *Beyond Band of Brothers.* New York: Berkley Caliber, 2006.

Wolfe, Martin. *Green Light!* Philadelphia: University of Pennsylvania Press, 1989.

Zaloga, Steven J. *The Battle of the Bulge (2) Bastogne.* Oxford, UK: Osprey, 2004.

———. *Panther vs. Sherman.* Oxford, UK: Osprey, 2008.

# NOTES

**PART ONE: WATCH ON THE RHINE**

1. George S. Patton, *War as I Knew It*, 340.

**CHAPTER ONE—STUCK IN THE MUD**

1. "George S. Patton in World War I," History on the Net, https://www.history onthenet.com/patton-wwl.
2. Stefanie Van Steelandt, "A Freak Accident, a Devoted Wife, and the Death of General Patton," The Cereal Reader, https://thecerealreader.com/2021/12/21 /a-freak-accident-a-devoted-wife-and-the-death-of-general-patton/.
3. Blumenson, *The Patton Papers*, 576.
4. George S. Patton, *War as I Knew It*, 178.
5. George S. Patton, *War as I Knew It*, 166.
6. Blumenson, *The Patton Papers*, 576.
7. Albin F. Irzyk, oral history, May 28, 2008, University of South Florida, Holocaust and Genocide Studies Center.
8. D'Este, *Patton*, 669.
9. D'Este, *Patton*, 664.
10. Blumenson, *The Patton Papers*, 577.
11. Sergeant Saul Levitt, "Capturing a Gestapo General," *Yank*, Old Magazine Articles, http://www.oldmagazinearticles.com/Gestapo_General_Anton _Dunckern_captured-pdf.
12. Blumenson, *The Patton Papers*, 577.
13. Blumenson, *The Patton Papers*, 700.
14. "General George Patton Interrogates a [*sic*] SS General, 1944," EyeWitness to

History, www.eyewitnesstohistory.com/patton.htm#:~:text=The%20pris
oner%20was%20Major%20General,%22He%20is%20a%20liar!%22.

15. Blumenson, *The Patton Papers*, 577–79.
16. D'Este, *Patton*, 669.
17. D'Este, *Patton*, 702.
18. Blumenson, *The Patton Papers*, 586.
19. George S. Patton diary, November 25, 1944, George S. Patton Papers, Library of Congress.
20. Robert G. Hays, "He Helped Decide to Hold Bastogne," *St Louis Post-Dispatch*, August 30, 1966, D3.
21. Captain Michael E. Bigelow, "Big Business: Intelligence in Patton's Third Army," *Military Intelligence*, April–June 1992, 31–36.
22. David T. Zabecki, "The Untold Story of Patton at Bastogne," *WWII*, November 2007, https://www.historynet.com/untold-story-patton-bastogne.htm.
23. Blumenson, *The Patton Papers*, 589.
24. D'Este, *Patton*, 672.

## Chapter Two—Dark December

1. Blumenson, *The Patton Papers*, 589.
2. Father James H. O'Neill, "The True Story of 'The Patton Prayer,'" The Imaginative Conservative, https://theimaginativeconservative.org/2022/03/true-story-patton-prayer-james-hugh-o-neill.html.
3. O'Neill, "True Story."
4. O'Neill, "True Story."
5. David T. Zabecki, "The Untold Story of Patton at Bastogne," *WWII*, November 2007, https://www.historynet.com/untold-story-patton-bastogne.htm.
6. Shirer, *Rise and Fall*, 1091.
7. Shirer, *Rise and Fall*, 1092.
8. Ward and Burns, *The War*, 307.
9. Toland, *Battle*, 21.
10. Parker, *Battle of the Bulge*, 73.
11. George S. Patton diary, December 11, 1944, George S. Patton Papers, Library of Congress.
12. Schrijvers, *Those Who Hold Bastogne*, 51.
13. Albin F. Irzyk, "Firsthand Account 4th Armored Division Spearhead at Bastogne," HistoryNet.com https://www.historynet.com/firsthand-account-4th-armored-division-spearhead-at-bastogne-november-99-world-war-ii-feature/.
14. Irzyk, "Firsthand Account."
15. "The 4th Armored: From the Beach to Bastogne," Lone Sentry, https://www.lonesentry.com/gi_stories_booklets/4tharmored/index.html.
16. Irzyk, "Firsthand Account."

17. Zabecki, "Untold Story of Patton."
18. O'Neill, "True Story."
19. O'Neill, "True Story."
20. Zabecki, "Untold Story of Patton."
21. Beevor, *Ardennes 1944*, 97.
22. Oliver Pieper, "Battle of the Bulge Survivor's Last Offensive," Deutsche Welle, https://www.dw.com/en/a-german-battle-of-the-bulge-survivors-last-offensive-in-the-ardennes/a-51656325.
23. John Eisenhower, *The Bitter Woods*, 179.
24. MacDonald, *A Time for Trumpets*, 90.
25. Toland, *Battle*, 22.

### Chapter Three—Blitzkrieg

1. Toland, *Battle*, 23.
2. Schrijvers, *Those Who Hold Bastogne*, 55.
3. Neill, *Infantry Soldier*, 237.
4. Oliver Pieper, "Battle of the Bulge Survivor's Last Offensive," Deutsche Welle, https://www.dw.com/en/a-german-battle-of-the-bulge-survivors-last-offensive-in-the-ardennes/a-51656325.
5. Koch with Hays, *G-2*, 86–87.
6. Charles Roland, "Army Captain Details His D-Day Story from Basic Training to Nuremberg," Military.com, https://www.military.com/history/d-day-story-charles-roland.html.
7. Farago, *Patton*, 697.
8. Farago, *Patton*, 698.
9. Blumenson, *The Patton Papers*, 595.
10. Walter S. Zapotoczny Jr, "The 28th Infantry Division's Heroic Defense During the Battle of the Bulge," Warfare History Network, https://warfarehistorynetwork.com/article/the-28th-infantry-division-heroic-defense-during-the-battle-of-the-bulge/.
11. Sergeant 1st Class Aaron Heft, "Holding the Line: The 28th ID and the Fight for the Ardennes," DVIDShub.net, https://www.dvidshub.net/news/435280/holding-line-28th-id-and-fight-ardennes.
12. John Eisenhower, *The Bitter Woods*, 81.
13. Hastings, *Inferno*, 572.
14. Ward and Burns, *The War*, 313.
15. Ward and Burns, *The War*, 313.
16. Parker, *Fatal Crossroads*, 29.
17. Hastings, *Armageddon*, 571–72.
18. D'Este, *Patton*, 678.
19. John Eisenhower, *The Bitter Woods*, 215.
20. Bradley and Blair, *A General's Life*, 356–57.
21. MacDonald, *A Time for Trumpets*, 193.

## CHAPTER FOUR—BLOOD AND IRON

1. Astor, *The Mighty Eighth*, 291.
2. Larry Alexander, "Veteran Recalls Malmedy Massacre During World War II," Lancaster Online, https://lancasteronline.com/donegal/news/veteran -recalls-malmedy-massacre-during-world-war-ii/article_453a1638-8206 -11e4-a8f6-739fa8623153.html.
3. George Stockburger and Alex Peterson, "Harold Billow, Midstate WWII Veteran & Malmedy Massacre Survivor, Laid to Rest," ABC27.com, https:// www.abc27.com/local-news/harold-billow-midstate-wwii-veteran-malmedy -massacre-survivor-passes-away/.
4. Harold Billow, interview with author.
5. Atkinson, *The Guns at Last Light*, 424.
6. "Remember the 285th F.A.O.B. 12/17/1944 Part One," Capital Cichlid Associ- ation, https://www.capitalcichlids.org/forums/threads/rember-the-285th-f -a-o-b-12-17-1944-part-one.36824/.
7. Bill Merriken, interview with author.
8. Kershaw, *The Longest Winter*, 149.
9. Atkinson, *The Guns at Last Light*, 425.
10. Ward and Burns, *The War*, 315.
11. Edward G. Lengel, "Sacrifice: The 333rd Field Artillery at the Battle of the Bulge," The National World War II Museum, https://www.nationalww2mu seum.org/war/articles/african-american-333rd-field-artillery-battle-of -bulge.
12. Schrijvers, *Those Who Hold Bastogne*, 33.
13. Ward and Burns, *The War*, 318.
14. Heinz Kokott memoir, Eisenhower Center, University of New Orleans.
15. Ward and Burns, *The War*, 319.
16. Dwight Eisenhower, *Crusade in Europe*, 345.
17. D'Este, *Patton*, 678.
18. D'Este, *Patton*, 678.
19. Frankel and Smith, *Patton's Best*, 107.
20. Carlo D'Este, "December 16, 1944: Ardennes Offensive Begins, An 'Abysmal Failure of Allied Intelligence,'" The History Reader, https://www.thehisto ryreader.com/military-history/december-16-1944-ardennes-offensive -begins-abysmal-failure-allied-intelligence/.
21. Koskimaki, *Battered Bastards of Bastogne*, 31.
22. Koskimaki, *Battered Bastards of Bastogne*, 28.
23. Koskimaki, *Battered Bastards of Bastogne*, 27.
24. Koskimaki, *Battered Bastards of Bastogne*, 40–41.
25. Koskimaki, *Battered Bastards of Bastogne*, 47.
26. Collins and King, *Voices of the Bulge*, 119.
27. Mitch Kaidy, "Who Really Liberated Bastogne? A Probe of History," 87th In- fantry Division Legacy Association, http://87thinfantrydivision.com/mitch -kaidy/who-really-liberated-bastogne-a-probe-of-history.
28. Collins and King, *Tigers of Bastogne*, 48.

29. Farago, *Patton*, 704.
30. Map: The Sixth Panzer Army Attack, https://history.army.mil/books/wwii /7-8/notes/MapII.jpg.
31. Barron, *Patton at the Battle of the Bulge*, 56.
32. Bradley, *A Soldier's Story*, 465.
33. Bradley, *A Soldier's Story*, 465.
34. Farago, *Patton*, 705.
35. D'Este, *Patton*, 678.
36. George S. Patton, *War as I Knew It*, 190.
37. Beevor, *Ardennes 1944*, 173.
38. Blumenson, *The Patton Papers*, 597.
39. Farago, *Patton*, 706.
40. Corsi, *No Greater Valor*, 105.
41. McAuliffe's citation reads: "For gallantry in action. On 6 June 1944, Brigadier General McAuliffe, without having received formal instruction in parachuting, volunteered to drop with the parachute echelon of the Headquarters Battery of the Division Artillery of the 101st Airborne Division in order to organize his artillery expeditiously. Landing far from the prescribed drop zone, he organized the scattered individuals of his Headquarters and joined with elements of Division Headquarters south of St. Marie du Mont. In conjunction with the latter, he led his artillery against the causeway at Pouppeville and assisted in capturing the town and beach defile against strong enemy resistance. The speedy juncture of airborne and sea borne forces at this point was in large measure due to his leadership. His conduct was in accordance with the highest standards of military service." Source: "McAuliffe, Anthony Clement, Silver Star Medal (SSM)," https://www.tracesofwar.com/persons /35018/McAuliffe-Anthony-Clement.htm.
42. "Anthony C. McAuliffe," Veteran Tributes, http://veterantributes.org/Tribute Detail.php?recordID=1081.
43. Jack Anderson, "Twenty Years After He Told the Nazis 'Nuts,'" *Parade*, December 20, 1964.
44. Toland, *Battle*, 123.

## CHAPTER FIVE—CRISIS AT VERDUN

1. Farago, *Patton*, 707.
2. Reminiscences of Karl R. Bendetsen, October 24, 1972, 129–30, Oral History Collection, Harry S. Truman. Library, Independence, MO.
3. Farago, *Patton*, 707.
4. Reminiscences of General Otto P. Weyland, 1960, 25–26, Oral History Research Office, Columbia University Library, New York City.
5. Astor, *The Mighty Eighth*, 392.
6. Codman, *Drive*, 231.
7. Dwight Eisenhower, *Crusade in Europe*, 350.
8. Codman, *Drive*, 231–32.

9. In September 1943, Eisenhower had written to George Marshall, US Army chief of staff, about Patton. "Many generals constantly think of battle in terms of, first, concentration, supply, maintenance, replacement, and second, after all the above is arranged, a conservative advance. This type of person is necessary because he prevents one from courting disaster. But occasions arise when one has to remember that under particular conditions, boldness is ten times as important as numbers. Patton's great strength is that he thinks only in terms of attack as long as there is a single battalion that can keep advancing." Source: Rickard, *Advance and Destroy*, 103.

10. D'Este, *Eisenhower*, 645.

11. Rickard, *Advance and Destroy*, 107.

12. Codman, *Drive*, 232.

13. Atkinson, *The Guns at Last Light*, 447.

14. Allen, *Lucky Forward*, 33.

15. "Lieutenant General Walton H. Walker," The Army Historical Foundation, https://armyhistory.org/lieutenant-general-walton-h-walker/.

16. D'Este, *Eisenhower*, 681.

17. D'Este, *Eisenhower*, 682.

18. Blumenson, *The Patton Papers*, 836.

19. "Andrew Roberts Paints the Fullest Ever Picture of Churchill," *Economist*, October 4, 2018, https://www.economist.com/books-and-arts/2018/10/04/andrew-roberts-paints-the-fullest-ever-picture-of-churchill.

20. "News 2008," 10th Armored Division Veterans, https://10tharmored.com/news2008.html.

21. Collins and King, *Voices of the Bulge*, 114–15.

22. Richard Winters, interview, National WWII Museum, New Orleans.

23. Walter Gordon, interview, National WWII Museum, New Orleans.

24. "VIII Corps After Action Report November 1944," Record 208, RG 407, National Archives II, 3.

25. Toland, *Battle*, 131.

26. MacDonald, *A Time for Trumpets*, 343.

27. MacDonald, *A Time for Trumpets*, 343.

28. Toland, *Battle*, 131.

29. MacDonald, *A Time for Trumpets*, 345.

30. Astor, *A Blood-Dimmed Tide*, 194.

31. Chaplain Paul W. Cavanaugh, SJ, "Chaplain Prisoner," *Woodstock Letters* XC, no. 1 (February 1961): 21.

32. Cavanaugh, "Chaplain Prisoner," 21.

33. Cavanaugh, "Chaplain Prisoner," 22.

34. Cavanaugh, "Chaplain Prisoner," 23.

35. Koskimaki, *Battered Bastards of Bastogne*, 54–57.

36. Koskimaki, *Battered Bastards of Bastogne*, 220.

37. In freezing conditions on the battlefield, the wounded were often doomed. "What worked against the soldier was shock," remembered medic Private Richard Roush of the 84th Division. "It didn't really make much difference

whether a soldier was barely or severely wounded in that extremely cold weather, he would immediately go into shock. We couldn't do anything for him because we didn't have any means to warm a wounded soldier. We could not save him." Source: Ambrose, *Citizen Soldiers*, 319.

38. Gordon Carson, oral history, National WWII Museum, New Orleans.
39. Codman, *Drive*, 233.
40. George S. Patton diary, December 19, 1944, George S. Patton Papers, Library of Congress.
41. "Patton's Near-Death Experience in World War One," History on the Net, excerpted from Keane, *Patton*, https://www.historyonthenet.com/pattons -near-death-experience-in-world-war-one.
42. "Patton's 'Blood and Guts' Speech," History on the Net, excerpted from Keane, *Patton*, https://www.historyonthenet.com/pattons-blood-and-guts-speech.
43. "SHAEF Main to Exfor for Field Marshal Montgomery," https://www.eisen howerlibrary.gov/sites/default/files/research/online-documents/ardennes -battle-bulge/033-038.pdf.
44. Beevor, *Ardennes 1944*, 203.
45. Ambrose, *Citizen Soldiers*, 217–18.
46. Keane, *Patton*, 161–62.
47. Keane, *Patton*, 161–62.
48. Lande, *I Was with Patton*, 290.
49. Ayer, *Before the Colors Fade*, viii.
50. Whiting, *Patton*, 94.
51. John Eisenhower, *The Bitter Woods*, 334.
52. MacDonald, *A Time for Trumpets*, 515.
53. Toland, *Battle*, 163–64.
54. MacKenzie, *The Men of Bastogne*, 110.
55. Summersby, *Eisenhower Was My Boss*, 20.
56. D'Este, *Eisenhower*, 651.
57. D'Este, *Patton*, 682.
58. D'Este, *Patton*, 682.
59. George S. Patton diary, December 20, 1944.
60. Caddick-Adams, *Snow & Steel*, 483.
61. Simpson, *Selected Prose*, 138.

### PART TWO: DAYS OF THUNDER

1. "Patton's 'Blood and Guts' Speech," History on the Net, excerpted from Keane, *Patton*, https://www.historyonthenet.com/pattons-blood-and-guts-speech.

### CHAPTER SIX—"DRIVE LIKE HELL"

1. "When Patton Enlisted the Entire Third Army to Pray for Fair Weather," History on the Net, https://www.historyonthenet.com/when-patton-enlisted -the-entire-third-army-to-pray-for-fair-weather.

2. Reynolds, *Men of Steel*, 120.
3. John Eisenhower, *The Bitter Woods*, 31.
4. Atkinson, *The Guns at Last Light*, 455.
5. Ambrose, *Citizen Soldiers*, 220.
6. Bradley, *A Soldier's Story*, 479.
7. Codman, *Drive*, 234–35.
8. George S. Patton, *War as I Knew It*, 355.
9. Ellis, *The Sharp End*, 161.
10. George S. Patton diary, December 21, 1944, George S. Patton Papers, Library of Congress.
11. According to Hubert Essame, a British major general in WWII who later studied Patton's leadership in detail, Patton worked "in the light of the cavalry tradition—quick decision, speed in execution, calculated audacity; better a good plan violently executed now than a perfect plan next week." Source: Richard Sassaman, "Patton: Loved, Hated, Appreciated," *America in WWII*, http://www.americainwwii.com/articles/patton-loved-hated-appreciated/.
12. Blumenson, *The Patton Papers*, 603.
13. George S. Patton, *War as I Knew It*, 197–98.
14. Bradley and Blair, *A General's Life*, 367.
15. Codman, *Drive*, 234–35.
16. Ellis, *The Sharp End*, 103–5.
17. Ellis, *The Sharp End*, 152–54.
18. Chester B. Hansen diaries, December 21, 1944, Chester B. Hansen Collection, Box 5, The United States Army Military History Institute at US Army Heritage and Education Center, Carlisle, PA.
19. David H. Lippman, "Clear Skies over Bastogne: Patton's Prayers Answered," *Warfare History Network*, https://warfarehistorynetwork.com/article/clear-skies-over-bastogne-pattons-prayers-answered/.
20. Mark Stout, "Patton's Christmas Prayer and the Reality of War," *War on the Rocks*, December 19, 2014, https://warontherocks.com/2014/12/warchives-pattons-christmas-prayer-and-the-reality-of-war/.
21. "Patton's Fair Weather Prayer Paid Off," Knight-Ridder News Service, *Times-News* (Twin Falls, ID), December 27, 1994, 5.

### CHAPTER SEVEN—THE HOLE IN THE DOUGHNUT

1. Koskimaki, *Battered Bastards of Bastogne*, 220.
2. Koskimaki, *Battered Bastards of Bastogne*, 222.
3. John Hanlon, "A Bell Rings in Hemroulle," *Reader's Digest*, December 1962, 8–10.
4. Hanlon, "A Bell Rings."
5. Koskimaki, *Battered Bastards of Bastogne*, 231.
6. Toland, *Battle*, 210–11.
7. MacKenzie, *The Men of Bastogne*, 163.

8. Kenneth J. McAuliffe Jr., "The Story of the NUTS! Reply," US Army, December 8, 2013, https://www.army.mil/article/92856/the_story_of_the_nuts_re ply. See also: "Surrender? 'Nuts!' Gen. Anthony McAuliffe's 1944 Christmas Message to His Troops," National Archives Foundation, https://www.ar chivesfoundation.org/documents/surrender-nuts-gen-anthony-mcauliffes -1944-christmas-message-troops/.

9. Marshall, *Bastogne*, 151.

10. MacKenzie, *The Men of Bastogne*, 164–65.

11. Barron, *Patton at the Battle of the Bulge*, 100–103.

12. MacDonald, *A Time for Trumpets*, 510.

13. Zaloga, *The Battle of the Bulge*, 57.

14. Irzyk, *He Rode Up Front for Patton*, 246.

15. Reminiscences of General Jacob L. Devers, November 18, 1974, P92, Dwight D. Eisenhower Library, Abilene, KS.

16. Life inside a tank was hazardous indeed. "We generally wore a crash helmet with goggles and carried a .45-inch calibre Browning pistol in a shoulder holster which fitted neatly under our armpits," recalled Captain Horace R. Bennett of the 4th Armored. "Wearing one on the hip, like a gunslinger, or General Patton, may have looked fine, but in a burning tank with seconds between life or death, none of us wanted to lose our lives because of a pistol getting caught in a hatch. We were slim in those days, but it was always a tight squeeze wriggling in and out of those hatches. I also got a 'Grease Gun' from another knocked out tank. It was a small and cheap version of a Thompson sub-machine gun, like Al Capone and his gangsters used, and chambered for the same calibre as my pistol. We liked it because it was light, you could stow it anywhere, and its magazine held 30 rounds—enough to get you out of trouble. It was a copy of the German Schmeisser, and I took it everywhere I went at night, just in case." Source: Caddick-Adams, *Snow & Steel*, 431.

17. A. Harding Ganz, "Breakthrough to Bastogne," *Armor*, November/December 1981: 37.

18. David H. Lippman, "Clear Skies over Bastogne: Patton's Prayers Answered," Warfare History Network, https://warfarehistorynetwork.com/article/clear -skies-over-bastogne-pattons-prayers-answered/.

19. "Patton's Fair Weather Prayer Paid Off," Knight-Ridder News Service, *Times-News* (Twin Falls, ID), December 27, 1994, 5.

### CHAPTER EIGHT—BLUE SKIES

1. David H. Lippman, "Clear Skies over Bastogne: Patton's Prayers Answered," Warfare History Network, https://warfarehistorynetwork.com/article/clear -skies-over-bastogne-pattons-prayers-answered/.

2. "When Patton Enlisted the Entire Third Army to Pray for Fair Weather," History on the Net, https://www.historyonthenet.com/when-patton-enlisted -the-entire-third-army-to-pray-for-fair-weather.

3. Beevor, *Ardennes 1944*, 245.

4. John Eisenhower, *The Bitter Woods*, 338.
5. John Eisenhower, *The Bitter Woods*, 338.
6. Monsignor James H. O'Neill, "The True Story of the Patton Prayer," The Patton Society, http://www.pattonhq.com/prayer.html.
7. Lippman, "Clear Skies over Bastogne."
8. Moorehead, *Eclipse*, 228.
9. Ambrose, *Citizen Soldiers*, 225.
10. Jack Barensfeld memoir, Eisenhower Center, University of New Orleans.
11. Schrijvers, *Those Who Hold Bastogne*, 142.
12. Brigadier General Albin F. Irzyk, oral history, United States Holocaust Memorial Museum, 2007, https://collections.ushmm.org/search/catalog/irn 530883.
13. Barron, *Patton at the Battle of the Bulge*, 137.
14. Barron, *Patton at the Battle of the Bulge*, 137–40.
15. Irzyk, *He Rode Up Front for Patton*, 252.
16. Don Moore, "Fighting for Gen. George Patton at the Bulge," War Tales, https://donmooreswartales.com/2010/05/26/john-beck-jr/.
17. Lande, *I Was with Patton*, 232.
18. Lande, *I Was with Patton*, 232.
19. D'Este, *Eisenhower*, 654.

### CHAPTER NINE—MANNA FROM HEAVEN

1. Tony Reichhardt, "The Pilot Who Led the D-Day Invasion," *Smithsonian*, June 6, 2014, https://www.smithsonianmag.com/air-space-magazine/pilot -who-led-d-day-invasion-180951679/.
2. Koskimaki, *Battered Bastards of Bastogne*, 254.
3. Koskimaki, *Battered Bastards of Bastogne*, 256.
4. Wolfe, *Green Light!*, 348.
5. Collins and King, *Voices of the Bulge*, 185.
6. Koskimaki, *Battered Bastards of Bastogne*, 257.
7. Collins and King, *Voices of the Bulge*, 189.
8. MacKenzie, *The Men of Bastogne*, 181.
9. Koskimaki, *Battered Bastards of Bastogne*, 257–58.
10. Koskimaki, *Battered Bastards of Bastogne*, 257–58.
11. David H. Lippman, "Clear Skies over Bastogne: Patton's Prayers Answered," Warfare History Network, https://warfarehistorynetwork.com/article/clear -skies-over-bastogne-pattons-prayers-answered/.
12. Parker's arrival in Bastogne was later described: "On the night of 18 December a Forward Air Control Team from the 393rd Squadron was sent to Bastogne to assist the 101st Airborne Division. The team consisted of an experience [*sic*] flight commander, Captain James Parker, a radio operator, a driver and a radio equipped jeep. The team joined the 101st just an hour before the last road to Bastogne was cut." Source: "367th Fighter Group," Fandom, https://mili tary-history.fandom.com/wiki/367th_Fighter_Group.

13. The attacking pilots came under considerable flak in some areas. One pilot, Lieutenant Howard Park, remembered "slipping and skidding as streams of flak fire reached for me, sometimes within three feet of my wing surfaces. Despite skill, a lot of luck was needed to escape unscathed. The flak took a toll. It seemed as if the 513th was always first out and it seemed we lost one in four in lead flight every time. Actually, we lost five of the 513th in three days, and seven in a week during which the group lost a total of 10 pilots. Most of those who didn't return were recently transferred to us from the States and had no feel for the flak as those of us who dealt with it regularly." Source: Lippman, "Clear Skies over Bastogne."
14. Koskimaki, *Battered Bastards of Bastogne*, 252.
15. MacKenzie, *The Men of Bastogne*, 197–98.
16. Simpson, *Selected Prose*, 138–39.
17. MacDonald, *A Time for Trumpets*, 521.

## CHAPTER TEN—CHRISTMAS EVE

1. H. P. Hudson, "The Intervention of the Third Army: III Corps in the Attack," National Archives, College Park, MD.
2. Zaloga, *Panther vs. Sherman*, 46.
3. Lewis Sorley, "The Way of the Soldier: Remembering General Creighton Abrams," Foreign Policy Research Institute, May 30, 2013, https://www.fpri .org/article/2013/05/the-way-of-the-soldier-remembering-general-creighton -abrams/.
4. "Army Chief Abrams Dies at 59, Directed U.S. Forces in Vietnam," *New York Times*, September 4, 1974, https://www.nytimes.com/1974/09/04/archives /army-chief-abrams-dies-at-59-directed-us-forces-in-vietnam-tough.html.
5. Sorley, *Thunderbolt*, 53.
6. "Nation: Pattern's Peer," *Time*, April 14, 1967, https://content.time.com/time /subscriber/article/0,33009,836935,00.html.
7. Sorley, *Thunderbolt*, 57.
8. "Army Chief Abrams Dies."
9. Sorley, *Thunderbolt*, 73.
10. David H. Lippman, "Clear Skies over Bastogne: Patton's Prayers Answered," Warfare History Network, https://warfarehistorynetwork.com/2016/11/29 /clear-skies-over-bastogne-pattons-prayers-answered/.
11. Freeman, *The Mighty Eighth*, 201.
12. Astor, *The Mighty Eighth*, 393.
13. "Oskar-Heinz 'Pritzl' Bär," Aces of WW2, https://acesofww2.com/germany /aces/bar/.
14. Astor, *The Mighty Eighth*, 393.
15. Freeman, *The Mighty Eighth*, 201.
16. Sorley, *Thunderbolt*, 70–74.
17. Collins and King, *Voices of the Bulge*, 201–3.
18. Toland, *Battle*, 248.

19. Egger and Otts, *G Company's War*, 110.
20. Clair Galdonik, oral history, Eisenhower Center, University of New Orleans.
21. MacKenzie, *The Men of Bastogne*, 204–5.
22. MacKenzie, *The Men of Bastogne*, 204–5.
23. Koskimaki, *Battered Bastards of Bastogne*, 289.
24. Koskimaki, *Battered Bastards of Bastogne*, 105.
25. Koskimaki, *Battered Bastards of Bastogne*, 291–92.
26. Koskimaki, *Battered Bastards of Bastogne*, 203.
27. Collins and King, *Voices of the Bulge*, 246–47.
28. Caddick-Adams, *Snow & Steel*, 431–32.
29. MacDonald, *A Time for Trumpets*, 525.
30. Corsi, *No Greater Valor*, 256.
31. Allen, *Lucky Forward*, 184.
32. McDonald, *Remembered Light*, 29.
33. Codman, *Drive*, 235.
34. Atkinson, *The Guns at Last Light*, 465.
35. John Eisenhower, *The Bitter Woods*, 340.
36. George S. Patton diary, December 24, 1944, George S. Patton Papers, Library of Congress.
37. Weintraub, *11 Days in December*, 136.
38. MacDonald, *A Time for Trumpets*, 525.
39. Weintraub, *11 Days in December*, 136.
40. Koskimaki, *Battered Bastards of Bastogne*, 285.

### CHAPTER ELEVEN—CHRIST'S BIRTHDAY

1. Koskimaki, *Battered Bastards of Bastogne*, 292–93.
2. Blumenson, *The Patton Papers*, 606.
3. George S. Patton diary, December 25, 1944, George S. Patton Papers, Library of Congress.
4. MacKenzie, *The Men of Bastogne*, 234.
5. Barron, *Patton at the Battle of the Bulge*, 294.
6. The London meteorological report for Monday, December 25, 1944, read: "Some cloud clearing by early afternoon. Fog overnight and ground frost. Winds from the north at 15–35 km/h. Chance of snowfall amounts near 0.8 mm." Source: Collins and King, *Tigers of Bastogne*, 190.
7. Astor, *A Blood-Dimmed Tide*, 330–31.
8. Walter Lipinski, personal narrative, Walter Lipinski Collection, Library of Congress, https://www.loc.gov/item/afc2001001.13727/.
9. Collins and King, *Tigers of Bastogne*, 192–95.
10. MacKenzie, *The Men of Bastogne*, 216.
11. MacKenzie, *The Men of Bastogne*, 228.
12. MacKenzie, *The Men of Bastogne*, 216.
13. MacKenzie, *The Men of Bastogne*, 216.
14. MacKenzie, *The Men of Bastogne*, 228.

15. MacKenzie, *The Men of Bastogne*, 228.
16. Zaloga, *The Battle of the Bulge*, 60.
17. Zaloga, *The Battle of the Bulge*, 61.
18. Koskimaki, *Battered Bastards of Bastogne*, 304.
19. Koskimaki, *Battered Bastards of Bastogne*, 331.
20. MacKenzie, *The Men of Bastogne*, 228.
21. Barron, *Patton at the Battle of the Bulge*, 235.
22. Beevor, *Ardennes 1944*, 283.
23. Jack Anderson, "Twenty Years After He Told the Nazis 'Nuts,'" *Parade*, December 20, 1964.
24. Koskimaki, *Battered Bastards of Bastogne*, 312–13.
25. Anderson, "Twenty Years."
26. Lande, *I Was with Patton*, 215–17.
27. Allen, *Lucky Forward*, 184.
28. D'Este, *Patton*, 691–92.
29. George S. Patton, *War as I Knew It*, x.
30. D'Este, *Patton*, 692.
31. Rickard, *Advance and Destroy*, 304.
32. George S. Patton diary, December 25, 1944.
33. Green and Brown, *War Stories*, 164–65.
34. Summersby, *Eisenhower Was My Boss*, 204.
35. Weintraub, *11 Days in December*, 170.
36. Weintraub, *11 Days in December*, 160.
37. MacKenzie, *The Men of Bastogne*, 232.
38. Marshall, *Bastogne*, 169.
39. George S. Patton, *War as I Knew It*, 201.
40. Weintraub, *11 Days in December*, 152.
41. Leif E. Maseng, "Bulge Memories," *The Bulge Bugle* 13 (Spring 2022): 18.

### PART THREE: SALVATION

1. "Patton's 'Blood and Guts' Speech," History on the Net, excerpted from Keane, *Patton*, https://www.historyonthenet.com/pattons-blood-and-guts-speech.

### CHAPTER TWELVE—"LET 'ER ROLL"

1. Collins and King, *Tigers of Bastogne*, 199.
2. MacKenzie, *The Men of Bastogne*, 244.
3. MacKenzie, *The Men of Bastogne*, 244.
4. MacKenzie, *The Men of Bastogne*, 244.
5. Dick Habein, "Tank Veteran Recalls Yule Dash to Bastogne," *Stars and Stripes*, December 27, 1949.
6. Barron, *Patton at the Battle of the Bulge*, 298.
7. Toland, *Battle*, 285.

8. Michael D. Hull, "Colonel Creighton Abrams at the Battle of the Bulge," Warfare History Network, https://warfarehistorynetwork.com/2017/05/26/colonel-creighton-abrams-at-the-battle-of-the-bulge/.
9. Toland, *Battle*, 285.
10. Frankel and Smith, *Patton's Best*, 120.
11. Toland, *Battle*, 285.
12. Adam Bernstein, "Medal of Honor Winner James R. Hendrix, 77, Dies," *Washington Post*, November 19, 2002, https://www.washingtonpost.com/archive/local/2002/11/19/medal-of-honor-winner-james-r-hendrix-77-dies/e72b7ca6-c85f-4791-a566-3a9b409c3222/. Hendrix would go on to survive the war and then remain in the army. He would gain press coverage again in 1949 when he amazingly survived an incident during paratrooper training when his "main parachute became ensnared in his boot buckles, and the emergency chute got caught up in the main chute. He cried out in terror as he fell, hoping the remaining flapping silk would save him. Moments before hitting the ground, he formed a 'V' with his body—keeping head and feet high, grabbing his ankles. He landed on his back in a plowed field, cushioned enough by the remnants of the chutes to escape with severe bruises but nothing more serious. The press of the day called it a 'miracle fall,' and Mr. Hendrix never discounted the power of prayer in his ordeal. His drop was featured in a 'Ripley's Believe It or Not' cartoon. He also served in the Korean War as a paratrooper." Source: Bernstein, "Medal of Honor Winner."
13. Frankel and Smith, *Patton's Best*, 120.
14. Michael E. Ruane, "A Battered World War II Hero of Bastogne Gets a New Home, and a Museum Built Around It," *Washington Post*, August 3, 2017, https://www.washingtonpost.com/news/retropolis/wp/2017/08/03/a-battered-world-war-ii-hero-of-bastogne-gets-a-new-home-and-museum-built-around-it/.
15. Sorley, *Thunderbolt*, 77.
16. Koskimaki, *Battered Bastards of Bastogne*, 353–58.
17. Collins and King, *Tigers of Bastogne*, 197.
18. Sorley, *Thunderbolt*, 77.
19. Astor, *A Blood-Dimmed Tide*, 359.
20. Astor, *A Blood-Dimmed Tide*, 359.
21. Ward and Burns, *The War*, 322.
22. Koskimaki, *Battered Bastards of Bastogne*, 353–58.
23. Koskimaki, *Battered Bastards of Bastogne*, 353–58.
24. Sorley, *Thunderbolt*, 80.
25. Hull, "Colonel Creighton Abrams."
26. Collins and King, *Tigers of Bastogne*, 200.
27. Don Moore, "Fighting for Gen. George Patton at the Bulge," War Tales, https://donmooreswartales.com/2010/05/26/john-beck-jr/.
28. Irzyk, *Patton's Juggernaut*, 261–62.
29. Sorley, *Thunderbolt*, 81.

30. The 37th Tank Battalion would receive the Presidential Unit Citation for its actions in the relief of Bastogne.
31. Hull, "Colonel Creighton Abrams."
32. Hull, "Colonel Creighton Abrams."
33. Blumenson, *The Patton Papers*, 606.
34. Allen, *Lucky Forward*, 186.
35. Rickard, *Advance and Destroy*, 178.
36. Hull, "Colonel Creighton Abrams."
37. Blumenson, *The Patton Papers*, 607.
38. Stanley Weintraub, "Patton and the Battle of the Bulge: 'As Soon As You're Through with Me, I Can Attack the Day After Tomorrow Morning,'" HistoryNet.com, https://www.historynet.com/general-george-s-patton-and-the-battle-of-the-bulge-2.htm.

### CHAPTER THIRTEEN—HIS FINEST HOURS

1. Toland, *Battle*, 294.
2. Shirer, *Rise and Fall*, 1094–95.
3. Collins and King, *Voices of the Bulge*, 283.
4. Hastings, *Armageddon*, 572.
5. "Harold Lindstrom's Remembrance," https://hldnoqtr.tripod.com/roh10.htm.
6. Gerald Nelson fought under Patton with the 7th Armored Division. He recalled: "Talk about praying. I used to pray the 23rd Psalm—'Yea, though I walk through the valley of the shadow of death. . . .' I'd pray that a lot during combat. But I'd pray only half of it. I'd say, 'I fear no evil because thou art with me. Thy rod and thy staff comfort me.' But I'd stop there. The rest goes on like the future: 'Thou preparest a table before me in the presence of my enemies; thou anointest my head with oil, my cup runneth over. . . .'" That's all in the future, and I stopped before that thought. All I could pray for was courage for the here and now—that I'd be able to do my job. Somehow, I couldn't say the rest until I was safe back home." Source: Lande, *I Was with Patton*, 294.
7. Jason Koebler, "Study: World War II Soldiers Relied on Prayer, Not Returning Home to Loved Ones, for Motivation," *US News & World Report*, May 28, 2013, https://www.usnews.com/news/articles/2013/05/28/study-world-war-ii-soldiers-relied-on-prayer-not-returning-home-to-loved-ones-for-motivation.
8. Blumenson, *The Patton Papers*, 609–10.
9. Koskimaki, *Battered Bastards of Bastogne*, 391.
10. Collins and King, *Tigers of Bastogne*, 200.
11. Koskimaki, *Battered Bastards of Bastogne*, 390. Hans Wiesman, "Where Patton Awarded McAuliffe: The 101st Airborne HQ Chateau in Bastogne Revisited," War History Online, https://www.warhistoryonline.com/guest-bloggers/patton-awarded-mcauliffe-101st.html?chrome=1&M3c=1&A1c=1.
12. "A Gunner's Story," Battle of the Bulge Association, excerpted from Valera, *My Father's War*, https://battleofthebulge.org/2018/08/01/a-gunners-story/.

13. Koskimaki, *Battered Bastards of Bastogne*, 390.
14. John Eisenhower, *The Bitter Woods*, 416.
15. Koskimaki, *Battered Bastards of Bastogne*, 393–94.
16. Rickard, *Advance and Destroy*, 239.
17. George S. Patton, *War as I Knew It*, 211.
18. Ambrose, *Citizen Soldiers*, 367–70.
19. George S. Patton, *War as I Knew It*, 211.
20. Stargardt, *The German War*, 480.
21. Toland, *Battle*, 324.
22. Toland, *Battle*, 326.
23. Schrijvers, *Those Who Hold Bastogne*, 289.
24. Astor, *A Blood-Dimmed Tide*, 364.
25. Astor, *A Blood-Dimmed Tide*, 364.
26. Blumenson, *The Patton Papers*, 611.
27. Blumenson, *The Patton Papers*, 612.
28. Blumenson, *The Patton Papers*, 613.

### Chapter Fourteen—Bloodred Snow

1. Dwight Eisenhower, *Crusade in Europe*, 363.
2. Rickard, *Advance and Destroy*, 246.
3. Schrijvers, *Those Who Hold Bastogne*, 205.
4. George S. Patton diary, January 3, 1945, George S. Patton Papers, Library of Congress.
5. "Combat—The Battle of the Bulge," Scions of the 17th Airborne, https://www.17thscions.org/history.
6. George S. Patton diary, January 4, 1945.
7. 17th Airborne after action report, National Archives, College Park, MD.
8. Gabel, *The Making of a Paratrooper*, 172–75.
9. "Isadore Seigfreid Jachman," Congressional Medal of Honor Society, https://www.cmohs.org/recipients/isadore-s-jachman.
10. "Division Battles," Scions of the 17th Airborne, https://www.17thscions.org/history.
11. Blumenson, *The Patton Papers*, 615.
12. Beevor, *Ardennes 1944*, 342–43.
13. "Battle of the Bulge," American Experience, https://www.pbs.org/wgbh/americanexperience/films/bulge/.
14. Wilson, *The 761st "Black Panther" Tank Battalion*, 53.
15. Abdul-Jabbar and Walton, *Brothers in Arms*, 187–204.
16. Arnold Blumberg, "The End of the Battle of the Bulge," Warfare History Network, https://warfarehistorynetwork.com/the-end-of-the-battle-of-the-bulge/.
17. Beevor, *Ardennes 44*, 347.
18. George S. Patton, *War as I Knew It*, 215–16.
19. Schrijvers, *Those Who Hold Bastogne*, 235.
20. Rickard, *Advance and Destroy*, 304.

21. Rickard, *Advance and Destroy*, 280.

22. Beevor, *Ardennes 1944*, 347.

23. That day was especially cruel for Ronald McArthur, serving in a Heavy Weapons Company: "At the beginning of the Battle of the Bulge, our outfit was a good many miles southeast of the breakthrough point. I was the first gunner in our section of water-cooled 30 caliber machine guns. We were a Heavy Weapons Company of the 45th Division, part of General Patch's 7th Army. We were ordered out between Christmas and New Year's to help close the gap in the line. We traveled nearly a day and a night in a northwesterly direction to our assigned area. We were attached to a rifle company to replace their light 30 caliber machine guns that had been knocked out in the attack. We set our guns up on the high ground on each side of a trail in the woods. There were several tanks with us in the attack. It was all quiet nearly all afternoon, only a few small arms fired at us during the day. Then, all of a sudden at about four o'clock, we were hit with a terrific artillery barrage. The shells were coming in hitting the trees and exploding. We were exposed to vicious tree burst shrapnel coming down on us. After some time, I told my assistant gunner to man the gun as I was going out to cut some large branch logs that had been knocked down from the shelling. This was afternoon, January 11, 1945. The logs were to be placed over our foxhole to protect from further shell bursts. I left the gun and went about 100 yards toward the lead tank that had been knocked out during the battle. I got about four logs cut when WHAM, I was shot through the face by a German sniper. He had been left behind as we drove Germans off the hill. He was out in front of the knocked out tank. I fell flat on my face in about 15" of snow. My only thought was, 'When will he let me have it again?' The bullet must have been a soft-nosed one as X-rays later revealed that I had pieces of shrapnel in my cheek and the roof of my mouth. The bullet had gone through my left cheek just below the jaw bone and exited out my right cheek, taking nearly all of [my] upper teeth and gums as well as most of the lowers. I remember feeling numbness in my mouth. I thought my tongue was gone. I put my hand in the opening and was relieved to find it intact. The opening of the right cheek was up to under my eye and back nearly to my right ear. Our medic was nearby. He came and patched the wounds with sulphadiazine powder. In short order, our jeep was there (each section of machine guns had its own jeep). They took me and another GI out to be evacuated to an aid station and several hospitals on my way finally to England and later home, the good old USA." Source: "Soldiers' Battlefield Accounts," American Experience, https://www.pbs.org/wgbh/americanexperience/features/bulge-dispatches/.

24. *Patton 360*, episode 9, "Battle of the Bulge," The History Channel, aired June 18, 2009.

#### CHAPTER FIFTEEN—HOUFFALIZE

1. George S. Patton diary, January 13, 1945, George S. Patton Papers, Library of Congress. That same day Patton wrote to the editor of *Stars and Stripes*,

"protesting against his paper as subversive of discipline. I sent a copy of my letter to general Lee. . . . I stated that unless there is an improvement, I will not permit the paper to be issued in this Army, nor permit his reporters or photographers in the Army area. It is a scurrilous sheet." Patton was particularly upset by the work of cartoonist Bill Mauldin. He was in fact so incensed that he made a complaint about Mauldin's irreverent cartoons to SHAEF. A meeting was suggested between Mauldin and Patton. Patton was having none of it, snapping: "If that little son of a bitch sets foot in Third Army I'll throw his ass in jail." Even so, Mauldin did meet with Patton. Mauldin remembered: "There he sat, big as life even at that distance . . . his collar and shoulders glittered with more stars than I could count, his fingers sparkled with rings, and an incredible mass of ribbons started around desktop level and spread upward in a flood over his chest to the very top of his shoulder, as if preparing to march down his back too." Mauldin would later describe Patton's features in vivid detail: "His face was rugged, with an odd, strangely shapeless outline; his eyes were pale, almost colorless, with a choleric bulge. His small, compressed mouth was sharply downturned at the corners, with a lower lip which suggested a pouting child as much as a no-nonsense martinet. It was a welcome, rather human touch. Beside him, lying on a big chair, was Willie, [Patton's] bull terrier. If ever a dog was suited to master this was one. Willie had his beloved boss's expression and lacked only the ribbons and stars. I stood in that door staring into the four meanest eyes I'd ever seen." Mauldin got a dressing-down but he continued to draw his cartoons. Patton, surprisingly, took no further action. Source: D'Este, *Patton*, 693.

2. "Jack's Wood," Europe Remembers, https://www.europeremembers.com/pois/386/jacks-wood.
3. George S. Patton, *War as I Knew It*, 220.
4. George Arnstein, interview with author.
5. Astor, *A Blood-Dimmed Tide*, 375.
6. Reynolds, *Men of Steel*, 113.
7. George S. Patton, *War as I Knew It*, 220.
8. Arnold Blumberg, "The End of the Battle of the Bulge," Warfare History Network, https://warfarehistorynetwork.com/the-end-of-the-battle-of-the-bulge/.
9. Brigadier General Michael J. L. Greene, "Contact at Houffalize," The 11th Armored Division Legacy Group, http://www.11tharmoreddivision.com/history/Link-up_History.html.
10. Greene, "Contact at Houffalize."
11. Greene, "Contact at Houffalize."
12. Toland, *Battle*, 360–62.
13. Blumberg, "The End of the Battle of the Bulge."
14. Greene, "Contact at Houffalize."
15. Blumberg, "The End of the Battle of the Bulge."
16. Toland, *Battle*, 362–64.
17. Greene, "Contact at Houffalize."

18. Toland, *Battle*, 364.
19. Green and Green, *Patton and the Battle of the Bulge*, 150–51.
20. Dwight Eisenhower, *Crusade in Europe*, 364.
21. "Martyred Town of Houffalize," Liberation Route Europe, https://www.liberationroute.com/pois/387/martyred-town-of-houffalize.
22. D'Este, *Patton*, 697.
23. Blumenson, *The Patton Papers*, 625.

### Chapter Sixteen—Battered Bastards

1. Schrijvers, *Those Who Hold Bastogne*, 250.
2. Michael D. Hull, "Bravery in Embattled Bastogne," Warfare History Network, https://warfarehistorynetwork.com/article/bravery-in-embattled-bastogne/.
3. Blumenson, *The Patton Papers*, 626.
4. George S. Patton, *War as I Knew It*, 222.
5. D'Este, *Patton*, 690.
6. Stiller would be wounded and earn the DSC on March 27, 1945.
7. George S. Patton, *War as I Knew It*, 627.
8. Blumenson, *The Patton Papers*, 630.
9. Monsignor James H. O'Neill, "The True Story of the Patton Prayer," The Patton Society, http://www.pattonhq.com/prayer.html.
10. George S. Patton, *War as I Knew It*, 207.
11. George S. Patton, *War as I Knew It*, 222.
12. D'Este, *Patton*, 701.
13. "Battle of the Bulge Memorial," Arlington National Cemetery, https://www.arlingtoncemetery.mil/Explore/Monuments-and-Memorials/Battle-of-the-Bulge.
14. D'Este, *Patton*, 700–701.
15. Lieutenant Colonel Freiherr von Wangenheim, Box 16, George S. Patton Papers, Library of Congress.
16. MacDonald, *A Time for Trumpets*, 618–19.
17. Poling, *Faith Is Power for You*, 190–92.

### Part Four: Victory in Europe

1. "11 Gen. George Patton Quotes That Show His Strategic Awesomeness," Military.com, https://www.military.com/history/2021/08/05/11-general-george-patton-quotes-show-his-strategic-awesomeness.html.

### Chapter Seventeen—To the Rhine

1. Codman, *Drive*, 252.
2. Codman, *Drive*, 252.
3. Farago, *Patton*, 743–44.

4. Farago, *Patton*, 743–44.
5. Richard Sassaman, "Patton: Loved, Hated, Appreciated," *America in WWII*, http://www.americainwwii.com/articles/patton-loved-hated-appreciated/.
6. Lande, *I Was with Patton*, 239–40.
7. Weigley, *Eisenhower's Lieutenants*, 595.
8. Ambrose, *Citizen Soldiers*, 413.
9. Ambrose, *Citizen Soldiers*, 413.
10. Hirshson, *General Patton*, 602.
11. George S. Patton, *War as I Knew It*, 243.
12. Ambrose, *Citizen Soldiers*, 413.
13. Codman, *Drive*, 259.
14. Codman, *Drive*, 260.
15. Codman, *Drive*, 255.
16. Codman, *Drive*, 257.
17. "Medal of Honor Recipients, World War II (A–F)," Internet Archive Wayback Machine, https://web.archive.org/web/20080616211621/http://www.history .army.mil/html/moh/wwII-a-f.html.
18. George S. Patton, *War as I Knew It*, 245–46.
19. Lande, *I Was with Patton*, 241.
20. George S. Patton, *War as I Knew It*, 249–50.
21. Toland, *Last 100 Days*, 175.
22. George S. Patton, *War as I Knew It*, 251–52.
23. Harry Fisher, "Israel: Offensive or Defensive," The Jewish Magazine, February 2008, http://www.jewishmag.com/121mag/patton-harry-fisher/patton-harry -fisher.htm.
24. Ayer, *Before the Colors Fade*, 193.
25. Koch with Hays, *G-2*, 162.
26. George S. Patton, *War as I Knew It*, 253.
27. George S. Patton, *War as I Knew It*, 253.
28. Codman, *Drive*, 264.
29. D'Este, *Eisenhower*, 685.

### CHAPTER EIGHTEEN—THE CROSSING

1. Speer, *Inside the Third Reich*, 437–40.
2. Toland, *Last 100 Days*, 256.
3. "George Patton's US 5th Division crossed the Rhine River during the night of 22 Mar 1945, establishing a six-mile-deep bridgehead after capturing 19,000 demoralized German troops. Patton, who actually did not have the orders to cross the river, did so under an extremely low profile: quietly, his troops crossed the river in boats without artillery barrage nor aerial bombardment. His commanding general Omar Bradley, who issued the order for him not to cross to avoid interfering with Bernard Montgomery's operations, did not know of the crossing until the next morning. Bradley did not announce this

crossing until the night of 23 March; Patton had wished the Americans to announce that they had crossed the Rhine River before the British. This was the first crossing of the Rhine River by boat by an invading army since Napoleon Bonaparte. Within three days Patton's troops were rapidly approaching Frankfurt, Germany, capturing bridges intact as the German defenses began to fall apart." Source: C. Peter Chen, "Crossing the Rhine, 22 Mar 1945–1 Apr 1945," World War II Database, https://ww2db.com/battle_spec.php?battle_id=134.

4. Lande, *I Was with Patton*, 249.
5. Weigley, *Eisenhower's Lieutenants*, 648.
6. Major General Michael Reynolds, "George S. Patton's End Run: The Story of His Final Days," Warfare History Network, September 2009, https://warfarehistorynetwork.com/article/george-s-pattons-end-run-the-story-of-his-final-days/.
7. "Patton's Entrance into Germany in 1945," History on the Net, excerpted from Keane, *Patton*, https://www.historyonthenet.com/pattons-entrance-into-germany-in-1945.
8. George S. Patton diary, March 24, 1945, George S. Patton Papers, Library of Congress.
9. Blumenson, *The Patton Papers*, 661.
10. Cadet G. S. Patton to General George S. Patton, March 25, 1945, George S. Patton Papers, United States Military Academy, West Point.
11. Province, *Patton's Third Army*, 226.
12. Codman, *Drive*, 269.

### CHAPTER NINETEEN—HUBRIS

1. Lande, *I Was with Patton*, 251.
2. "Harmonicas, Onions, and Patton—Harry Feinberg, 4th AD," Battle of the Bulge Association, excerpted from Joanne Palmer, "From Minsk, to Hollywood, to Buchenwald," *Jewish Standard*, December 13, 2013, https://battleofthebulge.org/2014/08/29/harmonicas-onions-and-patton-harry-feinberg-4th-ad/.
3. Bourke-White, *"Dear Fatherland, Rest Quietly,"* 230–33.
4. Toland, *Last 100 Days*, 285.
5. Baron, Baum, and Goldhurst, *Raid!*, 6–7.
6. Baron, Baum, and Goldhurst, *Raid!*, 8.
7. Abraham Baum, interview with author.
8. Kershaw, *The Longest Winter*, 203.
9. Blumenson, *The Patton Papers*, 666.
10. Blumenson, *The Patton Papers*, 676.
11. Blumenson, *The Patton Papers*, 676.
12. Bradley, *A Soldier's Story*, 542–43.
13. Kershaw, *The Longest Winter*, 222.

CHAPTER TWENTY—THE FINAL STRAIGHT

1. Atkinson, *The Guns at Last Light*, 568.
2. George S. Patton, *War as I Knew It*, 284.
3. Codman, *Drive*, 281.
4. Farago, *Patton*, 797.
5. Codman, *Drive*, 281–82.
6. Dwight Eisenhower, *Crusade in Europe*, 407.
7. Codman, *Drive*, 281–82.
8. "Ohrdruf," Holocaust Encyclopedia, United States Holocaust Memorial Museum, https://encyclopedia.ushmm.org/content/en/article/ohrdruf.
9. "Ohrdruf," Holocaust Encyclopedia.
10. Codman, *Drive*, 283.
11. Hobart R. Gay diary, April 12, 1945, National Archives, College Park, MD.
12. Toland, *Last 100 Days*, 371.
13. D'Este, *Eisenhower*, 689.
14. Blumenson, *The Patton Papers*, 686–87.
15. Farago, *Patton*, 195.
16. William E. Leuchtenburg, "Franklin D. Roosevelt: Death of the President," UVA / Miller Center, https://millercenter.org/president/fdroosevelt/death-of -the-president.
17. D'Este, *Eisenhower*, 689.
18. Blumenson, *The Patton Papers*, 685.
19. D'Este, *Eisenhower*, 689.
20. Farago, *Patton*, 765.
21. George S. Patton, *War as I Knew It*, 304.
22. George S. Patton, *War as I Knew It*, 782.
23. Codman, *Drive*, 293.
24. Ayer, *Before the Colors Fade*, 189.
25. Ayer, *Before the Colors Fade*, 203.
26. Ayer, *Before the Colors Fade*, 203–4.
27. Farago, *Patton*, 776.
28. Lande, *I Was with Patton*, 254.
29. According to one young officer, Patton's strict rules grated on many men: "If you drove in the Third Army sector without steel helmet, sidearms, necktie, dog-tags, everything arranged according to some forgotten manual, Patton's fiercely loyal M.P. gorillas would grab you. You could protest, but say one word against their pigheaded general?—I never had the nerve . . . there is no doubting his sincerity, and no doubt that compared to the dreary run of us, General Patton was quite mad." Source: John Phillips, "The Ordeal of George Patton," review of *Patton*, Farago, *New York Review of Books*, December 31, 1964 https://www.nybooks.com/articles/1964/12/31/the-ordeal-of-george -patton/.
30. Lande, *I Was with Patton*, 254.
31. Lande, *I Was with Patton*, 256.

32. "Stalag VII A: History, 1939–1945," Moosburg Online, http://www.moosburg
    .org/info/stalag/st95eng.html.
33. Lovoi, Listen . . . My Children, 143.
34. Nichol and Rennell, The Last Escape, 284.
35. Nichol and Rennell, The Last Escape, 284.
36. Lovoi, Listen . . . My Children, 162.
37. Chesterfield Smith, of the 94th Infantry Division, remembered how proud
    men were to serve under Patton: "We had to censor the mail for our troops. I
    had about 140 troops. We had to look at the mail and almost every letter I saw
    go home to wives and children and friends, but especially wives, would start
    off with the most unbelievable compliments and bragging like 'I'm a Patton
    man.' They were all so proud. They wanted to be a fighter because of him. They
    wanted to win that damn war because of him. And they'd put it in their
    letters . . . they'd brag, brag, brag. They'd say, 'I'm a Patton man!' I heard a lot
    of people who questioned Patton that were serving under him—like, 'That
    bastard is going to kill us. He doesn't care a damn thing about us. He just
    wants to win the war and be in a book or something.' But when they would
    write home, they'd brag endlessly. It's just kind of the way people are. I think,
    frankly, they all admired him every way as a soldier. Maybe they were think-
    ing, 'I don't have to be myself with this good of a soldier. Yes, I could do quar-
    termaster work, moving supplies. But I should be up here dodging bullets.
    Patton wants me to dodge bullets.'" Source: Lande, I Was with Patton, 286–87.
38. Graham, No Name on the Bullet, 95.

### Chapter Twenty-One—The End

 1. "The Death of Hitler," The History Place, https://www.historyplace.com
    /worldwar2/timeline/death.htm.
 2. Blumenson, The Patton Papers, 695.
 3. Blumenson, The Patton Papers, 677–78.
 4. Blumenson, The Patton Papers, 695.
 5. Codman, Drive, 296.
 6. George S. Patton, War as I Knew It, 324–25.
 7. Farago, Patton, 784.
 8. Farago, Patton, 787.
 9. Bradley and Blair, A General's Life, 436.
10. Atkinson, The Guns at Last Light, 626.
11. Egger and Otts, G Company's War, 252–53.
12. Farago, Patton, 790.
13. Allen, Lucky Forward, 379.
14. Lande, I Was with Patton, 264–65.
15. Farago, Patton, 791.
16. Allen, Lucky Forward, 394.
17. Lande, I Was with Patton, 264–65.
18. Allen, Lucky Forward, 379.

19. George S. Patton, *War as I Knew It*, 330.
20. Codman, *Drive*, 297.
21. George S. Patton, *War as I Knew It*, 308.
22. George S. Patton, *War as I Knew It*, 308.
23. Larry G. Newman, "Gen. Patton's Premonition," *American Legion Magazine*, July 1962: 12–13.
24. Newman, "Gen. Patton's Premonition."
25. Codman, *Drive*, 298–301.

## PART FIVE: A WARLORD NO MORE

1. "Patton's 'Blood and Guts' Speech," History on the Net, excerpted from Keane, *Patton*, https://www.historyonthenet.com/pattons-blood-and-guts -speech.

## CHAPTER TWENTY-TWO—PEACE BREAKS OUT

1. Harkins, *When the Third Cracked Europe*, 64–65.
2. Farago, *Patton*, 803.
3. Farago, *Patton*, 807.
4. D'Este, *Patton*, 746.
5. Codman, *Drive*, 318.
6. Blumenson, *The Patton Papers*, 720.
7. D'Este, *Patton*, 747.
8. Codman, *Drive*, 319.
9. Farago, *Patton*, 793.
10. Ayer, *Before the Colors Fade*, 243–44.
11. "President Truman Greeting General Patton in the United States, June 1945," The Digital Collections of the National WWII Museum, https://www.ww2on line.org/image/president-truman-greeting-general-patton-united-states -june-1945.
12. Odom, *General George S. Patton and Eisenhower*, 74.
13. Major General Michael Reynolds, "The Real Story of General George Patton Jr.'s Death & Final Days," Warfare History Network, https://warfarehisto rynetwork.com/real-story-general-george-patton-jr-death-final-days/.
14. Blumenson, *The Patton Papers*, 720–23.
15. Codman, *Drive*, 319.
16. Farago, *Patton*, 796. Bradley himself was rated by Eisenhower as the best of his most senior generals. "In my opinion," Eisenhower wrote Bradley that July, "you are pre-eminent among the Commanders of major battle units in this war. Your leadership, forcefulness, professional capacity, selflessness, high sense of duty and sympathetic understanding of human beings, combine to stamp you as one of America's great leaders and soldiers." Source: Cole Kingseed, "General Omar Bradley: Dwight D. Eisenhower's Indispensible [*sic*] Lieutenant," Warfare History Network, https://warfarehistorynetwork

.com/article/general-omar-bradley-dwight-d-eisenhowers-indispensible
-lieutenant.

17. Blumenson, *The Patton Papers*, 725.
18. Reynolds, "Real Story of General George Patton."
19. Farago, *Last Days of Patton*, 67.
20. Blumenson, *The Patton Papers*, 735.
21. George S. Patton diary, August 10, 1945, George S. Patton Papers, Library of Congress.
22. George S. Patton diary, August 10, 1945.
23. Farago, *Patton*, 811–13.
24. Walter Bedell Smith press conference transcript, September 26, 1945, Box 17, George S. Patton Papers, Library of Congress.
25. Summersby, *Eisenhower Was My Boss*, 278.
26. Reynolds, "Real Story of General George Patton."
27. Dwight Eisenhower, *At Ease*, 307–8.
28. Reynolds, "Real Story of General George Patton."
29. Eisenhower's son John later stated that his father told him that there was no "personal animosity" about the events of September 28. Source: John Eisenhower, *Strictly Personal*, 44.
30. Reynolds, "Real Story of General George Patton."
31. Farago, *Last Days of Patton*, 216–17.
32. Farago, *Last Days of Patton*, 216–17.
33. Ayer, *Before the Colors Fade*, 255.
34. Ayer, *Before the Colors Fade*, 255.
35. John Eisenhower, *Strictly Personal*, 114.
36. Dwight Eisenhower, *At Ease*, 307–8.
37. John Eisenhower, *Strictly Personal*, 114. John Eisenhower later remembered Patton in telling detail: "There was something a bit scary about Patton. . . . To pretend to love war like he did, there had to have been a screw loose somewhere. For some people the Army was a vocation—a paycheck—but Patton was one of those for whom it was an avocation. . . . One thing that I noticed about Patton . . . he was a very generous man, with courtly manners . . . when he was away from the front. At the front he was very aware that he was playing a certain role. . . . He was very excitable, though. Very high-strung. When I was with him at dinner one night he broke into tears twice, listening to what he himself had just said." Source: D'Este, *Patton*, 816.
38. Doolittle with Glines, *I Could Never Be So Lucky Again*, 363.
39. Reynolds, "Real Story of General George Patton."
40. George S. Patton, *War as I Knew It*, 389–90.
41. D'Este, *Patton*, 777.
42. D'Este, *Patton*, 777.
43. Farago, *Patton*, 819.
44. Robert Patton, *The Pattons*, 279.
45. Truscott, *Command Missions*, 508.
46. One of his staff, Robert S. Allen, later recalled with some bitterness how

Patton had been treated. He believed Patton "took the heartbreaking blow" of being relieved "in silence. But while outwardly subdued, inwardly he seethed in anguished fury and searing despair. He was baffled as to just where and how he had erred. He could not understand the rancorous storm of abuse and castigation. He had done no more than other Allied commanders administering occupied areas! So why pick him? If he was wrong, why weren't they? Particularly he was cut to the quick by Eisenhower's stinging rebuke in their talk. Patton felt that not only was that wholly uncalled for, but grossly ungrateful and unfair. From Africa to the ETO, he had given Eisenhower the utmost in loyal, unstinting and peerless service. . . . Surely simple gratitude alone warranted more than a humiliating verbal spanking in private and condemnation in public." Source: Allen, "The Day Patton Quit," *Army*, June 1971.

47. Reynolds, "Real Story of General George Patton."
48. William Kepner, oral history, The United States Army Military History Institute at US Army Heritage and Education Center, Carlisle, PA.
49. Richard Sassaman, "Patton: Loved, Hated, Appreciated," *America in WWII*, http://www.americainwwii.com/articles/patton-loved-hated-appreciated/.
50. Farago, *Patton*, 824.
51. Farago, *Patton*, 824.
52. George S. Patton diary, December 3, 1945.
53. D'Este, *Patton*, 780–82.

### CHAPTER TWENTY-THREE—THE LAST DAYS

1. D'Este, *Patton*, 783–85.
2. Lande, *I Was with Patton*, 269–72.
3. Lande, *I Was with Patton*, 269–72.
4. D'Este, *Patton*, 783–85.
5. *After the Battle* 7 (1975): 46.
6. Lande, *I Was with Patton*, 272.
7. Farago, *Patton*, 826.
8. Blumenson, *The Patton Papers*, 818–19.
9. Farago, *Patton*, 827.
10. Blumenson, *The Patton Papers*, 820.
11. Farago, *Patton*, 828.
12. Blumenson, *The Patton Papers*, 823.
13. Monsignor James H. O'Neill, "The True Story of the Patton Prayer," The Patton Society, http://www.pattonhq.com/prayer.html.
14. Blumenson, *The Patton Papers*, 827.
15. Blumenson, *The Patton Papers*, 831.
16. O'Neill, "The True Story."
17. Blumenson, *The Patton Papers*, 851–52.
18. Blumenson, *The Patton Papers*, 832–33.
19. Many of Patton's men were intensely proud that they had served under him. He gave them pride. As one veteran recalled after the war: "The fondest

memory I have of the war just finished is the thought that I was a member of the Third Army. In the earliest days of the Ardennes, we were green troops fighting with desperation, and in the darkest moments of the worst hours, the news came that we were in the Third Army and that help was coming. It would have warmed your heart to see the hope that came with that simple announcement. The Third Army meant the 'old man,' and he meant hope, success, and victory. . . . I feel that I am a better man because of the General, and . . . he will be a source of strength for the rest of my life." Source: Blumenson, *The Patton Papers*, 837.

20. Farago, *Patton*, 831.
21. D'Este, *Patton*, 802.
22. D'Este, *Patton*, 803–4.
23. Gavin, *On to Berlin*, 296.
24. Richard Sassaman, "Patton: Loved, Hated, Appreciated," *America in WWII*, http://www.americainwwii.com/articles/patton-loved-hated-appreciated/.
25. Robert Patton, *The Pattons*, 285.
26. "Beatrice Banning Ayer Patton," Find a Grave, https://www.findagrave.com /memorial/243009284/beatrice-banning-patton.
27. Blumenson, *The Patton Papers*, 844.
28. Robert Patton, *The Pattons*, 284.

# INDEX

# ABOUT THE AUTHOR

Alex Kershaw is a journalist and a *New York Times* bestselling author of books on World War II. Born in York, England, he is a graduate of Oxford University and has lived in the United States since 1994.